Arthur Phillip

Arthur Phillip

SAILOR
MERCENARY
GOVERNOR
SPY

Michael Pembroke

hardie grant books
MELBOURNE · LONDON

All the world's a stage,
And all the men and women merely players,
They have their exits and entrances,
And one man in his time plays many parts,
His acts being seven ages.

William Shakespeare,
As You Like It, Act 2, Scene 7

Botany Bay, it has been
argued, was meant as a
Gulag before Gulag …
Nothing could be further
from the truth.

Alan Atkinson
The Europeans in Australia

Published in 2013 by Hardie Grant Books

Hardie Grant Books (Australia)
Ground Floor, Building 1
658 Church Street
Richmond, Victoria 3121
www.hardiegrant.com.au

Hardie Grant Books (UK)
Dudley House, North Suite
34–35 Southampton Street
London WC2E 7HF
www.hardiegrant.co.uk

A Cataloguing-in-Publication entry is available from the catalogue of the National Library of
Australia at www.nla.gov.au
Arthur Phillip: Sailor, Mercenary, Governor, Spy
ISBN 978 1 74270 508 8

Publisher: Pam Brewster
Cover and text design: Nada Backovic
Typeset in 11/18pt Bell MT by Kirby Jones
Printed in the UK by the CPI Group (UK) Ltd, Croydon, CR0 4YY

CONTENTS

For Gillian Rose

and

Olivia, Harriet, India & Nick

PREFACE

My object in writing this book has been threefold – to convey something of the elusive character of Arthur Phillip, to bring to life his career in the Royal Navy and to explain the culture, values, fashions and features of the Georgian society in which he lived and died. I have endeavoured to do so with an eye to the picturesque and with appropriate focus on the scientific and natural world where it forms part of the narrative. This is not just a book about wooden ships and big guns, although they certainly feature. It is a story of privation and ambition, of wealthy widows and marriage mistakes, of money and trade, of espionage and mercenaries, of discovery and exploration, and of hardship and illness. It is also a story of the extraordinary idealism that inspired and accompanied the founding of Australia. Inevitably there is loneliness and desperation, war and disappointment. Eventually there were the rewards of re-marriage and genteel living in Regency Bath. At his peak, in mid-life, Phillip seemed almost perfectly suited to the role that history and circumstance presented to him. He was 'a man with a good head, a good heart, lots of pluck, and plenty of common sense'. To those qualities he brought an uncommon amount of integrity, intelligence and persistence. He was after all a captain in the Georgian navy, the type to whom British governments so often turned two centuries ago when they wanted a job well done in a distant part of the world. At the end, however, Phillip's story is one of loss of contemporary relevance and the painful decline into obscurity that comes with old age.

Easter 2013
Hawthorn, Mount Wilson

PHILLIP'S NAVAL RANKS

Captain's Servant	16 October 1755
Midshipman	3 February 1757
Fourth Lieutenant	7 June 1761
First Lieutenant	9 October 1778
Master & Commander	2 September 1779
Post Captain	30 November 1781
Rear Admiral of the Blue	1 January 1799
Rear Admiral of the White	23 April 1804
Rear Admiral of the Red	9 November 1805
Vice Admiral of the Blue	13 December 1806
Vice Admiral of the White	25 October 1809
Vice Admiral of the Red	31 July 1810
Admiral of the Blue	4 June 1814

PHILLIP'S SHIPS

Buckingham	1755
Princess Louisa	1756
Neptune	1757
Union	1757–58
Aurora	1759
Stirling Castle	1760–62
Infanta (captured Spanish vessel)	1762
Egmont	1770–71
Belém (Portuguese)	1775
Pilar (Portuguese)	1775–77
San Agustin (captured Spanish vessel)	1777
Santa Antonio (Portuguese)	1777–78
Alexander	1778
Basilisk	1779
Ariadne	1781
Europe	1782–84
Sirius	1787–88
Alexander	1796
Swiftsure	1796
Blenheim	1797

CHAPTER 1

NAVAL EDUCATION

Phillip's formative years – his parents, birth, education and apprenticeship

Arthur Phillip was born in the City of London in October 1738 during the reign of Britain's last foreign-born monarch, George II. It was a time of ebullient confidence, buoyant economic conditions and growing favourable trade balances. Englishmen exhibited a breezy, bigoted chauvinism towards the rest of the world. In 1707, their country had united with Scotland and became known as Great Britain but the new name was little more than a euphemism for greater England. France and Spain were the traditional foes. The citizens of the former were popularly seen as 'starveling, barefoot, onion-nibbling peasants oppressed by a lecherous clergy and a callous nobility'. Those of the latter were regarded with perennial suspicion as mysterious, black-robed, papist idolaters. On the other hand, when the French philosopher Voltaire visited England in the decade before Phillip's birth, he was dazzled by the extent of tolerance, political enlightenment and freedom of expression. But there was a darker side. London's urban proletariat was the gin-sodden sump of Georgian society – mercilessly satirised by the artist William Hogarth and justly described by a later French visitor as 'lazy, sotted and brutish'.

The fear that France and Spain might unite under one Bourbon monarch was the reason for the war that marked the beginning of the century – the War of Spanish Succession (1701–14). In 1738 the country was on the verge of another conflict with Spain. For years London merchants had been looking to expand their commercial interests in the Spanish territories of the Americas. Fuelled by avarice, their campaign was reinforced by discontent with Spain's use of *guarda costas* to board, search and frequently harass British merchant vessels on the high seas. One English captain named Robert Jenkins claimed that his ear had been sliced off when his ship was boarded. Reputedly, he produced his pickled ear to a committee of the House of Commons. The prominent Whig statesman, William Pitt the elder exhorted the government: 'Where trade is at stake, we must defend it or perish'. The whole tumultuous year was marked by loud and increasing demands for war. When it came in 1739, it was known as the War of Jenkins' Ear. The British public enthusiastically assumed that victory would be 'easy, glorious and profitable' and that there would be little more to do than usher Spanish galleons laden with gold and silver into home ports. And within a month the City bells tolled to celebrate Admiral Vernon's capture of Porto Bello on the Spanish Main – an event that was so joyous it led to Thomas Arne's song *Rule, Britannia!* and Portobello Road. English boys ached to go to sea.

Phillip was born amid this din and clamour for war. But the circumstances of his birth were inauspicious. His father Jacob is a mystery who has been repeatedly cast as an 'obscure German wanderer, teacher of languages and native of Frankfurt'. Phillip himself was once likened in appearance to 'a kapellmeister in some little Bavarian court'. Another writer referred to his 'un-English physiognomy', and another, surely lapsing into parody, to his 'long hooked fleshy nose and dark eyes with a hint of the orient about them'. Some have pointed to the Palatine migration as the occasion for Jacob Phillip's arrival in England. In 1709, many thousands of mostly Protestant refugees did come to London from the Rhineland Palatinate. But the evidence that Jacob was among them is speculative. The lists of Palatine refugees include Schneiders and Schaeffers, Hermanns and Mullers, but there is no surname similar to 'Phillip', except possibly Pfeiffer. John Jacob Pfeiffer is recorded in the first list of 6 May 1709. He was 42 years old and arrived with his wife, eight-year-old son and three-year-old daughter. But the conclusion that the son of John Jacob Pfeiffer, who arrived in London with his family in 1709, is the same person as Jacob Phillip, the father of Arthur Phillip born in London in 1738, rests on coincidence and the rudimentary anglicisation of Pfeiffer to Phillip. This is too slender a reed.

More is known about Phillip's mother. She was Elizabeth Breach, born in 1707 in the London parish of St Botolph without Aldgate.

From his mother Phillip acquired an English lineage and a modest naval connection. Her family lived in Stoney Lane, around the corner from St Botolph's Church near the old gateway leading from the City of London to Whitechapel. The Everitt family also lived in Stoney Lane, and Elizabeth's cousin Michael Everitt would in due course be influential in her son's early career. At the age of 21 Elizabeth Breach married a seaman named John Herbert. There were no banns, no public announcement, and the marriage was short-lived. He was an ordinary seaman destined for foreign service in what was then the most dreaded foreign station of all – the West Indies. When he made his will on 6 February 1729, a few months after the wedding, its time-honoured opening words betrayed a sense of foreboding – 'Mindful of the perils and dangers of the sea and other uncertainties of this transitory life'.

Two years later, on 18 October 1731, John Herbert died in the British naval hospital at Port Royal, Jamaica. Yellow fever was almost certainly the cause of his death, as it was for thousands of other British soldiers and sailors in the Caribbean in the eighteenth century. In Port Royal, the slave ships brought West African mosquitoes and larvae bearing the yellow fever virus from across the Atlantic. Newly arrived seamen with no immunity, crowded in damp and fetid places, did not stand a chance. In June 1732, John Herbert's ship returned to England without him. Elizabeth Breach could not have known of her husband's death before the ship's arrival. But when she did, she moved quickly to realise his meagre effects and collect his pay. By 1 August 1732 she had obtained probate of his will.

Just how Elizabeth Breach came to meet Jacob Phillip, or when they married, is uncertain. But two children, Rebecca and Arthur, were baptised in 1737 and 1738 at All Hallow's Church in Bread Street in the City of London. Bread Street is one of those lanes running off Cheapside in the shadow of St Paul's that still carry the names of the trades and enterprises that were once undertaken there – bread, wood, honey, milk and poultry, among others. There is even a Friday Street where fishmongers congregated. The church of St Mary le Bow is around the corner, from where its 'Bow Bells' could be heard daily, sounding a curfew at night to mark the end of the working day for the City apprentices. St Mildred's church was also in Bread Street, as well as the Three Cups Inn from where the stagecoach to Bristol would depart and return three times each week. Nearby was the parish workhouse for the poor. From Cheapside a labyrinth of narrow alleys and lanes led down to the broad River Thames. To the west of St Paul's, just a few streets away, was that place of misery and despair, the old Newgate Prison. Its stench pervaded the neighbourhood. The Italian chronicler and adventurer Casanova described Newgate as 'a hell such as Dante might have conceived'. Daniel Defoe, the English writer and author of *Robinson Crusoe*, thought it 'an emblem of hell itself'.

Jacob Phillip was a tenant of Martha Meredith's house in Bread Street. His contributions to the parish poor fund suggest that, at least for a few years, the family's circumstances were modestly comfortable. In 1736–37 his contribution was 19s 6d and in each of the next two years it was £1.19s. These amounts indicate an income that compared favourably with the rates of pay for farm labourers, ordinary seamen, weavers and teachers. Poor funds were administered by parishes, of which there were more than a hundred within the walls of the City of London. Some, like All Hallows, built workhouses to accommodate the poor. There, the infirm and elderly, the sick, senile, diseased and mad, were all housed together as objects of charity, supported by the parish with contributions from the residents.

After 1739, Jacob Phillip's name ceased to appear in the All Hallows poor rate register and he is never heard of again. Elizabeth's subsequent movements can be traced to Whitechapel and then to Rotherhithe, a docks area on the south side of the Thames, upstream from the naval yard at Deptford. It is reasonable to infer Jacob's death or disablement in the Sea Service, as the navy was then commonly called, because this was the primary qualification that entitled his son to be admitted some years later to the Charity School of the Royal Hospital for Seamen at Greenwich. Entrance was limited to 'the Sons of disabled Seamen, or whose Fathers were slain, killed or drown'd in the Sea Service', and who were 'objects of charity'.

It is more difficult to be certain about the precise cause of Jacob Phillip's death or disablement. But dockside areas like Rotherhithe were notorious hunting grounds for press gangs, a fact that might explain his disappearance and subsequent death during a time of recruitment for war. Press gangs were usually led by a junior naval lieutenant who reported to an officer of the Impress Service known as a 'regulating captain'. Often the press gang was just a group of rouseabouts who sallied from a rendezvous, usually an alehouse, with clubs, short curved cutlasses and the questionable authority of an Admiralty press warrant. Some regulating captains were failed officers and navy derelicts. The system was open to abuse and injustices were certainly perpetrated. Admiralty lawyers were kept busy defending the numerous legal challenges brought on behalf of pressed men. But the system was regarded as a necessary public policy and the only practical expedient for ensuring that there was sufficient manpower to man the fleets and protect the realm.

Although the usual form of Admiralty press warrant empowered only the pressing of 'seamen, seafaring men and persons whose occupations and callings were to work in vessels and boats', others who strayed into the path of a press gang could be swept away. And typhus, known as ship fever or jail fever, was the scourge of impressment. It proliferated where men, lousy and in rags, were crowded together in confined spaces lacking proper ventilation and sanitation. In fact, 1740 saw the worst naval typhus epidemic of all time. Although 15,000 men were quickly recruited at the outbreak of war, only 1000 men could be mustered six months later – and no fewer than 25,000 were sent to hospital ships, sick quarters and hospitals.

In an age before widow's pensions, Elizabeth Breach was again left without a husband. Stoney Lane near St Botolph's Church was familiar home territory. The Everitt family was there, including Michael Everitt, who in 1747 would be appointed to the rank of post captain in command of a rated naval vessel. In this capacity, Everitt was entitled to a number of 'servants' – four for every 100 of the ship's authorised complement.

A captain's servant was not a servant in the conventional sense but a boy bred up for seafaring life, almost as an apprentice to his master. The naval regulations stated that officers' servants should not be younger than eleven, but it was a regulation often ignored and boys as young as six were known to be at sea. A captain's servant could come from any background, and not all were noted in the muster books. Some were young gentlemen; others were not. Many were relatives and some were taken on as a favour to master shipwrights and dockyard officials. It was a small favour to grant, for the only risk a captain ran was that he would be given a troublesome or useless boy who would have to be returned to his parents. For many boys, it was the making of them, but the quality of their education and instruction at sea depended on the captain. A benevolent and enlightened captain would arrange tuition in mathematics, astronomy, reading, writing and drawing; a schoolmaster might even be part of the ship's complement. But on the worst ships, a boy might receive more gin than instruction, and pass his time sleeping and playing, or walking the decks with his hands in his pockets.

We know that Phillip went to sea in a British naval vessel at nine years of age. A testimonial about Phillip's service from the Viceroy of Brazil noted that Phillip's practical experience began at the age of nine as a *'guarda de Pavilhâo'*. This was the Portuguese equivalent of the most junior rank of cadet officer. At that age, Phillip could only have done so in the capacity of an officer's servant. And the source of the Viceroy's information must have been Phillip himself. The inference that he was taken on by Captain Everitt in 1747 has a reasonable basis. Not only did Phillip turn nine in the year that Everitt received his first command but it seems likely that by that time he was fatherless. Elizabeth Breach no doubt encouraged her cousin Michael Everitt to take her orphaned only son under his wing, and the official naval records show that Phillip spent a large part of his subsequent early naval career on ships under Everitt's command.

Everitt may have been one of the better captains. His portrait, painted in 1747 by Richard Wilson, a founder member of the Royal Academy, hangs in the National Gallery of Victoria. It suggests a corpulent, confident and self-satisfied man of his time. The Admiralty records indicate that his punishments of difficult and unsavoury seamen were frequent and severe, much more so than Phillip's would ever be, but not unusual among his contemporaries. There is no official record of Phillip's service with Everitt in the 1740s, though this is not surprising given that the system existed on patronage and preferment. Record keeping was often deliberately incomplete and it would not have been prudent to include in the muster book a boy younger than the minimum age prescribed in the naval regulations.

On 22 June 1751 Phillip commenced a more formal process of naval education when he was accepted for admission to the Charity School of the Royal Hospital for Seamen at Greenwich. The hospital, situated on the south bank of the Thames about five miles east of the City, was the dream of Queen Mary. As joint sovereign with her husband William of Orange, she made the hospital 'the darling object of her life'. When she died suddenly from smallpox in December 1694, William carried on the project in her memory, commissioning the celebrated architects Sir Christopher Wren and Nicholas Hawksmoor to design and build the four main buildings. Their prospect from the river, so famously painted by the Venetian artist Canaletto, is regarded as 'one of the most sublime sights that English architecture affords'. In this magnificent setting, Britain's sick and disabled seamen were housed and cared for, and the 'orphans of the sea' – the boys whose fathers were slain or disabled in the Sea Service and who were objects of charity – were maintained and educated.

By 1748 there were a hundred poor boys housed in a dormitory in the attic of the Queen Mary Court – the last of the four great buildings to be completed. All around them were the injured, aged and frequently decrepit pensioners. By day, the boys attended school at nearby Weston's Academy, where the headmaster in Phillip's time was the Reverend Francis Swinden. The boys were constantly supervised and could not leave the hospital grounds unless in the company of the official guardian or his assistants, who escorted them to and from the school, whipped them when required and presided at their table in the dining hall.

Phillip's entry to the school is recorded in the entry register and his departure appears in the binding out. In the former, his father is described as 'steward' – a likely occupation for a man with no particular seafaring skills who may have been pressed. In the latter, his father's occupation is listed as able seaman. Whether steward or seaman, Phillip satisfied the first criterion for admission, namely that he was the son of a seaman. The other criteria were that he be between eleven and thirteen years of age, of sound body and mind, and able to read. And of course, he must have been an 'object of charity' whose father had been 'slain or disabled in the Sea Service'. These conditions for admission were required to be proved 'by proper Certificates' and one of the school's articles provided that, 'If any Boy shall get in by false Testimonials, or other indirect means, upon Discovery thereof, he shall be stripped of his clothing and turned out of the hospital, never to be re-admitted.'

Once admitted, the boys were lodged, clothed and maintained at the expense of the hospital for up to three years. A nurse was appointed for every 30 boys to keep them clean, to ensure their hair was combed and free of vermin, to take care of their clothes, to make their beds if they were unable to do so, and to attend to their meals. Each boy was supplied with a bible, a book of common prayer and other books and instruments necessary for education. All the boys received instruction from the chaplains in the principles of religion and from the schoolmaster in writing, arithmetic and navigation. As for necessities, the boys were given linen and woollen clothing of the same quality as the pensioners, as well as a pair of hard-wearing ram skin leather breeches. They slept in hammocks rather than beds, presumably as practice for sea life.

The articles prescribed the routine of the boys' daily lives with resolute strictness. Each day followed the familiar, well-recognised patterns of institutional living that Charles Dickens later depicted in *Nicholas Nickleby*. The boys' diet was parsimonious: four ounces of bread and one of cheese for breakfast; five ounces of bread and one of cheese for supper; a daily quart of beer, of which half a pint was for breakfast, a pint for dinner and half a pint for supper; mutton with broth on Sunday; beef with broth on Tuesdays and Thursdays; and pease pottage on Fridays. Saturday's dinner was particularly spartan – water gruel with sugar and currants.

Education focused on arithmetic and navigation – the extraction of square and cube roots, trigonometry, plain sailing and oblique sailing, the doctrine of currents, sailing by middle latitude, Mercator sailing and, not the least important, the times of high water at various ports. Drawing was also central to the curriculum. The ability to draw landscapes and coastlines accurately was a crucial skill for naval officers and those involved in engineering and artillery. Indeed, training apprentices to become good artists as well as good seamen was a standard commitment to which masters agreed in their indentures. In his later life, Phillip would display a graphic talent in his chart work that must have been fostered at an early age. In the classroom, and if one account can be accepted, Phillip appears to have been a

11

good student. In his report of 22 June 1753, the Reverend Swinden is reputed to have made the observation that 'Arthur Phillip is noted for his diplomacy [and] mildness. [He is] nervously active, unassuming, reasonable, business-like to the smallest degree in everything he undertakes, always seeking perfection'. These traits would be apparent throughout Phillip's life.

Upon completion of his education, each boy was bound out with a sea chest, all necessary clothing and the books and instruments he used at school. He was fitted with a double-breasted pea jacket, a serge waistcoat, a Kersey waistcoat, good cloth breeches, ordinary shag breeches, a Drugget coat and further breeches, white shirts and cotton check shirts, yarn and worsted stockings, silk handkerchiefs, shoes and hat. In the usual case, this would have been the extent of each boy's worldly possessions. When a master could be found to take him on, the boy's apprenticeship would begin.

Phillip left the Charity School at the end of 1753. William Readhead, master of the 210-ton whaling ship *Fortune*, bound himself to instruct Phillip in 'the best Way and Manner for making him an able Seaman and as good an Artist as he can'. The indenture of apprenticeship was dated 1 December 1753 and was for a term of seven years. It included a further promise by Readhead not to 'immoderately beat or misuse' his apprentice. Depending on the master, an apprenticeship at sea could be onerous. But an apprenticeship on a whaling ship in the Arctic was particularly tough. The rations were austere, the physical conditions unhealthy and the work dangerous. And the apprentice could expect the worst and the last of everything.

Phillip embarked on his first whaling expedition in the spring of 1754 to Spitsbergen (now Svalbard) in the Barents Sea – within the Arctic Circle between 76° and 80°N. Apart from the far northern extremities of Greenland and Ellesmere Island, there is almost no land quite as close to the North Pole. The whaling ships went to Spitsbergen in the eighteenth century because its unique location made it a cradle of life for large numbers of whales, especially the Greenland Right whale or bowhead whale (*Balaena mysticetus*), which feed on the massive plankton that blooms in spring. For centuries these feeding grounds were a stopping point on the whales' circumpolar migratory route through the northeast Atlantic and Russian Arctic. Of all the whales, bowheads were the most valuable as their blubber was the thickest. And they were easy to hunt and harvest: they moved slowly, swimming languorously, feeding near the surface, sometimes literally basking in the seasonal warmth. Their immense quantity of blubber also meant that they floated readily when killed.

It is no surprise that Phillip's apprenticeship was on a whaling ship. At that very time, British whaling had emerged from a period of slumber to become a major industry operating from northern coastal ports such as Whitby, Hull and Yarmouth and from the Greenland Dock at Rotherhithe on the south bank of the Thames. From these places, dozens of whaling ships and hundreds of men were despatched to the Arctic each year. Their business was to bring back cargoes of blubber and baleen. The latter, often mistakenly described as 'whale bone', was much in demand in the eighteenth century for corset stays and skirt hoops, among many other things. The whale oil on the other hand, obtained by boiling and reducing the blubber, was an elemental necessity of life. It was the fuel for lamps and the primary substance from which soap and candles were manufactured. But what made British whaling sufficiently commercially attractive to generate its resurgence was the government bounty. By 1750 the owner of a whaling ship of 200 tons or more became entitled to £2 per ship ton. In the case of the *Fortune*, this amounted to £420 – enough to underwrite the basic cost of a whaling expedition and payable irrespective of the quantity of baleen, blubber or oil carried home. Although the apprentice's role in the whaling process was limited, the fifteen-year-old Phillip would have seen it all from the ship's rails. More often he would have been employed in fetching and carrying. Whenever necessary he would have been required to wash the deck clear of slippery and hazardous whale blood.

Only the strongest and fittest men manned the small boats known as 'whalers' that were despatched to hunt, harpoon and lance the whales. The work was too dangerous and physically demanding for a boy apprentice. A whaler needed to come close, very close indeed, to its quarry and great strength and power were needed to hurl the harpoon. At the right moment, the bow oarsman would draw in his oar, move forward and stand poised with the harpoon. It was about three feet long, made of iron with a wooden handle and attached to a hemp rope approximately 120 fathoms long. Each whaler carried six of these ropes, making well over 4000 feet in all. A hatchet was always on hand to cut the rope in case of entanglement. When a strike occurred, the whale might flick its tail perilously. Frequently it dived. Barring mishap, there would then follow a long and arduous process, over many hours, of wearing down the whale. When the whale was exhausted, it was repeatedly lanced until its death was certain. Other whalers would come to assist. The lances were thin and exceedingly sharp and penetrated deep into the whale, into its lungs and liver, causing blood to spout high in the air. The sea would become the colour of vermillion.

As its life drained away, the whale sometimes let out a mournful groan, lashing the water with its tail before it expired. Sometimes it raged, battering the sea with its fins and tail before losing all strength and turning over on its side.

The next stage was the strenuous and bloody business of stripping and flensing – the process of separating blubber from bone using large curved blades attached to long wooden handles. The blubber was then cut into strips and packed into barrels or 'blubber butts' to be transported to port. There the blubber was boiled and reduced to a fine waxy oil in grimy Georgian factories known as 'blubber boiling houses'. In London, they proliferated around Rotherhithe.

This was the experience of Phillip's Arctic apprenticeship. It was the toughest of schools in the harshest of environments. Phillip would have learned the rudiments of seamanship and seen firsthand the operation of a whaling ship. During the winter he would have had a different experience. Returned whaling ships such as the *Fortune* set off on the Mediterranean trade. This was a commercial circuit in which vessels sailed between the principal ports of northern Europe, the Iberian peninsula and the western Mediterranean, transporting goods and maximising revenue on each leg of the voyage. The winter voyage of the *Fortune* in 1754–55 conforms to this pattern of Mediterranean trading. The pass that William Readhead obtained from the Admiralty gave his first destination as Barcelona and the second as Livorno, or Leghorn as the English called it. *Lloyd's List* records that the vessel then returned via Sète and Rotterdam. Its outward cargoes were probably cloth, grain, fish and manufactured goods. Its Mediterranean cargoes were likely olive oil, currants, salt and silk. On the *Fortune*'s return to London from the Mediterranean in April 1755, she set off on a second whaling expedition to Spitsbergen. In July, at the end of the summer whaling season, when the ship once again returned to London and the crew was paid off, Phillip quit his apprenticeship and was released from his indentures. He had not served his seven years but there were moves afoot to advance his career in other ways. And Captain Michael Everitt was well placed to assist him.

CHAPTER 2

JUNIOR OFFICER

The Seven Years War and Phillip's service in the Mediterranean and the West Indies

The conflagration that became the Seven Years War (1756–63) was brewing throughout 1755. During that year Great Britain and France were engaged in constant skirmishing, moving publicly and ineluctably towards the first world war. Although formal declarations of war did not come until May and June 1756, the impending conflict had been inevitable for some time. In due course, Spain, Austria, Sweden, Portugal, Prussia and Hanover all joined in. Sensing the opportunities that lay ahead, some young Englishmen changed course and joined the navy. One such man, with a later connection to Australia, was James Cook, a seaman in the merchant service who signed up as an able seaman in June 1755. Another was Arthur Phillip, ten years younger than Cook, who abandoned his apprenticeship on a whaling vessel to join Captain Everitt on a ship of the line. He first appears in official naval records in October 1755 when he was entered in the muster book of the *Buckingham* as a member of the ship's complement. This was the start of his formal naval career.

Phillip was seventeen years old and one of Captain Everitt's official servants. It was the beginning of the road to becoming a midshipman. The naval regulations required that a candidate for commission as a lieutenant must have undertaken six years service at sea, at least two as a midshipman. Phillip's official time commenced to run from 16 October 1755 – ignoring what informal service he may have had with Everitt from the age of nine. Everitt's other servants on the *Buckingham* included his two sons Robert and George and two young boys who were, it seems, relatives of Vice-Admiral Temple West. Phillip was fortunate to be in the company of these boys for Everitt was naturally mindful of their education. In June, a few months before Phillip joined the ship, he requested from the Admiralty a schoolmaster to assist in the naval education of his 'young gentlemen'.

From modest beginnings, the Seven Years War fanned rapidly throughout Europe, the West Indies, North and South America, Africa, India and the Philippines and its outcome would permanently alter the world map. The origins of the war lay in rivalry between Great Britain and France over their competing colonial and trade empires and in antagonism between the Hohenzollerns and the Habsburgs, which pitted Prussia against Austria and the Holy Roman Empire. The antagonists and their allies coalesced into two camps: Anglo-Prussian and Austro-French. Portugal and some small German states aligned themselves with the former and Sweden, Saxony and later Spain with the latter. Throughout the war, Great Britain adopted a distinctive strategy, limiting her military commitment on the continent and subsidising her allies to engage the enemy on that front, while establishing naval supremacy on the high seas, controlling trade routes and plundering foreign colonies. But the campaign did not start well.

The opening sea battle of the Seven Years War occurred off the island of Minorca in the Mediterranean Sea. Minorca is the most northerly of the Balearic Islands, approximately 250 miles south of Toulon. It is rocky and sparsely cultivated and less well known today than its larger brother Majorca. But in 1756 it was a British frontier garrison, protected by a fort known as St Phillip at the entrance to its harbour. The township of Mahon was situated inside the harbour.

Britain had seized Minorca from Spain in 1708 for essentially the same strategic reasons as the Phoenicians, Greeks, Carthaginians, Romans, Arabs and Catalans had invaded it in earlier times. In the eighteenth-century, most of the British inhabitants on Minorca were soldiers and sailors, support personnel and their families. The island's strategic significance lay partly in its nearness to the French naval base and dockyard at Toulon and partly because it was at the crossroads of Mediterranean trade. As one contemporary British writer recorded: 'All ships sailing up the straits of Gibraltar, and bound to any part of Africa, east of Algiers, to any part of Italy, or to any part of Turkey, either in Asia or Europe, and all ships from many of those places, and bound to any port without the straits-mouth, must and usually do pass between this island and the coast of Africa'. Control of Minorca meant that Britain could intervene in the commercial and naval activities of its major imperial competitors – France, Spain and the Ottoman Empire.

In April 1756 the rumours about France's intention to invade Minorca became a reality. This act of French belligerence before the declaration of hostilities marked the real beginning of the war. When the island was overrun by French troops, the British residents in the township withdrew inside the fort, sheltering behind its stone walls and in its dungeons and damp subterranean passages. For weeks the French besieged the fort with cannon and artillery, battering its walls and confining the entire population of men, women and children within it. To relieve the British residents and the garrison, the Admiralty despatched a dozen line-of-battle ships from the Western Squadron under the command of Admiral Byng, who had been patrolling in the Bay of Biscay. Among them was the 70-gun *Buckingham* on which Phillip served. She was the flagship of Vice-Admiral Temple West and was commanded by Michael Everitt.

On 20 May, to the great relief of the besieged British residents, Byng's ships appeared on the horizon off Minorca and that afternoon engaged with a slightly more numerous French squadron. When the two lines of battleships engaged, the British line's approach to the enemy was oblique, so that its vanguard or 'van' closed with the enemy before its centre and rear. The *Buckingham*, in the middle of the British van, and the *Defiance*, whose captain was killed and replaced by the dashing Augustus Hervey, were exposed to the most intense French fire. But the centre and rear of the line under Byng's command remained out of range three miles back. The French fired high, as was their usual practice, seeking to dismast the British ships. But the British van under the command of Temple West aimed low and were faster and more effective.

During the engagement, Phillip and the other servants, together with the lieutenants, most of the midshipmen and the majority of the seamen, would have been confined to the gun decks. Here amid the deafening noise and choking smoke of the great guns, boys like Phillip were the powder monkeys. Their role was to fetch the gunpowder cartridges from the magazines for the gun crews. Each great gun – weighing up to two tons each – was manned by a crew of six or more seamen who were supervised by a midshipman. Their barrels, about ten feet long, bellowed like a booming thunderclap; each explosion accompanied by a flash of light and billowing clouds of acrid smoke. After discharge the huge weapon would recoil with a force that could kill a man caught in its path. When the gun came to rest at the end of its breeching, the gun crew would begin a rapid and precisely timed series of movements to reload and fire again. The bore hole was swabbed. Gunpowder, bound in a cloth cartridge, was rammed into the muzzle. A wad was rammed on top of the powder. Then cannonball and another wad were rammed down on top of that. Priming powder was poured into the touch hole, then the gun crew heaved in unison on the tackle and ran the weapon out through its port. A match lit the primer, the gunpowder would ignite and the gun would roar, recoil and the process would begin again.

If the enemy fire were directed at the guns, rather than at the masts, the gun deck could become a charnel house. If a cannon scored a direct hit, the gun crew would be eviscerated – killed, maimed and splattered with blood, brains, gristle and bone. If the oak hull was strong enough to stop the ball, an eruption of splinters on the inside wall might mutilate any man in near proximity. This is where Phillip and the other boys worked – crouching, flinching and hauling gunpowder amid the horror and darkness, where everyone was blackened and the deck was 'so completely filled with smoke that no one can see two yards before him'.

By mid-afternoon the fourth and fifth French ships, the *Sage* and the *Guerrière*, were driven out of the line and the French van began to disintegrate. This was the moment for the British squadron to press home its advantage, but the ships in the rear under Byng's command failed to join the battle. Byng's flagship, the *Ramilles*, barely fired a shot. Despite this half-hearted response, late in the afternoon the whole French line unexpectedly broke off and sailed away. But instead of advancing on Minorca to relieve the residents and troops in the garrison, Byng directed his squadron to Gibraltar. The survivors held out in Fort St Phillip until 28 June, inflicting many casualties on the besieging French, who lost almost 5000 men. But the hardship to the British residents, their eventual surrender and the loss of Minorca were inevitable.

After the battle, Phillip wrote to his sister Rebecca. His letter captures the essence of the engagement:

> When Admiral Byng hoisted the Red Flagg a signal to Engage, we with our Division bore down to the Enemy, and with Six Ships engaged their Van, (as we led the Van) which He (ie., Admiral Byng) instead of doing the Same with the Rear, layed his Main Top-Sails aback, then all his Division was obliged to do the like.
>
> The French began fireing at us, Some time before we fired at them, as their aim was to engage at a distance, and ours to engage them as close as we could. But when we began, we played upon [them] very briskly, and Soon drove

the 4th and 5th Ships out of the line & Raked them fore & aft as they went. One of them was their Rear Admiral, whose Stern was Shattered very much, & by this time our Van had a very great advantage over theirs, which we was hinder'd from making use of, by their Rear coming up. For all this time Admiral Byng lay with his Top Sails aback, and only fired now & then, & that at too great a distance to doe, or Receive any damage. But we gave them So brisk a fire that they declined coming to a close engagement tho' they had it in their power; So they filled their Sails and edged away to the rest of the Fleet, who altogether stood towards the Island of Minorca, and Soon after we tacked, and lay too.

We received but very little damage considering what a hot Fire we was exposed to ... But then we can give very good reasons for it, every man in our Fleet burned with the greatest ardour imaginable, and theirs by their behaviour i.e. the French with a great dastardness, for their not coming to a close engagement when they had Such Odds as their Whole Fleet against our [Division] plainly Shewed that most of them had rather Run than Fight. And it is very certain, that their fear kept them from taking proper Aim, which Saved Us a great many Men, as well as our Masts and Rigging. I need not mention the great Courage & conduct of our Admiral [ie. West] and Captains Shewed that Day in our Division, nor the Cowardice of the Only person Admiral Byng, that kept the French Fleet from being Distroyed, and the Island from being relieved. For no doubt all England will Soon be convinced of the merit of Admiral West, and the downright Cowardice of Admiral Byng.

There was national hysteria in England, fuelled by a press that was as jingoistic then as it is now. Byng was replaced, recalled and imprisoned under guard in Greenwich Hospital. Pamphlets and broadsheets accused and lampooned him; mobs burned and hanged his effigy. He was ridiculed as pompous and effeminate. In advance of his trial, George II unforgivably told a group of London merchants: 'Indeed he shall be tried immediately, he shall be hanged directly.' In that hyped state of affairs, Byng's court martial commenced on 27 December 1756 before a bevy of admirals and captains on board the *St George* moored in Portsmouth harbour. In happier days, Byng had been her captain.

Byng was charged under the Twelfth Article of War. It laid down that if any person in the fleet failed through 'cowardice, neglect or disaffection' to do his utmost to take, sink, burn and destroy the enemy's ships in battle, he shall receive the death penalty. The Article had once stipulated alternative penalties – either death or 'such other punishment as the court should judge fit'. But a recent amendment removed the discretionary alternative. This fatal amendment was introduced after an officer was controversially acquitted at an earlier court martial, over which Byng himself had presided. Ironically for Byng, he became the first officer to be tried under the amended Article. After a month of evidence, including from old General Blakeney, the commander of the garrison on Minorca, and Augustus Hervey, who was Byng's most valiant supporter, the court martial found the charge proved but specifically absolved Byng of any cowardice or disaffection. Byng was found guilty only of neglect. But it made no difference. Death was now the unalterable punishment for conviction, whether the finding was cowardice, disaffection or merely neglect. No senior naval officer thought this appropriate in Byng's case and those who constituted the court martial recommended clemency.

George II ignored the court martial's recommendation and refused to consider any leniency. He even rejected William Pitt the elder, who did all he could to obtain the King's pardon. Byng apparently bore the month-long court martial and sentence with great fortitude. But the sense of tragic theatre was exacerbated by the order to all the men-of-war at Spithead, the anchorage off Portsmouth, to send their boats with their captains and all of their officers to attend the execution. Byng was ceremoniously shot by a party of marines on the quarterdeck of the *Monarque* at 12 noon on 14 March 1757. The muzzles of their muskets were only three or four feet from his chest. He was kneeling and blindfolded. Voltaire was so provoked that he remarked in his novel *Candide* that 'in England it is thought necessary to kill an admiral from time to time to encourage the others'.

Phillip cannot have failed to have shared in this controversy, which engulfed England. Not only had he participated in the battle at Minorca, he was also at Spithead as a midshipman on the *Neptune* when her officers attended the execution. Phillip's own views on the appropriateness of the punishment are unknown but in his letter to Rebecca, he complained with youthful ardour of the 'downright cowardice of Admiral Byng', adding that 'no doubt all England will soon be convinced of the merit of Admiral West'. In truth, Temple West was so opposed to Byng's execution that he refused to sign the warrant and resigned his seat at the Board of Admiralty before the execution was carried out.

After Minorca, Phillip temporarily lost Everitt's patronage when he and the other captains were ordered home to give evidence at Byng's court martial. Phillip transferred briefly to the *Princess Louisa*, serving for a short time as the captain's clerk before returning to England in November 1756 on the *Ramilles*. There he rejoined Everitt on the *Neptune*, which was no ordinary warship. She was a massive 98-gun first-rate ship of the line, but she did not go to sea and Phillip's experience on her was brief and uneventful. From February until June 1757, the *Neptune* remained at anchor at Spithead. This was the period during which the trial and execution of Admiral Byng took place. In June, Phillip was discharged as 'unserviceable', connoting illness. By August, however, he was back with Everitt, but this time on the *Union*, another 90-gun battleship, in an apparent crew swap. The *London Chronicle* reported that the *Union*'s captain and officers 'are all turned over to the *Neptune*, and the *Neptune*'s to the *Union*'. A biographical note in the *Naval Chronicle* of 1812 confirms that although Phillip's name does not appear in the *Union*'s muster book he sailed with Everitt on the *Union* between August 1757 and November 1758. The absence of Phillip's name from the muster book is not unusual. There was often a degree of informality in the records kept of the captain's followers.

For his first four years Phillip followed Everitt, but by 1759, at the age of 21, he began to progress independently of his patron. In June, he was formally entered in the books of the 36-gun frigate *Aurora* as a midshipman. Her captain was Sam Scott. As a midshipman, Phillip was now a cadet officer and a candidate to become a commissioned officer. In this role he enjoyed his first formal responsibilities in the ship's hierarchy and became entitled to walk the quarterdeck and wear a midshipman's uniform. The midshipmen slept in hammocks on the gun deck, but in a separate section away from the officers, in an area towards the stern known as the gunroom. It was separated from the seamen by a canvas bulkhead. The daily role of the midshipmen was to direct the men's work, subject to the supervision of the lieutenants. They could give orders, even to much older seamen, and beat them if necessary. All midshipmen, regardless of their background, were referred to as 'young gentlemen' and were expected to behave like officers, but they were often treated like schoolboys – and naughty ones at that. Great enthusiasm, indeed dreams of glory, often accompanied a boy's appointment as a midshipman. After one boy received his midshipman's uniform, he wrote grandly: 'Brightly dawned the auspicious morning that beheld me habited in His Majesty's uniform and which, in my excited imagination, was at once to make a man and a hero of me.' Phillip would have been equally enthusiastic.

Frigates such as the *Aurora* were considered to be better schools for service than ships of the line. Many of the best captains for training boys commanded them. They were an intermediate class of warship that represented a compromise between power and speed. Lighter, more versatile and of shallower draft than a line-of-battle ship, a frigate could range ahead in search of the enemy, drop over the horizon, nose into bays and harbours, run up rivers and carry intelligence back to the flagship. Line-of-battle ships were huge, heavy and relatively slow. They carried at least 64 guns, often more, on two or three gun decks. A frigate on the other hand, commanded by a lieutenant or a recently appointed captain, mounted her battery of 24 to 36 guns on a single gun deck. And the officers and crew of frigates usually undertook more independent cruising and experienced more frequent action than those who sailed on men-of-war. With some justification, they tended to regard themselves as a professional elite. If a frigate could avoid it, however, it rarely engaged an enemy line-of-battle ship, for the frigate would be cruelly outgunned.

Phillip's service as a midshipman on the *Aurora* would have broadened his experience in valuable ways, advancing his seafaring skills and teaching him about the supervision of men. But the naval component of the war was now largely being fought in North America and the West Indies. In February 1760, Phillip chose once again to join his fortune to Everitt, this time on the *Stirling Castle*, a 70-gun third-rate ship of the line being fitted for service on the West Indies station. He was included in the ship's company as an able-bodied seaman but this was not a demotion, simply a customary means by which a captain such as Everitt might find a place for a young man whom he wished to favour when the ship already had her full complement of midshipmen. There was no immediate sailing, however, let alone any naval action, and Phillip was compelled to curb his enthusiasm during much of 1760 while the *Stirling Castle* was fitted out, first at Woolwich on the Thames and later at Spithead.

The fitting-out of vessels for West Indies service presented particular problems for the Admiralty. The warm waters caused ships to grow foul quickly with parasitic barnacles and weed on the ships' bottoms, inhibiting steering and slowing sailing. The marine borer known as the Teredo worm, endemic throughout the Caribbean, could render a ship unserviceable within two years – a problem so great the Admiralty would eventually introduce copper-sheathed hulls, but until then sailors made do by tarring and caulking the timbers of the hull and sometimes adding a temporary layer of wood planking over its underwater section. The annual hurricane season was another local problem. It imperilled the safety of the men and their ships, and drained supplies of spare masts, spars, rigging and sails stored in the British naval dockyards at Jamaica and Antigua.

The *Stirling Castle* eventually sailed from Spithead, arriving at the West Indies station in October 1760. There she stayed quiet until December, lying at anchor in the roadstead off St John's, Antigua until after the hurricane season. The preceding year had been a tale of British victories. It was known as the *annus mirabilis*. Horace Walpole, the social commentator and Whig politician, said that 'our bells are worn threadbare with ringing for victories'. By September 1760, Quebec had fallen and with it all of Canada. And in the West Indies, the French island of Guadeloupe had surrendered, although France still had a substantial presence on other islands. Between hurricane seasons, the *Stirling Castle* patrolled constantly among the slender archipelago of volcanic islands known as the Lesser Antilles, which stretch from Puerto Rico in the north to Trinidad and Tobago in the south. At the 'windward' end of this chain, closer to South America, the French island of Martinique remained a strategic British objective.

In the midst of its cruising the *Stirling Castle* captured a small French prize. But in a move of greater personal significance for Phillip, the commodore of the Leeward Islands station promoted him from midshipman to fourth lieutenant. Subject to the Admiralty's confirmation, Phillip became a commissioned naval officer from June 1761. Apart from six years' service at sea, including at least two as a midshipman, a candidate for lieutenant had to obtain a 'passing' certificate. This was a formidable examination in seamanship. Candidates had to prove that they could 'Splice, Knot, Reef a sail, work a Ship Sailing, Shift his Tides, keep a Reckoning of a Ship's way by Plain Sailing and Mercator, Observe by the Sun or Star, find the variation of the Compass and is qualified to do his Duty as an Able Seaman and a Midshipman'.

Contrary to popular misconception, the pool of lieutenants was not a socially exclusive club. The majority started their seagoing life as captains' servants, of whom a proportion was inevitably drawn from humble circumstances. As a lieutenant, Phillip became for the first time responsible for keeping a log and taking turns with the master to be officer of the watch. He was in charge of a division of the seamen and a group of the midshipmen, for whose welfare and efficiency he was responsible. He had to know his men as individuals, attend to their needs and endeavour to handle them in an intelligent and humane fashion. Unlike the midshipmen who slept on the gundeck, the lieutenants' sleeping quarters were below the great cabin near the wardroom. They graduated from hammocks and now slept in wooden cots with a mattress. All commissioned officers dined off china, drank from real glasses and used silver cutlery. Phillip was fortunate to have started his service in 1755 with Everitt, who saw him through to promotion to the first rank of a commissioned officer six years later. Then, as if he had done his duty, Everitt returned to England, leaving the new lieutenant to impress others under fire. Phillip was now available for promotion and advancement as and when any officers senior to him succumbed to death or disease or were themselves promoted. Hence the naval toast – 'To a bloody war or a sickly season.'

In January 1762 the *Stirling Castle* joined an invasion force consisting of eighteen ships of the line, 120 support vessels and 12,000 soldiers. She formed part of a renewed assault on Martinique, which the British had tried and failed to take in 1759. Phillip's ship bombarded the French batteries at Grand Anse d'Arlet and joined in the disembarkation of troops. Her role was modest but the expedition was successful and by February the French Governor had surrendered. In the meantime in London, while the British naval and military forces savoured their success in finally wresting Martinique from France, grander and more dramatic plans were being laid.

On 4 January George III, the 23-year-old grandson of George II, decided on war with Spain. The reason was the emergence of a secret pact between France and Spain that bound Spain to side with France against Great Britain if no peace had been concluded by May 1762. Within days, in a quiet room off Whitehall overlooking Horse Guards Parade, the Cabinet was deliberating over an ambitious strike force against Spain. London was soon full of talk about a mighty secret expedition against an undisclosed target. The target was Havana, Cuba, securely located within a deep harbour and guarded at its entrance by a mighty fort known as El Morro. It was Spain's strongest naval and military base in the Americas. It was also the most strategically important of all her colonial possessions. For all the Spanish galleons and treasure ships carrying the riches of Mexico, Peru and Columbia came to Havana before crossing the Atlantic on the return voyage to Europe.

Lord Anson, the old sailor who had circumnavigated the world in the 1740s and was now First Lord of the Admiralty, proposed a *coup de main* of astonishing boldness, to which the Cabinet agreed. The plan involved a surprise attack on Havana from an unexpected direction, with an expeditionary force of over 16,000 men carried in ships to be assembled from squadrons scattered right across the northern hemisphere – in British home waters, the Caribbean and off North America. It would be a race against time: the ships would be unable to operate off the coast of Cuba once the hurricane season resumed, and after a few weeks on land the army would be susceptible to a grim range of tropical diseases.

Once the decision to attack Havana was made, preparations were undertaken with impressive speed and efficiency. The meeting point for all the ships of the invasion force was off Cape St Nicholas, the western headland of the island of Hispaniola, immediately to the east of Cuba and separated from it by the Windward Passage. The *Stirling Castle* was part of this force, being one of eleven ships in a squadron commanded by Augustus Hervey. Her captain was now James Campbell. In late May 1762, the 156 transport ships carrying the huge expeditionary force of soldiers and slaves gathered together with the line-of-battle ships off Cape St Nicholas. In total, there were approximately 200 ships, formed into seven divisions. George Pocock, the son of a naval chaplain, was the admiral in charge of the fleet and George Keppel, the Earl of Albemarle, was the military commander. His two younger brothers, Commodore Augustus Keppel and Colonel William Keppel, also had prominent roles.

The most daring feature of the plan – intended to ensure the element of surprise – was the direction of approach to Havana, which is situated on the north coast of Cuba. Virtually all navigators approached from the west, after taking the southerly passage where there was deep and open water, rounding the western end of Cuba at Cape St Antonio and beating east into the prevailing wind along the north coast to Havana. The plan devised by Anson and Pocock was one of the riskiest feats of navigation of the age. They chose to approach from the east, through the virtually uncharted Old Bahama Passage along the north coast, where white surf marked the outer edges of the channel and the shallow aquamarine, cobalt and peacock green waters were perilously cluttered with reefs, shoals, cays and islands. And there were no reliable pilots available to assist. All that could be done was to send a frigate ahead to survey the channel, accompanied by cutters, tenders, longboats and other small craft to take soundings and mark shoals and hazards by anchoring over them or mooring buoys where reefs and cays broke the surface. At night, they lit bonfires on the coral. For a week this unwieldy secret flotilla edged forward warily, searching for a safe passage. Meanwhile in the troop transports, there was apprehension, not only of the enemy they would soon meet, but of the climate and tropical disease. As the tension and wariness of the men increased, Pocock and Albermarle attended to a matter of first importance. On the flagship they drew up and signed a long agreement providing for the allocation of prize money among the soldiers and sailors. After the two commanders and their deputies received their share, nine-fifteenths would be divided between the rest according to rank. If the expedition succeeded Phillip would be entitled to a lieutenant's proportion of the fabulous riches of Havana.

Phillip saw much action during the siege, both on board the *Stirling Castle* and also on shore. The coastline was rank and reeked of unseen pestilence. The heat was oppressive and the English had little resistance to the diseases carried by the ubiquitous mosquitoes. One army major lamented that the hardships sustained by his troops in their approaches against El Morro were 'altogether inexpressible'. Officers were distraught as men in their hundreds died on their feet or lay sick and diseased in makeshift hospital tents. The navy was called upon to assist the troops by providing cannon, which were landed three miles from El Morro and dragged by seamen along the foreshore on wooden sledges and then inland over steep rocky tracks. Over the same tracks, soldiers and slaves hauled ammunition, rations and kegs of water. The supply chain was congested, and the situation became worse as men stumbled and fell by the wayside, spilling the contents of their boxes, repeatedly halting the line.

It was debilitating and dangerous work, to which the seamen were unaccustomed. And as they approached the fortress, hauling the heavy cannon, they came under fire from Spanish guns occupying the high ground. On 21, 24, 25 and 26 June, Phillip noted that the *Stirling Castle* 'sent ashore a Lieut and forty men to hawl Cannon'. The work continued through July as more and more naval guns and seamen were sent ashore. On 8 July the *Stirling Castle* provided more 24-pound cannon. Increasingly, the naval detachments were employed 'in assisting to raise new batteries and in carrying up to them cannon, ammunition and stores'. Pocock reported to the Admiralty that 'the seamen have performed extremely well at the batteries … They have been commanded by Captains Lindsay and Douglas and lieutenants of the men-of-war'. Phillip was one such lieutenant, and must have witnessed much distress. The effect of yellow fever on such large numbers of exhausted and diseased men was indescribable. Almost nothing could be done for them. They were mired in filth and stench. Their diarrhoea and dysentery went unattended. The eyes of the dying protruded from their sockets; their blackened tongues lolled out of their mouths; their jaws clenched and their teeth rattled. In those pre-Crimea days, a century before Florence Nightingale's reforms, there was no adequate nursing and very little treatment. For the men who collapsed, the prospect of salvation was negligible.

At sea, there was another side to the siege. In early July, Phillip's ship joined in the memorable but ultimately unsuccessful naval bombardment of El Morro led by Augustus Hervey. At dawn on 1 July, four warships approached the fortress – the *Dragon*, the *Cambridge*, the *Marlborough* and the *Stirling Castle*. Their object was to use naval firepower to breach the castle's walls but things went wrong from the outset. Hervey's ship, the *Dragon*, lost her anchor when weighing. Phillip's ship, the *Stirling Castle*, lagged astern. When the ships opened fire, it soon became obvious that while the Spanish guns could not be lowered sufficiently to hit the ships' hulls, the British guns could not be elevated high enough to strike above the thick lower walls of the fortress. The booming guns and thick smoke created a mighty spectacle, recorded for posterity in the stirring painting by the British marine artist Richard Paton, but the bombardment achieved little. After three hours Commodore Keppel ordered the ships to withdraw. Only slight damage was inflicted on El Morro but the *Dragon* was badly damaged, the captain of the *Cambridge* was killed and there were many casualties among the crews. Hervey was so incensed by the conduct of Campbell, Everitt's successor as captain of the *Stirling Castle*, that he ordered that he be court-martialled. He was confident, he explained to Keppel, that Campbell's officers, presumably including Phillip, would 'represent his conduct more than adequately'. As Campbell was dismissed from the service, their evidence must have been damning. The whole incident is a curious echo of Phillip's experience at Minorca when Byng disgraced himself. This time, however, Phillip had the opportunity to do more than write to his sister.

On 13 August 1762, the Spanish finally surrendered Havana. But as Samuel Johnson sadly observed, it was 'a conquest too dearly obtained'. Approximately 8000 British soldiers and sailors had died from exhaustion and tropical disease. Relatively few were killed by the enemy. The riches that fell to the victors, or at least to those who survived, were stupendous. When accounts were finally settled, more than £737,000 was distributed in prize money. The Keppel family fortune was made by the campaign. And the victory was crowned by the capture of nine seaworthy Spanish ships of the line, on one of which – the 70-gun *Infanta* – Phillip returned to England. The siege was said to have been 'the most difficult since the invention of artillery'. In terms of lives lost, it was certainly one of the most costly. For Phillip, the campaign provided him with invaluable experience of artillery and ordnance and brought him into closer contact with Augustus Hervey. Their paths had already crossed at several points before Havana – 'off Minorca; in the Channel and the Bay of Biscay; at Martinique and Cap Francois' – and would do so again.

The peace settlement, ratified in February 1763 by the Treaty of Paris, represented an unparalleled triumph for Great Britain. The war had been her most successful of all time and she emerged as the world's leading colonial empire. When the treaty was finalised, the geopolitical landscape was set for the second half of the eighteenth century. The colonial world, as far as it was known, was effectively divided between Great Britain and France, Spain, Portugal and the Dutch republic. Great Britain owned Canada, and for the time being retained its thirteen colonies on the eastern seaboard of North America. It controlled the Mediterranean through Minorca and Gibraltar. It was the most powerful colonial force in India, especially at Calcutta, Madras and Bombay, and it had the lion's share of the fertile islands of the West Indies. The Dutch controlled the Cape of Good Hope and most of the East Indies, where they were the 'market maker' for the export of spices and dominated the trade from Java, Sumatra, the Moluccas and Borneo. The Portuguese not only owned Brazil but also Goa on the west coast of India and a series of colonies along the sailing route to the East, including the Azores, Madeira and the Cape Verde Islands in the North Atlantic; Angola on the South Atlantic coast of Africa; and Mozambique on its Indian Ocean coast. Spain dominated Central and South America, except for Brazil. Not only did it own Cuba, Mexico and the whole of Central America, but also those South American countries that we now know as Columbia, Venezuela, Chile, Peru, Ecuador, Paraguay, Bolivia and Argentina. In North America, Spain also possessed much of what is now Texas and New Mexico and in the western Pacific, it controlled the Philippines.

France, which had suffered most from the Treaty of Paris, still vied with Britain in India and the Caribbean but mourned the loss of its North American possessions, which once extended from the distant north of Canada through Quebec, Montreal, the Great Lakes and as far south as New Orleans. On the Indian subcontinent, it retained Pondicherry, south of Madras as well as the strategic Indian Ocean islands of the Seychelles, Mauritius and Reunion. And on the west coast of Africa, it still had a number of settlements that served an important role in the supply of slave labour for its sugar plantations on the French islands of the Caribbean, of which Martinique and Guadeloupe, which were returned to it, were the most prized.

Hand in glove with this division of colonial riches was the Atlantic slave trade, of which Great Britain was the leading exponent. The European colonies in the Americas and the Caribbean were economically slave-dependent. Their sugar and tobacco plantations and their gold and diamond mines could not be exploited without the powerfully built West African slaves who were shipped in their hundreds of thousands, and eventually millions, across the Atlantic. From Angola slaves were sent directly to Portuguese Brazil. And from Ghana, Senegal, Gambia and elsewhere along the west coast of Africa, British and French merchants despatched slave ships groaning with their tightly packed human cargo destined for plantations in the West Indies and North America. These plantations in turn produced the sugar and coffee that fuelled the salons and coffee houses of London and Paris – in which, ironically, Enlightenment aspirations, liberal ideas and rationalist thought politely fermented.

CHAPTER 3

GENTLEMAN FARMER

Phillip's first marriage, his period as gentleman farmer in Hampshire, his separation, the years spent in France and the beginnings of his career in espionage

The *Infanta* reached Portsmouth harbour in March 1763. Within days of Phillip's arrival, the Navy Board confirmed his appointment as a lieutenant and shortly afterwards his name was entered in the half pay register – not belonging to a ship, but paid two shillings per day. Phillip was able to add his share of the prize of Havana – £138.10s – but this was insufficient for him to make his way in the world or to establish himself as a gentleman. In the eighteenth century, a half pay lieutenant, even with a small prize, was usually a man in need of financial support. Phillip needed a wife, with means.

The postwar London to which Phillip returned was the same London to which James Boswell, the contemporary diarist and Samuel Johnson's constant companion, had arrived a few months earlier. Great Britain was 'master of the world' and stood at the apex of its international success. Among London's middle classes, the pervading atmosphere was one of unbridled confidence, prosperity and ostentation. The daily culture was one of sensation and celebrity, gossip and dispute, and relentless optimistic materialism. Affluent society was driven by fashion, consumerism and aspiration. Getting and spending was everyone's business. London pulsated with excitement. There was then 'no place on earth more tempting ... to a young man who longed to become somebody'. The prosperity was matched by an exorbitant national debt compounded by the cost of the war, but no one seemed concerned. Even the modestly affluent regarded a slice of serpentine river and a wood as an absolute necessity 'without which a gentleman of the smallest fortune thinks he makes no figure in his country'. There were 60 newspapers published every week, endless ephemera to buy and almost limitless amusements to enjoy. The pursuit of pleasure reached new levels of secular respectability. What the Victorians later regarded as debauchery was, if not de rigueur, almost commonplace. Calvinist taboos against indulgence were ignored and killjoy denunciations of the pleasures of the flesh were derided. Puritans were objects of ridicule. Boswell's 'whim' with an unidentified lady on Westminster Bridge would not have been an isolated incident.

The leading feature of female fashion was a low-cut and very conspicuous *décolletage*. The spirit of the age was so pervasive that even in the north of England a Whitby collier was named *The Free Love*. Nowhere was the morality of these times better exemplified than in the pleasure gardens of Vauxhall and Ranelagh and at the masked balls, ridottos and assemblies that were a feature of the social calendar. These were places to promenade – to see and be seen. In May 1769, a ridotto at Vauxhall Gardens was attended by more than 10,000 people. On his way there, Horace Walpole found himself stuck in a traffic jam of horses and carriages for an hour and a half. These libidinous gatherings were a mere front for assignations on a mass scale. Their *raison d'être* was orchestrated heterosexual sociability. Their size ensured a high degree of indecent ribaldry and licentiousness. Women were at the forefront and an air of feminine boldness was pervasive. Ladies were assumed to possess strong sexual appetites and the right to their gratification. Masquerades, with their strict anonymity and erotic frisson, promoted an abandonment of decorum – refined nonetheless, and accompanied by an atmosphere of gaiety, beauty and splendour. Older women were emboldened to seek young men of stamina and men of all ages routinely sought women of fortune. One of the chief dilemmas of the age was whether to marry for money or for love. Somewhere in this beguiling social context, at some point between March and July 1763, Phillip the half pay lieutenant found himself a wife. Her name was Charlott.

Charlott Tybott was born to a farming family in the county of Montgomery in North Wales in 1722. She married Arthur Phillip at St Augustine's Church in Watling Street on 19 July 1763 – four months after his return to England. On the day before the wedding she and Phillip signed a prenuptial agreement to which Charlott's sister Mary Thomas was also a party. The bride was 41. Her groom was just 24, a little pudgy and almost penniless. It was not Charlott's first marriage. In 1759 she had married John Denison but less than ten months later he was dead. Denison had been a prosperous cloth and wine merchant of King Street, Cheapside who owned property in Lambeth and farming lands in Dorset. Upon his death, Charlott inherited his vast estate including a £120,000 trust fund with the Bank of England. It was equivalent to about £200 million in today's money – depending on the methodology adopted.

Charlott Denison may have been an attractive prospect for a half pay lieutenant but the evidence suggests that she was no *ingénue*. She was either financially knowledgeable or was well advised, or both. Denison's will was proved and its validity established on 4 June 1760. Although it took another four years for the executors to compile and file a full statement of the assets of his estate, Charlott would have known from that date that she had become extremely wealthy. Paradoxically, the acquisition of significant wealth could be a serious problem for women of marriageable age in the eighteenth century. Georgian property law stipulated that upon marriage, the husband became entitled to all his wife's property, income and belongings. Male suitors with base motives were a social hazard. It was relatively common, at least at the wealthy end of the social scale, for women in Charlott's fortunate position to enter into a deed of settlement vesting in favour of trustees the legal title to their property. These deeds were protective measures – in substance prenuptial agreements – entered into either generally or in anticipation of a specific marriage. They prevented a putative husband from taking ownership of his new wife's property when the wedding vows were concluded.

In an age when the length of a person's rent-roll determined their attractiveness, marriage and settlement were bywords for negotiation and bargain. If a woman of means did not settle her property on trustees to remove it from the clutches of her future husband, she would at least usually require a marriage agreement carefully delineating the respective rights and property entitlements of bride and groom. Sometimes these prenuptial agreements would oblige the husband to secure annuities in favour of the wife or persons nominated by her. More often, the husband would disclaim his entitlement to the bride's property. By these means, or a combination of them, Charlott's marriage agreement entered into on 18 July 1763 – on the day before the wedding – protected her fortune.

The newly married couple lived fashionably. Charlott owned a residence at Hampton Court and she and Phillip appear to have resided there with all the trappings of wealth befitting someone of her financial standing – silver, china plate and carriages being much valued by the Georgians. In the 1760s Hampton was an Arcadian idyll on the Thames about fifteen miles upstream from the City of London. Henry VIII's palace stands there and in 1764 George III appointed Capability Brown as its master gardener. It was a residential area that attracted the well-to-do and the genteel. It was also David Garrick's world. Garrick was not only a famous actor and theatre owner but he was pre-eminently a leader of fashion. And he was one of the most well-known residents of Hampton. The locale conformed to the most romantic ideals of the eighteenth century. The paintings by the neoclassical artist Johann Zoffany, of Garrick and his family reposing on the sloping lawn running down to the river depict all those elements that were considered necessary for civilised living – a natural vista, a meandering stream and a home in the classical style.

In 1764, in accordance with the custom of the time, Charlott and Phillip had their portraits painted. The artist was George James, who had returned to England from Italy in 1760 and whose portraits, like so many others of the period, were in the style of Thomas Gainsborough. Charlott's portrait shows a fine-boned, elegant woman with low-cut bodice and slender waist. Her appearance is demure and youthful, her bearing gentle but upright. Her unblemished complexion is pearl white across the bosom and faintly coloured in her cheeks. She is a picture of controlled femininity and possibly of circumspection. Her chosen background reflects the romanticism of the age – a sky of Canaletto blue, light scudding cloud and the distant prospect of a grand house elusively concealed. In the foreground, prominence is given to her silver gown in shimmering silk edged with gold brocade and lace embroidery. Her regal, dusky pink cape is gathered at each shoulder by a bejewelled clasp and her tiara, with its substantial pearl drop as its centrepiece, sits ritually above her forehead. As was the fashion, her *décolletage* is unadorned, flat and cut as low as decency permitted.

Phillip's portrait conveys a different image. The newly married lieutenant appears somewhat jowly, even plump, and a little sallow. He wears a navy-coloured coat with gold braid and buttons, a style that was popular with naval officers. His shirt and ruffles appear to be of white linen, possibly of cotton. His solitary concession to fashion is a tangerine-coloured waistcoat edged in gold. It contrasts distinctively with the stark white of his shirt and the deep navy blue of his jacket. Somewhat portentously, he holds a chart, presumably naval. Behind him, the sea stretches limitlessly to the horizon.

The background sea of Phillip's portrait could not have reflected his life at Hampton Court, where there are no vistas of the sea. It is presumably aspirational, redolent of the view of the English Channel seen from the South Downs of Hampshire and Sussex. The Hampshire countryside, within an easy coach ride of Portsmouth, was a place where naval officers congregated in peacetime as gentlemen farmers. In about 1765 Phillip and Charlott came to Lyndhurst in the ancient New Forest. Their farm was known as Vernals. The road running past the door led to the Channel port of Lymington. Michael Everitt was not far away in Portsmouth. The tithe survey suggests that Vernals was a substantial establishment, consisting of a house, farm offices, garden and shrubbery, as well as 22 acres of adjoining pasture. Phillip diligently carried out the role and responsibilities of a country gentleman and became one of the parish's Overseers of the Poor. He also expended large amounts of his wife's capital. Some years later, the *London Observer* reported that while at Lyndhurst Phillip spent £2000 of his wife's money 'principally in domestic disbursements'. He also expanded their land holdings, acquiring a property known as Glass Hayes where the Lyndhurst Park Hotel now stands, another known as Black Acres or Blackacre and a third known as Coleman's. The term 'Blackacre' is a legal euphemism, coined by the Elizabethan jurist Lord Coke and still used as part of the arcana of the law to describe unnamed or fictitious estates in land. It may well have referred to the fields lying between Vernals and Glass Hayes.

The country Phillip farmed was moist, green countryside, shaded by trees of oak and beech, 'acquiescently fertile with the faithful tillage of hundreds of years'. The shaggy New Forest ponies that are indigenous to the area caused some degradation of the soil but in the main the land was deep-soiled and benign. The farming was gentle and the evenings peaceful. Most landowners kept horses, cattle, sheep, poultry and pigs on small holdings. Phillip was assisted in his rural endeavours by a man named Henry Dodd. The male farm workers were mostly ploughmen, carters, shepherds and horsemen; their major responsibilities were caring for the draught animals. The women carried out the lighter tasks associated with the household. They made cheese, managed the poultry and tended to the vegetable garden where they grew chard and spinach, swedes and turnips, onions and leeks, potatoes and carrots, cabbage and beetroot. In the orchard, the mainstays were apples, pears and quinces. Rural England was then a leisurely, well-mannered society: gentlemen raised their hats to one another; labourers touched their forelocks to their masters – and especially to the squire and his lady. In the rating book for the parish of Lyndhurst, Phillip was described as a substantial inhabitant and was accorded the status of 'Esquire'. With the accretions he added to Vernals, he had become, at a young age, the respectable squire of a considerable farming estate.

But Phillip's time as a gentleman farmer in the New Forest ended badly. And it may never have been the bucolic bliss that he and Charlott presumably wished it to be. The years 1766–68 happened to be tumultuous years for the rural community of southern England and the West Country. Harsh winters, record heavy snowfalls and flooding spring rains ruined crops and led to prohibitive prices for staple products. In the parish of Selborne, 30 miles to the east of Lyndhurst, the curate Gilbert White recorded that on one day the temperature was fourteen and a half degrees below freezing 'within doors'. He said that there was 'reason to believe that some days were more severe than any since the year 1739–40' – a winter when the Thames was frozen over from Christmas to February. In 1766–67, the winter hardship caused hunger and rioting in market towns in Devon, Somerset, Wiltshire and Hampshire. And at one stage, 3000 troops were sent in to quell looting and attacks on food stores. We do not know how Phillip's daily life and farming routine at Vernals were affected, but it is clear that by 1768 a great unhappiness had descended on the married couple. Phillip's life as a country gentleman was coming to an end.

In the eighteenth century, England was the only Protestant country in Europe without a specific divorce law. Germany, Scandinavia, the Netherlands, Scotland and even some of the English colonies in America all permitted divorce on grounds including adultery, impotence and desertion. Henry VIII had the opportunity to introduce a divorce law, and was encouraged to do so by several clerical advisers, but he did not grasp the nettle. Instead, he had his marriages to Catherine of Aragon and Anne of Cleves annulled. Divorce or annulment was not necessary in the case of his other wives. For the vast majority of English couples death was the only means of release from a miserable marriage. But there was another means for the well advised and well to do. Deeds of separation, drawn up by Chancery lawyers acting on behalf of the husband and the trustees of the wife – as she had no legal status – became widespread. They could provide for the division and settlement of matrimonial property, and even for the repayment to one party of monies expended by the other during marriage. These deeds were necessarily consensual and were ineffective without the cooperation of both parties. And of course they had no legal effect on the existence of the marriage, so that neither could re-marry while the other was still alive.

After six years of marriage, Phillip and Charlott concluded a formal 'Indenture of Separation' on 22 April 1769. It seems that the fatherly Michael Everitt supported Phillip in this dark time, for he was one of the signatories to the document on Phillip's side. The deed recites that Phillip and Charlott had 'lately lived separately and apart' – something which seems to be confirmed by the fact that Phillip resigned from the office of Overseer of the Poor at Lyndhurst during the previous summer and was replaced by a William Lake. The language of the deed contains the usual obscurities of which lawyers are so fond, but in essence, Phillip renounced any title or claim to 'all and every the Household, Goods, Plate, Chair, Horses, Furniture, fixtures and things whatsoever then in the possession or Use of the said Margaret Charlotte Phillip or in or about her Dwelling House or Place of abode at Hampton Court in the County of Middlesex and also all her Wearing Apparel, Jewels, Diamonds, Watches, rings and ornaments of her person'. But that was not all. Phillip had come into the marriage with nothing, but left with a continuing financial commitment to secure several annuities in favour of persons nominated by Charlott. This was a burden that was to dog him for more than twenty years until Charlott's eventual death and his release.

What caused the marriage to break down remains a matter for speculation. A newspaper later reported that 'some circumstances occurred which induced [him] to wish for a separation' – suggesting that Phillip may have been more wronged than wronging and may have sought the separation. He does appear to have acted honourably – the same newspaper reporting that he made enough money in the immediately succeeding years to pay his estranged wife what he had spent of her fortune. And he secured the annuities that Charlott stipulated. But what he did in the years following his separation, and how he made his money, are matters of mystery. These were his lost years in France.

In September 1769, a few months after the separation, Phillip obtained permission from the Admiralty to go to St Omer in Flanders. In fact, apart from a short period of service as the fourth lieutenant on the *Egmont*, Phillip spent most of the next five years on the continent at St Omer, Lille and St Amand les Eaux – towns of north east France that were central to the linen and wool trade. He seems also to have been at Toulon, France's principal naval base on the Mediterranean. The Admiralty records suggest that the purpose behind Phillip's extended sojourns in Flanders was for the benefit of his health. Indeed, the combined effect of the failure of his marriage and the loss of his wife's very substantial resources may have left Phillip feeling sickly, but the explanations appearing in the Admiralty records probably concealed the truth.

St Omer and Lille were not Flanders health resorts. They were textile trading towns in one of the most densely populated and urbanised regions of northern Europe. All of the region's principal cities – Bruges, Ghent, Ypres, Lille, Brussels and St Omer – had risen to prominence through international trade and the manufacture and sale of textiles. Nearby in Hainault, the small town of St Amand les Eaux had a reputation for its natural waters but in the eighteenth century its importance lay in cloth manufacture, and the local waters were essential to power the mills. The three towns (St Omer, Lille and St Amand les Eaux) are in close proximity to each other, connected by river and canal and beyond to the Channel port of Calais at the Strait of Dover – the gateway to English trade in the 1760s and 1770s. It is inconceivable that Phillip passed his time in those Flanders towns merely tending to the rejuvenation of his health. If that were his true object, there were better places to go.

The region's prominence in the textile trade provides a further clue as to Phillip's true activities. Charlott's first husband John Denison had been a prosperous cloth merchant. His business and connections are unlikely to have vanished upon his untimely death, and Phillip would not have been human if he were not naturally interested in the subject matter of his wealth. Phillip would later demonstrate that he was acquainted with the cloth trade – showing a keen interest in the cultivation of cochineal, the insect that is the source of the brilliant red dye that was essential to the eighteenth-century cloth trade. And courtesy of Michael Everitt, he had acquired a personal and professional connection with John Lane and his merchant banking firm Lane, Son & Fraser, which combined trade with banking and finance.

Phillip's time in Flanders between 1769 and 1774 is the period when he is supposed to have made enough money to repay Charlott what he had spent of her fortune. While we cannot be certain how he made this money – if it is true – we do know that St Omer, Lille and Hainault were not places of rest and recuperation. They constituted an axis of trade and commerce, with a heavy emphasis on linen and wool. And through marriage and circumstance, Phillip appears to have been well positioned to profit from the cloth trade. Mercantile connections like those with the Lane family would have been valuable to someone in Phillip's position. When this is added to John Denison's past commercial pedigree, and the spirit of the times, it would be surprising indeed if Phillip was merely resting in Flanders. The trade in linen and wool suggests the answer but the picture is shadowy.

Phillip's activities were not confined wholly to the cloth trade during these years. He still held the rank of fourth lieutenant, to which he had been appointed in the West Indies. When a Spanish force of more than

1000 men in five frigates took the British settlement of Port Egmont in the Falkland Islands in June 1770, a crisis erupted – British forces mobilised for war and Phillip returned to England in anticipation of conflict. In November he joined the *Egmont*, a 74-gun ship of the line, and for the next few months led a press gang in London. Augustus Keppel, under whom Phillip had served at Havana, was to lead the fleet if war were declared. However, in January 1771 an unsatisfactory compromise between Britain and Spain was reached, leaving for future resolution – and continuing dispute – the sovereignty of the islands that the Spanish called '*las Malvinas*'. As the need for recruitment dissolved, Phillip re-joined his ship, which gradually worked her way round from the Thames estuary to Spithead, from where he left her. His name was once again entered in the half pay register and in August he returned to Flanders to resume whatever activity had first drawn him there. The fact that he had returned to England because of the prospect of war against Spain, and had served for seven months until that prospect fully receded, tends to put the lie to the statement in the Admiralty records that in August 1771 he was going to Lille in Flanders 'for the benefit of his health'.

It is even less likely that the genuine reason for Phillip's third stint in France between July 1773 and August 1774 was 'for the recovery of his health'. In 1773 Lord Sandwich was the First Lord of the Admiralty and Augustus Hervey was the 'Naval Lord' – a serving naval officer on the Admiralty Board. Phillip was known to Hervey, especially from the siege of Havana, where he had served with distinction under his command. In mid 1773, there was considerable consternation and alarm in London at reports that the French were aggressively rebuilding their navy at Toulon. British state papers are replete with official correspondence recording the anxieties of ministers and public officials. Whitehall was in urgent need of intelligence concerning France's military intentions. In July, the Secretary of State requested the Chargé d'affaires in Paris to 'constantly attend to what is passing in the French ports, and lose no time in transmitting the earliest intelligence of what comes to your knowledge'. It may not have been a coincidence that in the same month, Phillip sought approval from the Admiralty to go to France for a third time. Hervey was one of the Lords of the Admiralty dealing with the alarm. He would have been aware of Phillip's request, quite probably conferred with him and may well have engaged him.

The Admiralty records in 1773 state that Phillip was going to St Amand les Eaux for 'the recovery of his health'. In truth, it appears more likely that he went to Toulon. A later remark by Phillip provides a clue as to where he may have been. In the mid 1780s when Phillip was undoubtedly engaged in professional espionage at the French naval base at Toulon, he reported that the French arsenal was 'superior to what it was when I saw it before the War'. His observations of Toulon 'before the War' could only have been surreptitious, for British naval officers were not welcome, to put it neutrally, at French naval ports. And we now know that from 1774 until 1784 Phillip was elsewhere engaged and could not have visited Toulon. The concern about the French naval build-up in 1773, the relationship between Phillip and Hervey and the fact that in July of that year Phillip sought and obtained permission from the Admiralty to go to France for a further twelve months, suggest that his earlier observations of the French arsenal at Toulon were likely to have been during the 1773–74 alarm. As a naval officer, with a discreet manner, fluent in French and German, and who had been living and travelling in France almost continuously since 1769, Phillip would have been a particularly suitable choice to carry out covert observations at the French naval dockyard at Toulon. The undisputed fact of his later espionage activities in 1784–86 suggests his secret life may have commenced at this time.

There is one more aspect to Phillip's lost years in France. In the book *Adventures and Recollections of Colonel Landmann*, published in 1852, the author GT Landmann explains that one summer in the 1790s his father paid him a short visit and there had 'the unspeakable pleasure of meeting his oldest and most intimate friend, Captain Phillip of the Royal Navy'. The author's father was Isaac Landmann. Like John Lane, Isaac Landmann was a similar age to Phillip. And he was of German origin. Landmann was the Professor of Fortification & Artillery at the Royal Military Academy, Woolwich from 1777 to 1815. But Phillip's relationship with him probably originated in the early 1770s when Landmann was attached to the École Militaire in Paris during a period that overlapped with Phillip's years in France. While in Paris, Phillip may have attended Landmann's well-publicised lectures. At a professional level at least, Phillip and Landmann would have had a natural affinity and much to offer each other. They certainly had mutual interests. One of Landmann's specialities, the science of fortification, included the manner of attacking and defending places and the use, conduct and direction of mines. His other speciality, the theory of artillery, included the doctrine of projectiles applied to gunnery and the principles on which ordnance and their carriages were constructed.

No practical experience of artillery and fortification could have been better than Phillip's participation in the siege and reduction of El Morro – 'the most difficult since the invention of artillery'. And at the time there was no more pre-eminent teacher of the theory of artillery than the renowned Isaac Landmann in Paris. It is probably no coincidence that after Phillip's return from France, Augustus Hervey enthusiastically promoted his credentials as a very good naval officer who combined theoretical knowledge with much practical experience – *'le Theorie avec beaucoup de Pratique'* as he quaintly described it. Hervey would have been well aware of the likely sources of Phillip's theoretical and practical knowledge – the former gleaned from Isaac Landmann and the latter obtained firsthand at Havana. And in the next decade, Phillip acknowledged his artillery experience, referring modestly but probably disingenuously to his 'own little knowledge as a field engineer'.

CHAPTER 4

MERCENARY

Phillip's service in the Portuguese navy, his secret charts and his surveillance of the South American coastline

Whatever the truth about Phillip's espionage activities in France in 1773–74, or the origins of his friendship with Isaac Landmann, by August 1774 he was back in London, deep in negotiation with Augustus Hervey about another assignment, involving more leave of absence, this time in service with the Portuguese navy. The two persons who were primarily responsible for this career move were Hervey, who encouraged and facilitated it, and Lord Sandwich, the First Lord of the Admiralty, who approved it.

The immediate cause of Phillip's service in the Portuguese navy was the war in South America between Spain and Portugal known as the Third Colonia War (1773–77). That war eventually led to the creation of the Republic of Uruguay, but the origins of the conflict can be traced to the Treaty of Tordesillas in 1494. Before then, Portugal and Spain divided the known world between them according to a line drawn by Pope Alexander VI down the centre of the Atlantic 'one hundred leagues west of the Azores or Cape Verde Islands'. New lands discovered to the west of that line belonged to Spain while those to the east belonged to Portugal. Under this Papal division, the bulge of South America would have been awarded to Spain. But by 1494, Portugal had discovered that part of the South American mainland now named Brazil. The Portuguese King therefore had good practical reasons to argue that the line of demarcation should be adjusted to the west, and in 1494 the Treaty of Tordesillas prescribed a new line 370 leagues west of the Cape Verde Islands, ensuring that Brazil would become Portuguese territory.

But this arbitrary line did not resolve all differences. To start with, there was constant disagreement about where precisely the line ran. Not only was the precise length of a league a matter for debate, but there was no consensus about the starting point in the Cape Verde Islands – the most westerly island or the most easterly? There was also no consensus about the particular parallel of latitude along which the measurement should be made, or even a precise way of calculating it. Unsurprisingly, there were constant boundary disputes in places where political or commercial advantage outweighed other factors.

One source of constant disagreement, of invasion and counter-invasion, was Colonia do Sacramento on the north shore of the Plate estuary – a hundred miles west of Montevideo and almost opposite where Buenos Aires now stands. Colonia was actually to the west of the line, in Spanish territory. But in 1680 the Portuguese boldly annexed it and founded an outpost there that was an invitation to trouble. For the next 100 years Colonia was the 'apple of discord' between the two Iberian nations. It was also a place in which Britain had a vested interest. For Colonia, part trading post and part Portuguese convict colony, was a foothold with access to Spanish markets in South America. And the Plate estuary was the confluence of three great rivers – the Paraguay, the Paraná and the Uruguay. Silver, cattle and hides were shipped down these rivers and slaves shipped upriver to the Spanish mines and agricultural enterprises in the hinterland.

For these reasons, Colonia became an important location for illicit trade with Spanish merchants. Whitehall connived at the trade, and even encouraged it. In 1761 the British ambassador reported that among the goods brought back by the Portuguese Rio fleet 'there are 4,000,000 cruzadas in silver, the produce of the trade at Nova Colonia in the river of Plate. This silver the government has ordered to be conveyed with the greatest secrecy not to give umbrage to the court of Spain'. And a few years later, when it was thought that the actions of the Portuguese prime minister were endangering British commerce at Colonia, the same ambassador said, 'The clandestine trade carried on … in the Brazils with the Spanish colonies, so very advantageous and profitable to this nation, will be infallibly lost … Consequently the consumption of British manufactures at Buenos Aires, and in the Spanish colonies adjoining the Colonia do Sacramento in the River of Plate, will be considerably lessened and diminished.'

Britain's commercial interest lay in the continuance of Colonia in Portuguese control, as a base from which its clandestine trade with Spanish merchants might continue. If Spain took control of Colonia, British access would be denied and its valuable trade diminished. Access to South American ports was already extremely difficult. Spanish colonies were strictly off limits, and the Portuguese jealously guarded their Brazilian ports against all comers including Britain, and especially at Rio de Janeiro. In 1768 during the visit of the *Endeavour* to Rio de Janeiro, the Viceroy of Brazil forcefully explained to Captain Cook that although British ships were permitted to enter Portuguese ports in Europe, Asia and Africa, access to Portugal's ports in the Americas was prohibited 'because on the contrary follows the ruin of our Commerce'. Only foreign ships requiring repairs or provisioning were permitted entry.

In late August 1774, at Hervey's behest, Phillip attended on Pinto de Souza, the Portuguese ambassador in London with a letter of introduction. It was an official letter, written by Hervey on behalf of the Admiralty, extolling Phillip as a '*très bon officier de Marine*' and adding that although he was a lieutenant he well deserved a command. Hervey had become known as the 'hero of Havana' after the Seven Years War and was well known in Lisbon. History now remembers him more famously as 'the English Casanova' whose published journal sets forth with startling frankness his amorous encounters with the ladies of the Mediterranean. His conquests included 'princesses, marchesas, countessas, a Portuguese royal duchess, the wife of the doge of Genoa and several nuns'. He and Lord Sandwich were significant figures within the Admiralty and both were members of the Society of Dilettanti.

When the diplomatic protocols were complete, the Portuguese King José was quite convinced by the recommendations of Hervey and Pinto de Souza. His Minister for Marine and Colonies, Mello e Castro, relayed an offer from Lisbon that was passed on to Phillip and Hervey as his patron and proposer. The offer included a captain's commission at double the remuneration received by Portuguese officers. Phillip's additional request for half pay when on the Portuguese retired list was too ambitious and was politely refused – Portuguese officers did not retire so long as they were able to serve. This was a highly satisfactory outcome from Phillip's perspective but Hervey went further still, revealing the strength of his patronage by reiterating to the ambassador that Phillip's pretension was to be a captain of a ship of the line which, he added deftly, 'in England, makes a great difference'.

Portugal had been an ancient ally of Britain ever since the fourteenth century, when English archers on their way to the Crusades helped overthrow the Castilian assault on the Portuguese throne. But during the 1760s tensions over access to trade in South America had led to a hardening of the relationship. Since at least 1767 Britain had begun to contemplate and prepare for the possibility of war in both Spanish and Portuguese America. Phillip's role would enable him to satisfy the administration's demand for information on South America, information that it had been seeking to obtain through more formal channels for some time. In 1767, for example, the British ambassadors to Spain and Portugal both received almost identical instructions relating to South America. The instructions to the latter were marked 'most secret'. Those to the former were as follows:

> apply yourself with diligence to procure the most exact information concerning the strength and weakness ... the state of the military and fortifications, the points which may

be supposed to be most open to attack, and the inclinations which may be expected to be found in such provinces in such cases. You will, likewise, procure any maps or charts of those provinces, either manuscript or printed, together with plans of their towns and fortifications, which you will transmit to us together with your opinion how far each is to be depended upon.

In the parlance of espionage, Phillip would be a sleeper. He would acquire the confidence of the Viceroy, make charts of the coastline and investigate the country's economic production. In his role in the Portuguese navy, he would have an unparalleled opportunity to survey thousands of miles of the South American coastline, to make observations and to report on the economies and policies of the Spanish and Portuguese colonies along the coast. His experience equipped him to assess accurately the effectiveness of fortifications, the layout of harbours and all the points of vulnerability. And his suitability was enhanced in other ways. Phillip was a linguist, intelligent and well travelled; he was subtle and discreet, his judgement measured. These qualities endeared him to the Portuguese Viceroy in Brazil, the Marquis of Lavradio, who later revealingly said of Phillip:

He gives way to reason and does not, before doing so, fall into those exaggerated and unbearable excesses of temper which the majority of his fellow countrymen do, more especially those who have been brought up at sea … saying what he thinks, but without temper or want of respect.

The Lords of the Admiralty, including Sandwich and Hervey, formally approved Phillip's service in the Portuguese navy on 1 December 1774. After final arrangements were made with the Portuguese, Phillip sailed for Lisbon from Falmouth, Cornwall on the regular packet service carrying the Post Office mail destined for British embassies, colonies and outposts in the Mediterranean. At that time, Lisbon was a famously sensual and complex city, unlike any other in Europe. The literary grand dame Rose Macaulay described it as 'a city of churches, convents, gold and jewelled ornaments, abject poverty, negro slaves, priests, friars, sumptuous processions, superstition, squalor, corruption, women eating sweets and playing guitars at windows, and rich galleons sailing in from Brazil'. The past successes of Portugal's merchants and navigators had ensured Lisbon's place as one of the great cities of the age and one of the undisputed capitals of Europe's overseas trade. Although its dominance of the Asian trade routes had declined with the rise of the Dutch and English East India companies in the seventeenth and eighteenth centuries, Portugal's South American territory was vast and rich. And Lisbon itself was uniquely placed to prosper because it was the *entrêpot* through which all riches of Brazil were funnelled before they were exported throughout Europe.

On arrival at Lisbon, Phillip was promoted to the rank of captain and the terms of his appointment, including his double pay, were recorded in a commission from the King. On 25 January 1775 a public announcement was made that he had been granted permission to go to Salvaterra de Magos, the royal hunting lodge 30 miles up the Tagus River. This was unusual but Phillip was a prize recruit. History does not record what Phillip did at Salvaterra, what entertainments he witnessed or what passed between him and the Portuguese monarch, but it would not be the only time that he received a royal audience before embarking on a major undertaking.

By April Phillip was in Brazil. Rio de Janeiro had recently become the centre of colonial administration and the seat of the Viceroy, the Marquis of Lavradio. Its most distinctive physical feature then as now was its harbour – then the finest in the known world. The headlands at the entrance to the harbour were guarded by the fortresses and batteries of Sao Joao at the base of Sugarloaf and Santa Cruz beneath Papagaio Peak. These headlands were like sentries, beyond which the unfolding expanse of Guanabara Bay stretched for twenty miles.

The cultural atmosphere that Phillip encountered in Rio de Janeiro in 1775 was different from that which he had known in Protestant northern Europe. The indigenous Indian peoples and the African slaves were easy converts for the Jesuit missionaries. And the Portuguese colonialists, remote from the security and worldliness of home, were intensely pious. A pervasive religiosity, even more fervent and confronting than in Lisbon, marked out the local society. The bells of the churches sounded morning, noon and night. Religious images, statues and icons were ever present. And at each intersection in the city stood a pole on which hung a crucifix or saint's image before which passers-by genuflected. Away from the crowded streets, behind the shutters of the private homes in which the colonial administrators and the wealthy merchants lived, there was the usual contrast. In his elegant chambers in the Viceroy's palace, Lavradio hosted regular meetings of the Scientific Society. And there was always the opera to attend. In

Phillip's case, there was also a new language to learn and within twelve months, he spoke and wrote Portuguese fluently.

Lavradio was a cultivated man who took an immediate liking to Phillip. He was no doubt encouraged by the recommendation from Mello e Castro that Phillip brought with him. The Minister for Marine and Colonies announced that he had received from London 'conspicuous information concerning Phillip's intelligence, ability and character, in which together he excelled all other of his countrymen recruited'. The source of this information was probably Hervey. Mello e Castro added that Phillip was an officer in whom Lavradio could confide, even suggesting that he might be retained in Rio de Janeiro for the constant benefit of his advice. Lavradio did not take long to form his own favourable assessment. Within weeks of Phillip's arrival, he described him in official despatches as a man of honour, one willing to conform to Portuguese custom and to respect authority. In turn Phillip handled himself wisely, lavishing praise on the enthusiasm and discipline of the city's volunteer guard and giving Lavradio the impression of being interested in continuing permanently in the service of Portugal.

Colonia do Sacramento is 1200 miles south of Rio de Janeiro. In 1775 it was a garrison outpost of about 2000 officials, soldiers, sailors, assorted smugglers and villains, free settlers and *degredados* – convicts, exiles, deportees, deserters and other undesirables who could be compelled to serve as soldiers. Apart from the Governor's house, the church, the hospital and the barracks, there were few amenities. And as the Spanish progressively tightened their blockade, the port, commercial houses and surrounding farms almost all ceased to function. At Buenos

Aires on the southern side of the Plate estuary, Spanish soldiers and sailors waited for the signal to cross the water and overwhelm the tiny Portuguese outpost. On the northern side, in the hills behind Colonia, Spanish cannon was trained on its fortifications.

Not surprisingly, morale was low and food was scarce. By 1775 the settlement had become entirely dependent on intermittent supplies of food and firewood brought in by sea. In April, the Governor Da Rocha complained bitterly to Lavradio that Colonia was not a fortified refuge but 'a prison and the ruin of its inhabitants'. To make matters worse, the hardships and dangers were exacerbated by the usual rigours and unpleasantness of such a place. Whether as a soldier or convict, a term of seven years' service at Colonia was regarded as a punishment. Against the odds, Portugal sought to hang on grimly to this outpost. And almost continuously from October 1775 to December 1776, Phillip was the commodore of the Portuguese naval forces at Colonia. Initially this involved only his ship the *Pilar* but during 1776 the frigates *Nazaré* and *Nossa Senhora da Gloria* were also within his command. In August 1776, Lavradio reported that the presence of the three vessels 'had effectually put a stop to all the acts of daring which [the Spanish] had practised'.

Phillip kept the peace, kept the sea lanes open and kept the Spanish commanders in check. Unrestrained, the Spaniards would swoop on Portuguese fishing and trading vessels, seizing goods and slaves and diminishing fragile Portuguese resources. Like coastal patrol operations all over the world, the circumstances required firmness and sound judgment, and occasionally courage. He was determined to extract good manners from the masters of Spanish vessels and to have them conform to the naval conventions that usually prevailed among civilised nations. More than once he showed that he was not afraid to act, opening fire on the enemy and causing great anxiety to the nervous Portuguese Governor Da Rocha, who feared Spanish reprisals. Phillip gave the forlorn community time, but the situation could not last.

In December 1776 Phillip was ordered to leave Colonia and rendezvous with the Portuguese squadron at Santa Catarina. Colonia was soon overrun by Spanish forces. Governor Da Rocha was predictably blamed, taken back to Lisbon, tried, convicted and sentenced to death. Fortunately for him, or perhaps unfortunately, his sentence was commuted to transportation to a convict settlement – from which he never returned.

These were momentous times. Britain was now embroiled in a costly revolutionary war with her thirteen American colonies and was unlikely to assist Portugal while engaged in her own dire conflict in North America. Spain took advantage of Britain's distraction and conceived a massive offensive against Portugal in South America, to be spearheaded by a naval and military strike at the island of Santa Catarina and at Colonia on the Plate estuary. In late 1776, an armada of over 100 ships assembled at Cadiz under the command of Admiral Casa Tilly and more than 10,000 Spanish soldiers and 8500 seamen soon sailed for South America. The proposed name of the territory that Spain intended to capture was 'La Plata'. The overall military commander and the would-be Viceroy was Zeballos.

On 17 February 1777, the pitifully small Portuguese squadron, which had sailed from Rio de Janeiro, and which Phillip had now joined from his station at Colonia, waited in one of the bays in the channel between Santa Catarina and the mainland. Soon a seemingly endless line of Spanish ships entered the channel. Within three hours there were so many sails that it was impossible to count them. The natural inclination of Robert McDouall, the commodore of the Portuguese squadron, was to avoid combat. He sought refuge in delay, fearing the decimation of the Portuguese squadron, and called a council of war, summoning all his captains to the *Santo Antonio* for a colloquy. But before it convened he privately consulted Phillip, who was horrified by McDouall's prevarication. In their conversation Phillip 'made every effort to induce the Chief to attack the enemy'. And on returning to his ship Phillip wrote to McDouall, 'imploring him for the sake of his own honour and that of the Nation, not to refrain from attacking them'.

The council of war did not take place until 20 February – three days after the first sighting of the enemy's fleet in the channel. The Spanish transports and men-of-war had already begun to unload their troops; McDouall had lost those most valuable military advantages – speed and surprise. Although Phillip's initial sentiments were heroic, the circumstances now called for sober realism. The Court Instructions from Lisbon required protection of the fleet, but the viceregal orders of Lavradio ordered the enemy be attacked. Six of the eight captains favoured protection of the squadron, stating that if they attacked the superior Spanish fleet, the Portuguese squadron would be destroyed. Only one captain, de Melo, favoured attack, expressly analysing the discrepancy between the orders. Phillip wanted to vote with de Melo, but it appears that McDouall showed him only the Court Instructions to protect the fleet and not Lavradio's order to attack. In Phillip's written opinion, unlike that of de Melo, he quotes from the former and does not mention the latter, of which he appeared to be unaware.

But it was now too late and the initiative had been lost. As Phillip observed, the enemy was now free of the encumbrance of its transports, and a strong fleet at anchor has a great advantage over a weaker one that goes to attack it. He concluded, reluctantly it seems, that there was now 'no advantage to be gained by disobeying His Majesty's orders'.

In the aftermath, Lavradio condemned the captains who voted against attacking the Spanish fleet but excused Phillip. He believed that Phillip had not been shown the full set of orders and had been tricked by McDouall into changing his mind – which he had only done, reported Lavradio, 'out of the great deference he renders to the orders of his superiors'. In the result, the Portuguese settlement at Santa Catarina was sacrificed with little resistance and Colonia followed soon afterwards. McDouall departed, taking his squadron north to Rio de Janeiro without offering a shot. It was no doubt out of a well-honed sense of self preservation that he sent Phillip ahead to deliver the distressing news to Lavradio. Later, when McDouall faced the Viceroy, Lavradio said that 'his countenance betrayed the anguish which every man ought to feel under such circumstances'.

Fortunately, the embarrassing capitulation at Santa Catarina and Lavradio's fury were soon followed by a naval success in which Phillip played a leading role, further raising his esteem in Lavradio's eyes, and for which he was amply rewarded. The result was the capture of a considerable prize – Spain's newest battleship, the *San Agustin*, a 70-gun ship of the line carrying 550 men and first-class munitions and accessories. Lavradio gladly appropriated her to his squadron and she became distinctly his most powerful ship. The *San Agustin* had not been ready to sail when the Spanish armada had left Cadiz and only followed a month later with despatches intended for the military commanders at Santa Catarina. At Montevideo the despatches were transferred to a fast-sailing guard ship the *Santa Ana*, which ran ahead. On 14 April 1776, in the coastal waters off Santa Catarina, the *Santa Ana* failed to identify the approaching Portuguese squadron and was duly intercepted and boarded and her crew taken prisoner. Her captain, Salcedo, threw the despatches overboard, but by one torturous means or another, the existence of the *San Agustin* following behind was extracted and the Portuguese waited, ready to pursue and attack when the unsuspecting battleship appeared.

On 19 April the *San Agustin* was sighted by the lookouts on de Melo's ship the *Prazeres* and on Phillip's ship the *Pilar*. On the signal to beat to quarters, nervous energy would have rippled through the crews on both ships; the gun decks would have been cleared for action and sail added for greater speed; all obstructions including animals had to be removed and bulkheads and partitions dismantled to provide maximum space for loading and firing the guns. Phillip and de Melo were eager for the hunt and soon outdistanced their colleagues. The *Prazeres* was larger and faster than the *Pilar* but the *San Agustin* was more powerful than both of them. Phillip pushed his vessel forward even though a frigate could expect to be heavily outgunned by an enemy battleship. When de Melo was within range he fired, inflicting some damage but from a considerable distance. Phillip then came up with his frigate and was allowed to get closer to the Spanish battleship.

The Spanish thought the *Pilar* was one of their own, unable to convince themselves that such a weak vessel, carrying only 26 guns, would venture to attack a 70-gun line-of-battle ship. Their mistake was soon followed by unmitigated surprise. On Phillip's command, her guns were run out through their ports and a broadside was poured into the *San Agustin*'s masts, rigging and sails. Phillip's intention in aiming high was to retard the *San Agustin* sufficiently to allow de Melo to approach and for the two of them to engage her. But the damage was insufficient and the Spanish ship fled, crowding on more sail. For the remainder of the day, the two Portuguese vessels chased their Spanish quarry through the southern Atlantic waters. When night fell, the eyes and ears of hundreds of experienced seamen would have strained for telltale signs of the enemy's presence, but darkness enveloped them both and the *San Agustin* escaped.

The next morning, as dawn broke and the pale light of early morning gradually strengthened, the *San Agustin's* crew were dismayed to find that their ship was floating within sight of the Portuguese squadron. The ensuing battle was marked by confusion and fright on the part of the Spaniards, and lasted just an hour and a quarter before the Spanish captain surrendered.

Lavradio showed his appreciation to Phillip by appointing him to command the captured *San Agustin*, which patrolled in the waters of the Southern Atlantic from late May until August 1777, when a truce was declared. Phillip appears to have slipped easily into his new role as captain of a 70-gun line-of-battle ship. A large ship of the line such as the *San Agustin* was a community of many hundreds of men, for whom the captain was patron and protector; the 'first after God' in the eyes of the seamen; responsible for their health, wealth and welfare and ultimately accountable for everything and everybody on his ship. Although he was assisted in the day-to-day operation of the vessel by the master and the ship's officers, the captain's conduct set the tone and his decisions could make the difference between a successful voyage and failure; between mutiny and harmony.

Phillip was never brutal, erratic or unfair, and on the *San Agustin* it no doubt helped that he had learned the Portuguese language. He had, it seems, the confidence of his superiors and the respect of his seamen. At the end of Phillip's service in Brazil, Lavradio's estimation of his character as a man and as a naval officer was unqualified. He reported to his superiors in Lisbon that Phillip was 'very clean-handed; an officer of great truth and very brave'. Truth and bravery are clear enough but the expression 'clean-handed' requires some explanation. It was a common form of praise in the eighteenth century, connoting honesty, trustworthiness, frankness and the absence of any behaviour that could be described as sneaky or underhanded.

Conveniently, the respect and freedom accorded to Phillip meant that whenever possible during assignments and between naval engagements, he was able to survey the coastline, draw maps and charts and observe the fortifications. And he investigated the commerce and structure of Portuguese and Spanish colonial settlements, keeping a weather eye on opportunities for the expansion of British trade. He displayed an interest in the manufacture of cochineal, the red crimson dye that was so essential to the eighteenth-century cloth trade, and acquired a detailed knowledge of the Brazilian diamond mines and their production processes. There was plenty of time to pursue these private and sometimes secret interests – four months in Rio de Janeiro when he first arrived in 1775, fifteen months at Colonia from 1775 to 1776 and nine months when he returned to Rio de Janeiro after the truce of August 1777. And considerable time also to enjoy the company of the urbane Lavradio.

Phillip's strategic observations were extensive. He gathered details of Spanish settlements and made charts of the coast between Rio de Janeiro and Colonia. He noted three good harbours along the coast 'where ships that wanted to wood and water, would find only a few settlers'. He drew charts of the harbour at Rio de Janeiro, another of Rio Grande and a third of Colonia including the adjacent shores and islands. He made enquiries about the Spanish settlement of Maldonado and the more substantial base at Montevideo. The former, he explained, had many defects and in any event was too shallow for large ships. Montevideo, he thought, was the key to control of the whole estuary. As well as military and strategic observations, Phillip investigated Spanish commerce and transport networks, reporting later on the trade to hinterland cities such as Cordoba, Santiago and San Miguel and the length of the journey to each of these places. At all times, however, it seems clear that his principal focus was on the fortifications and defences, and the vulnerability to attack of the Spanish towns and harbours along the Atlantic coast. He noted elliptically that the Spanish at Montevideo and Buenos Aires lived in constant fear of attack by bands of Indians.

Phillip's investigations and coastal observations established the groundwork for future British aspirations in the Plate estuary. In the coming years, all of these matters of geography and strategic vulnerability along the South American coastline would form part of Phillip's discussions with the administration – first with Lord Sandwich at the Admiralty and subsequently with Evan Nepean and his superiors at the Home Office. By his thorough investigations and his careful charts, Phillip soon made himself indispensable on any question concerning the Spanish settlements on the Atlantic coast of South America. He knew that charts and maps were intensely political; that they were 'keys to empire' and a 'way to wealth'; and that they provided opportunities for international advancement and professional success. In due course, when he later made his charts available to Lord Sandwich for use by ships of the Royal Navy and the East India

Company, he politely requested that his authorship be acknowledged – so 'that I may reap the Credit and Advantage that will naturally arise from them'.

International advancement meant new territories, new markets and the diversification of British trade. In the second half of the eighteenth century Great Britain's overall objective was worldwide economic suzerainty. The cochineal trade had returned great riches to Spain since the Spanish conquistadors first arrived in the new world and discovered the Aztecs using it. The name 'cochineal' is derived from the Latin word for scarlet – *coccinea* – which describes the indelible crimson dye obtained from the crushed bodies of a particular scale insect of Mexican origin. Spain soon created a near-monopoly in cochineal dye, which was in great demand in the European cloth trade. It had a symbolic and practical significance for the British as it was the colour source for the distinctive red coats of their soldiers and marines – the 'lobsters' as the navy disparagingly called them. In fact, brilliant dyes of scarlet and crimson had been sought-after symbols of power and authority since at least Roman times. If you were 'born to the purple' in ancient Rome, you belonged to the aristocracy. Cochineal insects produced a red of such intensity that nothing else could match it. All else was drab, dull and brown in comparison.

In Brazil the Portuguese sought to develop their own industry. Lavradio even established a cochineal plantation on the island of Santa Catarina from where host cactus plants with their accompanying cochineal insects were despatched to other parts of Brazil. While he was at Colonia, Phillip showed a keen interest in the commercial potential of this insect. So much so that he obtained specimens from the plantation established by Lavradio at Santa Catarina and bred cochineal insects in his ship's cabin, closely observing their cycle. He thought that their potential for breeding in the West Indies would be for 'the great advantage of the nation'. Sir Joseph Banks, the President of the Royal Society, was later so encouraged that he even developed plans for a cochineal industry in New South Wales.

The diamond trade was another well-recognised source of national wealth. Phillip investigated Portugal's diamond mines and production processes at Minas Gerais, a mountainous area approximately three hundred miles north of Rio de Janeiro. His journal contains detailed accounts, as well as what he describes as 'Views of the Diamond Works ... taken on the spot'. For centuries, vast supplies of rough diamonds had been shipped from India to Lisbon and London, from where they made their way to the skilled cutters, polishers and diamond bourses of Antwerp. In the mid eighteenth century, as the Indian diamond mines neared exhaustion, the Portuguese uncovered a new source of supply in Brazil. So important did Brazil's mineral wealth at Minas Gerais become, that the seat of Portuguese colonial government was moved from Bahia to the port city of Rio de Janeiro, closer to the diamond mines. From there the mineral riches of Minas Gerais were shipped to Lisbon. In the official regulations, the diamond-producing district was described as the 'Forbidden District', but it seems likely that with Lavradio's acquiescence Phillip had access to it. We know because of Phillip's journal of his Brazilian years. All that now remains of the journal is a five-page extract held at the William Clements Library at Ann Arbor, Michigan, which details a precise knowledge of the diamond works and production processes, as well as the work of the African slaves on whose labour the mines depended.

The slaves were a nagging and ever-present feature of the social structure in Brazil, which was a true slave society to which nearly five million slaves would eventually be imported. In Europe, however, the morality of slavery had commenced to be a topic of discussion. Slavery and the slave trade still flourished but the slow progress towards emancipation was underway, although in Brazil it would be more than a century before abolition was achieved. While Phillip was serving in South America, the heavy Portuguese dependence on slave labour was everywhere apparent. In Rio de Janeiro alone, slaves represented approximately half the total population, and the percentage was much higher on the plantations and in the mines. Many of the slave dealers in Rio de Janeiro lived and carried on business in large houses on Rua Vallongo. Each house had a 'ware room' in which three or four hundred slaves 'were exposed for sale like any other commodity'. The merchants lived on the first and second floors while the slaves were lodged on the ground floor. There they were prepared to be sold by being 'shaved, fattened, and if necessary, even painted' to give the illusion of health.

At the diamond mines, the slaves were an expendable and replaceable means to an economic end, as they have always been. There were so many thousands of slaves that it was possible to use their labour to turn whole rivers, manually redirecting watercourses to expose the diamond-bearing silt and rock. Phillip describes the slaves working in line after line, bent over with pick and hoe, raking, sifting and washing the gravel, searching for the elusive gemstones, all the time guarded by superintendents who used their whips freely. As one fell, another would take his place. Phillip's contemporaneous observations seem objective, eschewing judgment. But he would have been too discreet to record criticism of the Brazilian administration. It seems inevitable, however, that during his Brazil years he began to develop personal views about the institution of slavery.

When the war between Spain and Portugal in South America concluded, Phillip's Portuguese service also came to an end. The August truce was followed on 1 October 1777 by the Treaty of Santo Ildefonso. Among other things, the treaty provided for Spain to return Santa Catarina to Portugal, Portugal to relinquish Colonia and the *San Agustin* to be handed back to Spain. In the aftermath, McDouall was relieved of his command and despatched on the first ship to Lisbon to be court-martialled for his part in the loss of Santa Catarina. Phillip was given the command of McDouall's flagship, the *Santa Antonio*, in which he returned triumphantly to Lisbon in August 1778. He had decided to resign his Portuguese commission and rejoin the Royal Navy. The war front in which Great Britain was engaged was broadening as France had now taken the side of the rebellious American colonies, and Spain would soon follow. Phillip's final Portuguese assignment consisted of escort duty across the Atlantic with a convoy of merchant vessels. On board the *Santa Antonio* he carried five locked chests lined with velvet, each brim-full of diamonds destined for the Portuguese treasury. Phillip was merely a courier of the diamonds, but it seems likely that at this time he acquired and brought back from Brazil the 'Duncombe diamond', which he gave to Charles Slingsby Duncombe, who in turn bequeathed it to Phillip on his death 'as a token of my lasting friendship'.

CHAPTER 5

CAPTAIN OF THE *ARIADNE*

The American Revolutionary Wars including Phillip's secret missions in South America, his special operations on the Continent and the convict legend

The rebellion by the thirteen American colonies that began in 1775 spawned another global war – a war that was not settled until 1783. Just as the Seven Years War had done, the American Revolutionary Wars soon stretched across much of the world and were waged simultaneously in Europe, the Mediterranean, North America, the West Indies, the Indian subcontinent and Africa. France, Spain and the Dutch republic all secretly provided supplies, ammunition and weapons to the American rebels, whose turning-point victory at Saratoga in 1777 would never have been achieved without covert

French assistance. In March 1778 France entered the war openly and in the next year Spain followed suit. France's intention was not only to help the Americans win their independence but also to capture British territory in the West Indies. It constantly threatened an invasion of England, aiming to encourage the Royal Navy's ships to stay in the English Channel, while aspiring to take Britain's Caribbean colonies.

In April France dispatched the Toulon squadron to North America but retained a more powerful fleet at Brest. The Admiralty responded by sending half of its ships of the line to the West Indies while keeping back the remainder of the fleet to match the French squadron at Brest. In July at Ushant, the island that sits at the mouth of the English Channel and marks the north-westernmost point of France, the two fleets came together and the French inflicted considerable damage on the British. Admiral Keppel, who bore the brunt of the indignity, explained that the object of the French guns 'was at the masts and rigging and they have crippled the fleet in that respect beyond any degree I ever before saw'.

By the spring of 1779, a French invasion of England appeared imminent. In June, when Spain joined forces with France, it seemed certain. Their combined fleet in the English Channel numbered 66 ships of the line, while the Royal Navy could marshal only half that number. The threat of invasion was the most formidable that England had faced since the Spanish Armada in 1588. One commentator observed that there was 'great affright and terror in every part of the kingdom'. At Plymouth, many shopkeepers and their families fled inland. And a royal proclamation directed that all horses and cattle be driven from the coast.

In this war, unlike in the Seven Years War, Phillip would not participate in any of the major battles. The responsibilities given to him, initially by Lord Sandwich at the Admiralty, and later by Evan Nepean at the Home Office, would be more clandestine, reflecting his unique experience and his particular talents. But Phillip's first task was promotion. In Portugal's navy, he had held the rank of captain and commanded the best ship, but in Britain's navy he was still a mere lieutenant. And his patron Augustus Hervey had retired as a Lord of the Admiralty in 1775 and ceased to be influential. Despite a testimonial from his Portuguese service that described him as 'one of the officers of the most distinct merit that the Queen has in her service in the navy', Phillip could not assume that promotion and command would come easily or immediately. For in Great Britain's eighteenth-century navy, there were always 'many suitors and little to bestow' and many a talented junior officer would remain undistinguished.

For Sandwich, the distribution of promotion, employment and distinction was his most vexatious single responsibility. Nonetheless he had, it was said, a favourite type of sea officer: one who was able, hardworking, somewhat obscure and not closely linked with any obvious political rivals. Phillip fitted this description and wasted no time pressing his claims. In late 1778, on the final leg of his homeward voyage on the packet boat from Lisbon, he sighted more than 30 French ships sailing south from Brest. Immediately on the arrival of his coach in London, Phillip reported his observations to Philip Stephens, the Admiralty Secretary, announcing that he had returned to His Majesty's service and adding adroitly that he had most recently commanded the Portuguese *Santa Antonio*.

Having brought himself to notice, Phillip was suitably rewarded. On 9 October 1778, just four days after he arrived back in London, he was appointed as the first lieutenant of the *Alexander*, a 74-gun line-of-battle ship with a crew of over 600 men. For the next eleven months she cruised as part of the Channel fleet, sailing out to the western approaches to meet the threat from the combined French and Spanish navies. As first lieutenant, Phillip was the second in command – the highest-ranking officer below the captain and responsible for the ship's day-to-day operations. Of all the officers on a ship, the first lieutenant was the one subject to the crew's most constant scrutiny. They looked to him for his skill and professionalism because the safety of the ship often rested on his decisions. And they depended on his fairness, for among many other things, he devised the sleeping plan and determined how much living space each seaman would have and with whom he would share it. It was a saying among seamen:

> that every man's comfort afloat depended upon the kind of man a ship had for its first lieutenant, for that he was the Prime Minister of the small community over which the captain ruled as absolute Monarch, and as every measure and arrangement was to be carried out by him, it was better to sail with a bad captain and a good first lieutenant than to have the conditions reversed.

Phillip must have proved to be a worthy first lieutenant, for when the fleet returned to Spithead in September 1779, he was immediately promoted to the rank of master and commander. He was then 40 years old. His new rank was the navy's first position of independent command – effectively captain of a smaller vessel that was not rated. The rating system categorised all line-of-battle ships and frigates into six 'rates' that were nominally determined by the number of guns each ship carried. The first, second, third and fourth rates were the huge line-of-battle ships that carried between 50 and 100 guns. The fifth and sixth rates were the frigates. They were not 'ships of the line' and usually only carried between 24 and 36 guns. The non-rated vessels included sloops, brigs and fire ships. Phillip's first command in the Royal Navy was of the *Basilisk*, a fire ship. She carried eight guns and a crew of 45.

Fire ships were a permanent part of all eighteenth-century naval fleets and had been used since at least Alexander the Great's Siege of Tyre in 332 BCE. For understandable reasons, their command carried additional dangers and special rewards. When packed with explosives a fire ship could be used to devastating effect against a fleet at anchor. With the wind in the right direction, it would be cut loose and allowed to drift towards the target. If there were no wind, the crew would steer it towards the objective, before abandoning ship and escaping, all going well, in a small pinnace. If they were successful in destroying an enemy ship of over 40 guns, the crew would receive £10 each, and the commander had a choice between £100 and a medal with gold chain. Phillip's opportunity for derring-do, however, never arose. The *Basilisk* was too old and weak for immediate operations and required extensive fitting out and repairs to make her seaworthy. In fact, so much time was required to make the *Basilisk* seaworthy that after months of waiting, dockyard officials abandoned the ship in early 1780 as not worth repairing. Phillip's appointment was never consummated and the *Basilisk* did not put to sea under his command.

While Phillip waited for the *Basilisk* to be repaired, he took other steps to distinguish himself. On 5 September 1779, he wrote to Sandwich requesting permission to cruise as a volunteer on the *Victory*. We cannot be entirely certain that Sandwich acceded to Phillip's request. His name does not appear in the *Victory*'s muster book, although that by itself would not be determinative. If Phillip did serve on the *Victory*, it would have been an enviable experience for a man of his ambition. The *Victory* was the flagship of the Channel fleet; years later she would be Nelson's flagship at Trafalgar. The *Victory* was, in truth, a manoeuvrable floating weapons platform. She carried 100 great guns distributed across her three gun decks, the quarterdeck and the forecastle. The sheer weight of the largest of these great guns was enormous. But they were also a marvel of contemporary engineering. By the mid eighteenth century, foundries had begun to cast cannon in solid iron, without a barrel or bore hole, which would then be painstakingly drilled using a boring lathe linked to a horse-mill around which plodding horses endlessly circumvolved. The job could take weeks, but the result was a precisely machined barrel free of the usual imperfections that reduced the efficiency and accuracy of firing.

Phillip had an interest in naval ordnance but it was the *Victory*'s prestige and symbolism that must naturally have acted as a magnet for him. And if he did serve as a volunteer on the *Victory*, he may have come in contact with Evan Nepean, if he had not already done so. For there is a suggestion, of questionable veracity perhaps, that in late 1779 Nepean was the *Victory*'s purser. Nepean certainly served as a ship's purser, notably on the *Foudroyant*. In the coming years, he would become one of the most influential men in Whitehall.

Sandwich on the other hand had been First Lord of the Admiralty when Phillip was granted permission to travel to France during the 1773–74 alarm and again when Phillip took leave of absence to serve in the Portuguese navy in 1774. He was still there when Phillip returned from Brazil and continued in the position until the change of government in 1782. He was one of the dominant figures in the administration and was reputed to have been an excellent judge of men – and of himself. When Phillip came to know him, Sandwich was at the peak of his career. He presided over the whole of the operational strategy of the Georgian navy from the Admiralty building on Whitehall, a building that was constructed in 1726 as the first purpose-built government office in Britain. Symbolically, in the Admiralty Board Room, where the great discoveries of Cook were planned and Nelson's victories were later celebrated, the First Lord sat beneath a wind dial over a circular map of the world. The wind dial was connected to a weather vane on the roof. It informed the Sea Lords which way the wind was blowing, which in turn determined whether the fleet in the Solent could be ordered to sail. When a decision was made, the Admiralty's instructions were sent to the fleet by semaphore, relayed by teams of signalmen stationed on prominent points such as churches all the way to the Hampshire coast. By this means, a message from Sandwich at the Admiralty Board in Whitehall could reach Portsmouth in twelve minutes.

In March and April 1780, with the *Basilisk* unfit to go to sea and without a ship on which to serve, Phillip appears to have had the first of a series of private consultations with Sandwich. His euphemistic explanation was that private affairs took him to London. But it seems safe to assume that over a period of four weeks in the spring of that year, Phillip consulted Sandwich at the Admiralty, sharing his charts and his experiences of South America. Spain's recent entry into the war had generated renewed interest in the vulnerability of its South American possessions. In July Phillip wrote to Sandwich, reminding him of his promise that when an occasion offered he would be provided with 'an opportunity of getting what is due to me at Lisbon'. Pointedly, he added that service in any part of the world whatsoever would be agreeable to him. For the rest of 1780, however, there was no foreign service nor even Channel service. Phillip stayed in London, for at least part of the time with John and Eleanor Lane, from where he corresponded with Stephens, the Admiralty Secretary. His naval service was limited to light relieving duties for the captains of the *St Albans* and the *Magnanime* while their ships were being fitted out on the Thames.

January 1781 seems to have brought the reward that Phillip sought. During that month, he provided more private advice to Sandwich about the east coast of South America. He then disappeared until October. Significantly, his reappearance was promptly followed by his promotion to captain of the *Ariadne*. The inference is reasonable that his promotion was a reward for services rendered during these nine months.

There is a legend about Phillip that may have its genesis in these missing and undocumented months. According to the legend, when Phillip's ship's company and its cargo of Portuguese convicts were confronted with an epidemic of illness during a voyage across the Atlantic, Phillip persuaded the healthiest prisoners that if they assisted him in working the ship, he would in return represent their good behaviour to the Portuguese King. Not only was the voyage successfully completed and the prisoners subsequently emancipated, but they were also given small grants of land in Brazil. The provenance of this story may lie in the work Phillip did transporting troops, and possibly *degredados*, between Rio de Janeiro and Colonia during his Portuguese service between 1775 and 1778. But contemporary newspaper reports and respected historians speak uniformly of Phillip's trans-Atlantic transport of 400 criminals 'from Lisbon to the Brasils'. As Phillip's time during his service with the Portuguese navy is almost entirely accounted for, and there is no mention of any such assignment, or any time during which it might have occurred, it is likely that if there were a trans-Atlantic crossing with convicts, it occurred later and in different circumstances.

The evidence to support the legend is circumstantial but it is unlikely that the newspaper report is pure invention. The known facts are these. Throughout 1780 the Admiralty had been considering how Great Britain might most effectively wound Spain, which had joined in the war in 1779 on the side of France and the American colonies. In fact, the Spanish suspected an attack in South America and believed that Phillip would have command of any British expedition because of his known experience of Rio de Janeiro. Sandwich consulted Phillip in March and April 1780, no doubt discussing and reviewing with him the secret charts that Phillip had made of the South American coastline and harbours while serving in the Portuguese navy. By November 1780, the Cabinet had resolved to send a flying squadron to the Plate estuary under the command of Commodore George Johnstone. Its ambitious purpose was the sacking of the Spanish settlements at Buenos Aires, Maldonado and Montevideo and the capture of the Spanish treasure fleet. Advice was sought from Phillip and also from McDouall, Phillip's former commander in the Portuguese navy.

McDouall estimated the Spanish forces to be one line-of-battle ship, three frigates and 5000 troops. It is clear from later despatches that Phillip believed the Spanish forces were much weaker than that. The strategic objective of the proposal was the disruption of trade between Spain and Buenos Aires and the capture of Spanish bullion being transported from Peru and Chile around Cape Horn to Buenos

Aires. Before the plan could be implemented, however, there were complications as a result of the British declaration of war against the Dutch on 20 December 1780. This opened up a new front and as a result, the squadron's initial target became the Dutch-owned Cape Town. Only then, it seemed, would the squadron swing across the South Atlantic Ocean to the Plate estuary.

In January 1781 Sandwich called Phillip to London where his South American charts were again pored over. In his letter to Sandwich dated 17 January 1781, Phillip advised the First Lord that he had delivered sealed copies of the charts to his friend John Lane in Lombard Street. He clearly expected imminent orders, observing in his letter that 'it is probable that I may be call'd forth by your Lordship at very short notice'. At the time, the Portuguese were sending large numbers of recruits, including convicts and *degredados*, to India via Brazil. Johnstone's expedition sailed on 13 March but Phillip was not part of it and had probably already set off in January. At the Azores, Johnstone sent McDouall ahead to Rio de Janeiro, among other things, to enquire about a regiment of fusiliers 'being sent from Lisbon via Rio de Janeiro to Buenos Aires'. A fusilier was a common private soldier and the lowest rank of infantryman – the type that the Duke of Wellington would later describe as 'the scum of the earth … who enlist for drink'. Many of them were convicts and *degredados*.

This is where the legend about Phillip probably has its origin. It seems distinctly possible that Phillip may have sailed to South America ahead of Johnstone, transporting Portuguese troops or convicts. These were the fusiliers for whom McDouall was searching. If Phillip did do so, and if there were an outbreak of disease during the voyage, this would explain the legend and the later newspaper reports about Phillip's skill in handling convicts. The speculation gains credibility from the fact that Johnstone's initial recommendation was for 2500 troops, yet the Cabinet only agreed to 1000 troops. The need for additional troops was obvious and Sandwich may just have been sufficiently imperious to go about secretly procuring additional troops his own way, in league with Phillip and the Portuguese. The truth, however, is opaque.

In fact, circumstances conspired against Phillip. Johnstone's intended raid on the Spanish settlements in the Plate estuary never eventuated. The fleet under his command was mauled en route by a French squadron under Admiral de Suffren at the Cape Verde Islands and the planned attack on the Dutch at the Cape was abandoned. Instead of swinging across to South America, Johnstone sent the British troops onward to India and took his own damaged squadron to the safety of the harbour at Jamestown on the island of St Helena in the South Atlantic. For Phillip, this was a grand opportunity lost. Later reports confirm how ardently he felt about the intended raids on the Spanish settlements in the Plate estuary. On two subsequent occasions he expressed his regret, reiterating his keenness for the expedition and sighing for past disappointments, knowing that the Spanish forces had never been as numerous as McDouall had estimated. He later reminisced to Nepean with obvious feeling – 'You know how much I was interested in the intended expedition against Monte Video.'

Whatever Phillip had in truth been doing since January 1781, we do know that by October he was back in England and that early that month the Admiralty appointed him as acting captain of the *Ariadne*, a 24-gun frigate. In November he was confirmed in command of his ship and promoted to the rank of post captain. Promotion to the rank of post captain brought with it independence, prestige and the chance of wealth. There was no examination and seniority was not a determinative factor – just a good reputation for professional ability. Without it, even the well connected fared badly. The selection was made by the naval members of the Admiralty Board, who acted on recommendations and their own personal knowledge. In the case of ships on foreign service, the commander-in-chief of an overseas station might promote officers, subject to later confirmation by the Board. Officers distinguished in action were usually given priority, although no seaman, let alone the Admiralty Board, wanted 'a mere fighting blockhead without ten grains of commonsense'. That, in any event, was never Phillip's style.

When the *Ariadne's* fit-out was completed, she joined several squadrons patrolling in the Channel. Having already been a captain in the Portuguese navy, where he had commanded both a frigate and a line-of-battle ship, Phillip knew the responsibilities of leadership that were involved. He was the person responsible for the route the ship took, the food the men ate, the drink they were allowed and the discipline they received. If the men were fortunate, a bold captain might secure a 'prize' to be shared among them. On a well-run ship, united in the mutual experience of a dangerous profession, in which teamwork was essential to survival, and discomforts were shared, ties of personal loyalty to the captain often developed. If a captain were humane and successful, he generated trust and respect, even love, and men would follow him loyally from ship to ship.

On 30 November 1781 the *Ariadne* was ordered to proceed to the Elbe River to escort a transport ship bringing a detachment of Hanoverian troops to England en route to service with the British army in India. This would be a sensitive assignment requiring fortitude and flexibility, and Phillip's fluent German would be of undoubted assistance. The Elbe River meets the North Sea at Cuxhaven, a port town and a centre for shipping, shipbuilding and fishing. Its harbour was well known for its hazardous features; at low tide, its waters receded so far that the island of Neuwerk, several miles offshore, could be reached on foot. In winter the harbour froze, preventing the movement of inbound and outbound shipping and driving to pieces any wooden vessels still moored there.

George III was the third successive British Hanoverian monarch and the Elector of Hanover. Hanoverian troops were generally loyal to Great Britain and usually responded favourably to British requests for reinforcements. Among other engagements, the 15th and 16th Hanoverian Regiments were called upon in 1782–83 to serve under British command in India where the last distant battles of the American Revolutionary Wars were taking place against the French and Dutch. It was some of these troops that Phillip was to escort to England. But the assignment did not go smoothly.

Phillip reached Cuxhaven on 28 December 1781. It was late in the season and ice was expected at any moment. The transport ship that Phillip had been sent to escort was empty: the troops had mutinied and the harbour master had ordered her to be run ashore, out of the reach of the impending ice. Phillip moved swiftly to locate the troops, who had withdrawn to Otterdorf, and within 48 hours he had arranged with their commanding officer to embark them on his own ship, the *Ariadne*. He hoped to use his frigate to get the troops out of the harbour before it froze. But time and weather were against him, and the estuary filled with ice before he could act. As no wooden ship could withstand the inexorable pressure of the encroaching ice, the Cuxhaven pilots insisted to Phillip that he run the *Ariadne* into the mud to prevent her being crushed. They made clear that they would refuse to 'take any further charge of her if she remained at Anchor'. Phillip had no choice but to remove her guns and equipment and drive the *Ariadne* clear of danger. For the next two months, he waited out the winter in Saxony. He was not inactive, however, moving in influential circles and taking the opportunity to discuss the recruitment of German seamen for the Royal Navy with one of George III's Hanoverian Privy Councillors. When Phillip eventually returned with the Hanoverian troops in March 1782, he recommended to the Admiralty that it station an officer at Stade to recruit among the seamen of Hamburg and Hanover.

In the following months of 1782 the *Ariadne* cruised in the English Channel, patrolling along the southern coast and in the western approaches. Phillip brought on board a new lieutenant, Philip Gidley King, but then left his ship towards the end of summer to attend to 'private affairs' in London. Once again, Phillip was involved in consultations concerning possible intrigue in South America. The further occasion for doing so followed the change of government that occurred in March 1782. Sandwich retired at the Admiralty, Lord Shelburne became Home Secretary and Evan Nepean became his Under-Secretary. This was the beginning of Nepean's long reign of influence. Both Shelburne and Nepean maintained Sandwich's interest in attacking the Spanish in South America – and so did Thomas

Townshend (later Lord Sydney), who became Home Secretary in July when Shelburne moved to Prime Minister. Nepean naturally played a central role. Shelburne left a memorandum for Sydney listing matters requiring his urgent attention, including 'Preparations and Plans for W. India [Spanish America]. Expeditions require to be set forward – Major Dalrymple has a Plan against the Spanish settlements'.

Coincidentally, during August widespread reports emerged of insurrection by the native Indians and Creoles against the Spanish in South America. This seems to have been both the catalyst and the opportunity that Britain sought. On 13 August, Shelburne openly informed the Portuguese ambassador that Britain might try to capture the Spanish settlements on the Plate estuary and offer assistance to the rebellious Creoles and Indians against Spain. Phillip spent late August and most of September in London, again ostensibly on 'private affairs'. In reality he was in discussion about attacks on the Spanish settlements, offering private advice to the new administration about the Plate estuary and the strength of Spanish forces there. Just as had been done with Sandwich in 1780–81, Phillip's charts of the South American coastline were scrutinised. On this occasion, the consultations were not at the Admiralty but at the Home Office with Sydney and Nepean. These were the beginnings of a close relationship between the three men. And Shelburne, as Prime Minister, oversaw the proposal. In fact, Phillip was so extensively engaged in these consultations with the administration that by 25 September Augustus Keppel, who was by then the First Lord of the Admiralty, asked peevishly if he could have him back so that he could 'send him to his ship'. When Phillip eventually sailed downriver a few days later the Portuguese ambassador, aware of the latest intelligence, reported to Lisbon that there was good reason to suppose that Captain Phillip was going 'to investigate the situation in the River Plate'. Phillip's experience in Brazil was beginning to pay dividends, both for him and for the administration.

Keppel's inquiry as to whether the administration had finished with Phillip occurred on the same day on which the Cabinet, led by Shelburne, firmly decided to press ahead with the scheme to attack Spain in South America. One historian has referred to it as the 'Phillip plan'. The capture of some of Spain's South American settlements was seen as a means of breaking the impasse in the peace negotiations. On 26 September the Navy Board informed the Home Office that it would be necessary to have warships and transports, landing boats, artillery, ordnance and provisions including 'arms for the Chileans and presents for the Indians'. The expedition was known as the 'Southern Expedition' and its object was to 'give great alarm and probably do great Mischief in support of the Rebellion'. Not to put too fine a point on it, the British intended to foment an incipient insurrection in a foreign country as part of a wider diplomatic strategy. If all went according to plan, the expedition would eventually proceed to India and the East Indies to provide reinforcements of ships and troops to meet the French and Dutch threat faced by Admiral Hughes' India Squadron.

Progress was, however, slow. As events unfolded, anxiety about the urgent need for a swift increase in the naval forces in the East appears to have become the paramount consideration. The priority of the proposed attack on the Spanish settlements in the Plate estuary receded in importance. In November Nepean requested the Admiralty to prepare three line-of-battle ships and a frigate 'with all possible expedition'. Reserves of stores and provisions, and transports carrying troops, could follow later. Expedition, indeed haste, certainly seemed to be the order of the day. A few days before Christmas 1782, the Lords of the Admiralty ordered Phillip to hold himself ready for foreign service.

Two days later he was commissioned as captain of the *Europe*, a 64-gun line-of-battle ship, taking command a few days later and sailing on 16 January 1783. The squadron, under the command of Robert Kingsmill, consisted of the 74-gun *Elizabeth*, the 70-gun *Grafton*, the 31-gun *Iphigenia* and the *Europe*. The alacrity with which the expedition was despatched was counter-productive – winter conditions in the North Atlantic were never propitious for sailing.

CHAPTER 6

CAPTAIN OF THE
EUROPE

The American Revolutionary Wars in the East and Phillip's command of the *Europe*

The *Europe* was Phillip's first line-of-battle ship in the Royal Navy, something for which he had waited ever since completing his meritorious Portuguese service four years earlier. He was now 44, somewhat old for such an appointment, but more than ready to acquit himself. And his sense of the expedition's significance must have been reinforced by the urgency that accompanied his appointment as captain and the speed of the squadron's embarkation in mid winter. His charge was a third-rate line-of-battle ship with a complement of approximately 600 men. As a class, third-rates were not as large or as powerful as first- and second-rate vessels. They had fewer guns and only two gun decks, not three. But they were more numerous and more manoeuvrable than larger ships of the line and were often considered the optimal configuration.

In India and the East Indies, the war that had started as a rebellion by the thirteen American colonies had developed a distant and improbable life of its own. France's decision to help the American cause made its Indian territories and possessions a legitimate target. Within months of France joining the war in 1778, the British laid siege to the French port of Pondicherry and moved on French holdings on the west coast of India, including the key port of Mahé. When the French Admiral de Suffren was eventually despatched to India to redress the situation, the stage was set for a naval war between Great Britain and France in the Bay of Bengal. On four separate occasions in 1782, de Suffren's squadron and the British India Squadron under Sir Edward Hughes met in full battle – off Sadras on 17 February, Providien on 12 April, Nagapatam on 6 July and Trincomalee on 3 September. They would do so one more time, on 20 June 1783 off Cuddalore, unaware that by then the war had ended. Although he did not yet know it, this was the theatre of war to which Phillip was headed.

In late January 1783, when the violent gales and winter seas in the Bay of Biscay swept through Phillip's squadron, he lost sight of the other ships. The *Grafton* had lost her mainmast, the *Iphigenia* had sprung her bowsprit and Commodore Kingsmill's *Elizabeth* was in distress. Their captains, including Kingsmill, returned to England. The *Europe* pressed ahead alone. One seaman wrote subsequently, referring to Phillip, that 'our captain dreaded the idea of an order to return'. We will never quite know what motivated Phillip, but once he departed from Portsmouth, his return was a distant prospect. When he opened his first rendezvous directing him to Madeira, he did not know that approximately a week earlier at Versailles, the British government's emissary in Paris had exchanged peace declarations with the representatives of the new 'United States' for the mutual cessation of hostilities. The declarations were part of a general armistice between all of the belligerents except the Dutch republic, which held out until 2 September. The truce eventually led to the series of treaties that formally concluded the global war. Great Britain, France, Spain and the United States signed their treaties on 3 September 1783. The Dutch eventually signed a separate peace treaty on 20 May 1784. All of this passed Phillip by. Oblivious of the truce, he set his course for sun-drenched Madeira, the Portuguese island in the Atlantic 500 miles west of Casablanca. From the moment he separated from his squadron, and for the next fifteen months, while the western world readjusted to peace, he was alone at sea on the *Europe* – far from the intrigues of Whitehall, the demands of the Admiralty and the politics of the day.

Although the *Europe* was alone, Phillip was not without companions. He brought with him a number of followers including Gidley King, who had joined him briefly the year before on the *Ariadne* during her short period of Channel service. Gidley King was 20 years younger than Phillip and became his lifelong friend and admirer. The attractive aphorism describing Phillip as someone in whom 'is blended, which is not common with captains, the gentleman, the scholar and the seaman' has its origin with him. The ship's complement also included a number of captain's servants whose surnames suggest that Phillip exercised the same patronage that gave him a start 30 years earlier. There was a Harry Duncombe, presumably a relative of his friend Charles Slingsby Duncombe. There was a Thomas Lane, presumably a relative of Phillip's close friend and banker, John Lane. And there were family relatives too – Gayton (or Gaiton) and Herbert. Everitt's widow was Elizabth Gaiton Everitt and of course his mother's first husband was John Herbert.

It is also possible that a woman came on board in the Cape Verde islands for whom Phillip had a distinct partiality. The *Europe* had proceeded directly to Port Praia in the Cape Verde islands and never made the first planned rendezvous at Madeira. Philip subsequently provided a lengthy explanation to the Admiralty for the change of course – that the weather continued to be bad; that there were only two days when the lower deck ports could be open for fresh air; that scurvy had consequently appeared among the crew; and that a malfunctioning of the ship's compasses placed the ship 70 leagues off course. The passage to Port Praia does appear to have been difficult, for fresh water ran short, leading Phillip to put himself and his officers on two quarts of water a day, though he refused to ration the crew. However, the ship's boatswain Edward Spain said that Phillip had no intention of calling at Madeira 'lest there be orders there for us to return to England'. Whatever the reason, the *Europe* limped into Port Praia on 1 March 1783 where the ship was repaired as best it could and wood, water, food and livestock, including pigs, goats, fowls and turkeys, were taken on board. Also brought on board were four women, one of whom, a Mrs Brooks, is said to have captured Phillip's affection – and gained free access to the great cabin.

The presence of women on board fighting ships was not at all unusual in the eighteenth century. The practice was originally tolerated in peacetime but it continued during times of war too. Most common were the wives of warrant officers such as the gunner, carpenter or purser, all of whom had a higher status than the ratings. Like the boys and the captain's servants, women were often not entered on the ship's books and their status was unofficial. Sometimes they brought children with them and some even gave birth at sea. There was a supposed understanding that such women should be plain in order to avoid unwanted disruption. But any such restriction is doubtful and it certainly did not apply to senior officers who carried women to sea with them. Captains were in the best position to indulge themselves but other officers did so as well. And service in foreign stations naturally seemed to generate more liaisons. Augustus Hervey had a woman on board in the Mediterranean for some time. And in the North American station in the 1760s, Lord Colville showed a marked reluctance to investigate claims that his commanders were carrying 'lewd women' to sea. Invariably the practice was more likely on a distant ship, remote from an Admiral's eye. Providentially, this was the *Europe*'s situation when she called at the Cape Verde islands.

It is quite impossible, however, to be sure about Phillip's personal arrangements. No one refers to the woman except Spain, whose journal is not wholly reliable. He was a crew member of American origin who had been pressed into naval service and bore a grudge against Phillip. But his account cannot be entirely rejected. Unreliable witnesses more often embroider the truth rather than construct a wholesale fabrication. Elements of Spain's story, possibly much of it, may well reflect the reality. There was also something vaguely headstrong about Phillip's behaviour on this expedition, at least at the start. Perhaps it was simply overconfidence and impatience. He was, it seems, unwavering in his determination to complete the mission. When in the Bay of Biscay, prudence might have dictated that he return to Portsmouth with the rest of the squadron. And when, three months later, the *Europe* reached the harbour at Rio de Janeiro, he conducted himself with a distinct and uncharacteristic haughtiness – quite unlike the gentleman whom Lavradio had praised as not suffering from those exaggerated and unbearable excesses of temper for which English naval officers were renowned.

For reasons best known to himself, when the *Europe* entered the harbour at Rio de Janeiro, Phillip ignored the long-standing Portuguese regulations that applied at the port. Everyone knew that a visiting ship was required to stop off the fort at Santa Cruz and wait there for instructions. A boat would come out from the town with an official to ascertain the purpose of the visit. If permission were granted, the ship would be allowed to proceed to an anchorage under the guns on the island of Ilha das Cobras. Guard boats would then encircle the ship to ensure that no contraband changed hands. And a team of officials would then come on board to examine the captain, the senior officers, the ship's papers, the log book and the cargo, if any. Only when this process was complete would the Viceroy decide how long the ship should be allowed to stay and under what conditions.

Perhaps Phillip thought he was emulating Cook, who had a contretemps with the Portuguese authorities in Rio de Janeiro in 1768. Perhaps he thought that his illustrious record of Portuguese service entitled him to special treatment. Whatever the reason, he simply sailed past Santa Cruz and should not have been surprised when he was duly fired on. He then reacted like the excited Englishman that he was not, at least not usually. He had only himself to blame, but still protested vigorously and demanded satisfaction for the 'insult' to which he had been subjected. The language of his account of the incident seems almost laughingly inappropriate. He told the Admiralty that when the fort fired on him:

> I paid no attention, nor did I return the fort's fire; but after the ship was anchored, I waited on the Vice-King and informed him, that unless I received ample satisfaction for the insult offered to His Majesty's Colours, I should be obliged to fire on the fort.

When the commandant of the fort was sent on board 'to make an acknowledgement' to him, Phillip must have derived some satisfaction, but in truth he achieved little and could not avoid the usual interrogation. He duly answered all questions, co-operating willingly and avoiding further trouble. His failure to comply with the protocol was an error of judgment but any difference between him and the Portuguese officials was happily resolved and quickly forgotten. And in the end, he earned the enduring respect and friendship of the new Viceroy Vasconcelos, who had replaced Phillip's admirer, Lavradio. Strangely, however, Phillip's report to Stephens, the Admiralty Secretary, seems out of sync with the agreeable outcome that ensued. Its tone is unrepentantly self-righteous and belligerent – 'exaggerating the incident and magnifying his own conduct, perhaps to impress the authorities at home with his firmness and courage'. To similar effect was his reiteration in the same report of the missed opportunity of carrying out raids on the Spanish settlements in the Plate estuary a few years earlier – raids which he had plotted, first with Sandwich and then with Sydney and Nepean. He said the Spanish forces were 'such as I always thought them. Of five Companies of Regulars, sent out from Cordova only Seven Men returned, the rest were either killed or deserted to the Indians ... All the Regulars in Buenos Ayres, Monte Video, and the different Guards in the River of Plate do not amount to five hundred Men. No Ship of the Line and only two frigates in the River'.

Phillip remained at Rio de Janeiro for twenty days, unloading and repairing the *Europe* and restocking her with supplies and provisions. While there, he added to the menagerie of live animals on board by taking on 20 bullocks to supplement the pigs, goats, fowls and turkeys acquired at the Cape Verde islands. This was normal practice. Phillip's ship, like any eighteenth-century ship of the line, was not just a fighting machine, but also a floating farmyard carrying as many beasts as could be afforded and housed. Cattle and sheep, pigs and goats, hens and geese, and dogs and cats, were commonplace. Live animals were carried on warships for their milk and eggs, and were butchered for their meat. It was fashionable for senior officers to go to sea with their favourite greyhounds, and cats served a useful purpose in reducing the rat population below decks. On many ships, goats roamed freely. Fowl were generally kept in coops but sometimes also ran free. Below decks, where space was confined and the air frequently malodorous, cattle and sheep created formidable problems in the fodder they consumed, the dirt they produced and the miasmas they created. But they were an integral part of everyday shipboard life. They added a farmyard flavour to the sea air and were considered so natural that on another voyage, the seaman Aaron Thomas wrote approvingly in his journal that 'this morning when I first came on deck the smell from the livestock was almost as fragrant as a cow yard', adding that the aroma of their excrement and breath was 'that of nature'.

On 5 May 1783 the well-stocked and newly repaired *Europe* sailed from Rio de Janeiro. She would not make landfall again until mid-June in the Comoros Islands in the Indian Ocean. Phillip had no need to stop at Cape Town and good reason to avoid it. Cape Town was a Dutch possession and, as far as Phillip was aware, the British and the Dutch were still at war. News of the peace did not reach him until a few weeks later when the *Europe* had a mid-Atlantic encounter with some Indiamen coming from England. However, there was still no treaty – just a general truce to which the Dutch had not assented. It was no doubt for those reasons that Phillip pressed on, charting a course across the Atlantic well south of the Cape of Good Hope and then up through the Mozambique Channel to the Comoros Islands off the coast of Tanzania. This inner passage between the coast of Africa and Madagascar was the original Portuguese trade route to India and the East Indies. It hugged the African shoreline before heading northeast across the Indian Ocean towards the Seychelles and the Maldives. There was another available route, but sound and explicable reasons for avoiding it as well, truce or no truce. It involved skirting around the southern tip of Madagascar and travelling in a more northerly direction to India after stopping at the French-owned Mauritius. The Dutch had first opened this route to keep clear of the uncharted atolls of the Mozambique Channel. In time, Mauritius became a Dutch territory. Then in 1715 the French occupied it and renamed the island somewhat improbably 'Ile de France'. Phillip remained suspicious of the French, apparently taking the view that Mauritius was best avoided, notwithstanding the truce. This was reasonable, especially when one could not be certain whether a French ship bringing news from Versailles had yet reached the Indian Ocean outpost.

Phillip therefore made his way to the Comoros Islands, to a place that was rich in the Swahili influence of East Africa and much exposed to the cross-cultural currents of Arab, Persian and European civilisation. More importantly, the islands contained plentiful food supplies. One island, named Johanna, was particularly fertile and for ten days before continuing the journey to Madras, the crew of the *Europe* replenished wood, water and food there. Phillip even set up a tent on shore, receiving half a dozen small bullocks from representatives of the ruling family in return for muskets, ammunition and a brass box compass. From Johanna, the *Europe* set a course for Madras, threading her way northeast across the Indian Ocean. Her condition had now deteriorated and she began to feel the effects of the long voyage. The ship's timbers weakened, showing the strain of both the gales that she endured at the commencement of her voyage and her subsequent long crossings of the Atlantic and Indian Oceans. In the Arabian Sea, Phillip ordered that some of the great guns be stowed in the hold to increase the ship's ballast and enhance her buoyancy. Then one evening at about eight o'clock, still approximately 700 miles from the Maldives, there was a cry of fire. The flames, which had started in the purser's slop room, were swiftly extinguished. Edward Spain was this time rightly justified in his observation: 'I cannot help reflecting what would have been the consequence if the ship had burnt. We were 150 leagues from the coast of Arabia, which was the nearest land. We had near 600 men and 4 women on board. The boats would not have carried above 200 of us.'

As the *Europe* rounded Ceylon, heading for the Coromandel coast, the anxiety of all on board abated. From the land, they were greeted by fragrant scents wafting in the light airs – 'the aromatic smell of the cinnamon with which this island abounds' as one member of the crew described it. They were now near their immediate objective and reached Madras on 18 July, four weeks after Hughes had fought the last battle against de Suffren. Although Phillip had learned of the peace in May, the British and French naval commanders in the Bay of Bengal had only become aware of the January armistice on 29 June when a British ship flying a truce flag arrived. At Madras there was no harbour and the only anchorage was a mile or more offshore beyond the surf. Phillip presented Admiral Hughes with two of the bullocks from Johanna and several drawings of places that they had visited during the passage to India.

The condition of the *Europe* was now as precarious as that of some of Hughes' ships that had been damaged in battle with the French. A survey showed her to be so badly strained that she was compelled to undergo essential repairs. The carpenters stripped and fished the mainmast, the rigging was overhauled, more guns were stored in the hold and supplies of wood, water and food replenished. When she was ready to sail, Hughes ordered her home, in a squadron of eleven other ships under Sir Richard King's command. Phillip may have reached his destination but within three months of his arrival at Madras, he turned for England. On 2 October, Commodore King's squadron including the *Europe* sailed for Cape Town with a northeast monsoon at its back.

In late November, near the Cape of Good Hope, in the notoriously stormy seas off Cape Agulhas on Africa's southernmost tip, the squadron's progress was cruelly delayed. In this region, known to sailors as the 'Cape of Storms', the cold waters of the Atlantic meet the tropical waters of the Indian Ocean. And two great currents, one from the Equator and one from the Antarctic, collide – resulting in the warmer current turning back on itself. These are the wild seas where the legend of Wagner's Flying Dutchman had its origin. The meeting of the currents generates significant turbulence and contributes to a well-delineated change in the natural history of the area. One consequence is that the kelp beds that thrive in the cold Atlantic waters stop abruptly at Cape Agulhas where warmer water commences. The conjunction also contributes to periodical foul weather and occasional freak waves – to which the many shipwrecks in the surrounding waters attest. Here in these lumpy and dangerous conditions, a number of the ships were further damaged and the condition of the many scorbutic seamen on board worsened. When the twelve ships eventually sailed into Table Bay on 9 December 1783, an astonishing number of the crews had contracted scurvy. Approximately 1800 men were afflicted. One ship, the *Monarca*, had buried 180 men at sea since leaving Madras. Whether the four women were still on the *Europe* and, if so, whether they were also afflicted, remains a mystery.

This was Phillip's first visit to the Dutch-owned Cape Colony and it provided him with valuable insights that would stand him in good stead for the future. On this occasion, he was part of a squadron of twelve men-of-war whose first priority was the landing of a huge number of scurvy-ridden seamen. When the ships were moored, Commodore King sent Phillip ashore to request permission to land the sick. But the Dutch Governor had received no formal advice of the rumoured truce and refused the request. King sent Phillip back to reason with the Governor and gave him a copy of Sir Edward Hughes' order to cease hostilities against the Dutch. Only then was the Governor reluctantly persuaded to allow the scorbutic seamen to be landed. He stipulated Robben Island, five miles up the bay from the dock. For centuries this windswept, low-lying and barren island has served as a place of banishment, isolation and imprisonment. The Dutch quarried its stone and salt and incarcerated their political prisoners there. So did apartheid governments in more recent times. In the nineteenth century the British used it as a leper colony. For the scorbutic British seamen in 1783, it was a refuge of sunshine, clear air and above all, fresh food – whose supply was not without its logistical difficulties. For at that time of the year boats could only ply up and down the bay in the mornings before the winds blew up – winds that would prove to be an unpleasant characteristic of Table Bay on future visits during the southern spring and summer.

Phillip came ashore to reside in the township and to better supervise the resupply of the squadron. This was no easy task as the Dutch were obstructive and uncooperative. While he was there, he had the opportunity to familiarise himself with Cape Town's structure, its resources and its society. And he was able to observe its slave culture, which differed from that in Brazil. The Cape slaves were not the broad-shouldered West Africans who were sent to the Americas. They were more ethnically heterogeneous and came from diverse parts of the East – from Mozambique and Madagascar; from Java, Bali, Timor and Burma; from the Malay Peninsula; from the Coromandel and Malabar coasts of India; and even from China. While he was at the Cape, Phillip met and dined with the Dutch Governor and must inevitably have met the commandant of the garrison, Colonel Robert Gordon. Gordon was of Scottish descent but his service and loyalty were with the Dutch republic. He was also an amateur naturalist who shared his interest with the Scots gardener Francis Masson, whom Sir Joseph Banks had sent to the Cape to collect plants for the gardens at the Royal Palace at Kew.

The lack of cooperation from the Dutch at Cape Town was so great that Commodore King sent Phillip ahead in February to deliver Admiral Hughes' despatches and to inform the Admiralty of 'the difficulties which have attended the refitting of His Majesty's Squadron at the Cape of Good Hope'. The *Europe* sailed from the Cape on 20 February and reached Spithead on 22 April 1784. Phillip's voyage, which had started in great haste and almost never eventuated, thus ended on a personally triumphant note. Its original objective, to provide reinforcements to the India Squadron, was thwarted by the peace. But he had taken the *Europe* and the ship's complement of men and women across the Atlantic from north to south and from west to east; twice doubled the Cape of Good Hope; twice traversed the Indian Ocean from Cape Agulhas to the Coromandel Coast of India; and earned the honour of being sent ahead of the returning squadron with the Admiral's despatches.

CHAPTER 7

SECRET AGENT

Phillip's role as a secret agent and the reasons for British espionage during the 1780s

The peace to which Phillip returned in April 1784 was brittle and precarious. Anglo–French relations continued to be marked by mutual distrust and the administration in Whitehall remained wary. The immediate cause for British concern was France's apparent designs on India and the East. Intelligence reported disguised French warships sailing for the East with guns de-mounted and stored in the hold, as if they were merely cargo vessels or '*flûtes*'. The French expression for this subterfuge was '*armés en flûte*'. There were also reports that France intended to send Admiral de Suffren back to India; and other reports of increased activity in the French naval dockyards at Brest and Toulon. The British consul in Nice reported that the French were working day and night in arming their navy. And the consul at Genoa reported that all the caulkers and carpenters in Marseilles had been ordered to go to Toulon. In early October British agent Mevrow Wolters reported that the shipyard at Toulon had orders to fit all the line-of-battle ships and frigates for sea and that French naval officials expected to have 30 line-of-battle ships ready by the following January.

Ever since the indignity of France's losses in the Seven Years War (1756–63), successive French Ministers of Marine had taken the view that the renewal of the navy was a national *magnum opus* crucial to the restoration of French prestige and the recovery of its valuable overseas territories. At the end of the American Revolutionary Wars, France's net gains were minimal and its losses were only partly redressed. By 1784, in the months after Phillip returned to England, it had become clear that the upsurge in French shipbuilding activity had reached new heights and that the French and the Dutch were manoeuvring for advantage in India and the East. The administration of the 24-year-old Prime Minister William Pitt was under no illusion about the pretensions of its enemies. In early October 1784, Lord Carmarthen, the Foreign Secretary, stressed the necessity of knowing the extent of the proposed French and Dutch forces in India. The information was essential, he added, 'in order that we may ascertain the number of ships to be employed by us in that quarter of the world'. In November, Henry Dundas, possibly Pitt's closest advisor, warned that 'India is the first quarter to be attacked, we must never lose sight of keeping such a force there as will be sufficient to baffle or surprise'. As Sir James Harris, the foremost diplomat of the age and then British ambassador at The Hague, put it: 'Our wealth and power in India is their great and constant object of jealousy; and they will never miss an opportunity of attempting to wrest it out of our hands.'

Renewal of war with France was everywhere anticipated. While British diplomats strived to prevent any possible alliance between France and the Dutch republic, British intelligence simultaneously sought to obtain accurate information about the precise extent of the French naval build-up in the ports and arsenals. On 19 October 1784 Carmathen instructed the British ambassador in Paris to obtain 'the fullest and most accurate intelligence of the present state of the French marine, of the particular force now fit for, or preparations for service, both at Brest and Toulon, as well as what ships of war may have sailed from either of those ports since the last; and as far as possible, the respective destinations of such ships'.

In this state of heightened anxiety Nepean once again turned to Phillip. It was only a relatively short time since they had worked closely together on the planning and preparation for the proposed 'Southern Expedition' and on the voyage of the *Europe* to the India Squadron. And Phillip's fluency in French, German and Portuguese, his previous experience as a covert agent and his record of discretion, made him a valuable resource. On Nepean's instigation, Phillip was granted twelve months' leave from the navy. The official reason for his absence was absurdly meretricious: he was, it was said, travelling to Grenoble 'on account of his private affairs'. The truth was somewhat different. Nepean had commissioned Phillip on behalf of the Home Office 'to undertake a Journey to Toulon and other ports of France for the purpose of ascertaining the Naval Force, and Stores in the Arsenals'. On 11 November Nepean entered in the Secret Service Ledger, in his own hand, the details of the payment to Phillip of £150 from Secret Service funds for his salary and expenses.

In the 1780s the Secret Service operations of the British government were apportioned between the Foreign Office and the Home Office. Strange as it may now seem, the Home Office, not the Foreign Office, was primarily responsible for gathering intelligence on French and Spanish naval operations. This was in a sense a historical accident following a reorganisation in 1782 when the Home Office absorbed the responsibilities of what was known as the Southern Department. Until then, the foreign affairs of state were divided between the Northern Department and the Southern Department. Espionage was an essential allied component of the operations of both departments. The Northern Department's attention was directed to Russia, the Holy Roman Empire and the northern European states. The Southern Department focused on France, Italy, Switzerland, the Iberian Peninsula and Turkey. Significantly, responsibility for colonies, as well as voyages of discovery and settlement, also came under the umbrella of the Southern Department and therefore, in due course, of the Home Office.

Evan Nepean had been the Under-Secretary of the Home Office since March 1782. In the small and hierarchical world of the then British government, this was a position of considerable power and influence. Nepean's counterpart at the Foreign Office, William Fraser, had no naval experience and little involvement in gathering intelligence on French naval operations. And Nepean's Home Secretary from July 1782, Thomas Townshend, soon to become Lord Sydney, was supposedly not energetic. This may be debatable but it is entirely possible that Sydney was uneven in his attention to the quotidian affairs of the office. Whatever the truth, when it came to the collection of French naval intelligence, Nepean almost single-handedly directed the espionage operations of the Home Office with little oversight from Sydney. And there were no formal budgetary restraints. The Home Secretary, and therefore Nepean, had an unlimited entitlement to draw on the Treasury for Secret Service funds, provided the money was for national defence or the detection of treason. In fact, between 1782 and 1801 the Treasury disbursed over £1.3 million for Secret Service operations, of which a significant proportion was drawn by Nepean.

Nepean took an unusually active and personal role in gathering French naval intelligence. He was intensely security conscious, tightly controlled the service and gave many detailed orders himself. In fact, all surviving copies of Home Office letters, accounts and ledgers in connection with Secret Service activities of the period are in his own hand. Ordinarily, clerks would perform the menial chirographic functions – writing up ledgers and laboriously listing amounts in columns of figures. But in Nepean's time, he kept the business of the Secret Service effectively classified to himself.

The Home Office, from where Nepean conducted operations, was located on Whitehall. All of the British government departments were housed in a motley collection of buildings on or around Whitehall. None was purpose-built except the Admiralty. The Palace of Whitehall had once occupied much of the area but all except the Banqueting House went up in flames in January 1698 and was never rebuilt. In its time the palace had constituted the largest and most complex aggregation of government buildings in Europe. Although the palace ceased to exist, government offices continued to cluster around Whitehall and the name became a metonym for government. In Nepean's time, the Home Office carried on business upstairs in a nondescript and unpretentious two-storey building known as the Montague lodgings. Until 1782 the building had been occupied by the Board of Trade, and before that it had been the site of Henry VIII's real tennis court. The whole of the office occupied only the first floor where there were four rooms, each with its own fireplace. The private offices of the Home Secretary and Under-Secretary, but not that of the clerks, had carpets and curtains. The ten clerks shared a single room known as the boardroom where they sat at a long table with quill pens, ink and blotting sand, copying letters, papers and despatches. Correspondence was filed in leather-bound volumes stored in wooden presses around the room.

It was a small and intimate establishment. But notwithstanding its size, the Home Office handled a remarkable amount of business, all of which Nepean directed. In fact, during the 1780s decisions were made in the Home Office that affected every inhabited continent on earth. Nepean controlled the office and opened the incoming correspondence, deciding which letters and despatches should go to Lord Sydney. In turn, Sydney sent the most important ones to George III. With some exceptions, Nepean would sign the outgoing correspondence. He also drafted letters for Sydney, who customarily signed only those addressed to the heads of other government departments, colonial governors and most private citizens. Sydney did not concern himself with the Secret Service, leaving it to Nepean.

Espionage agents engaged by the Home Office had no recognised institutional existence. Many, like Phillip, were naval officers on half pay. Some were merchants with a penchant for adventure. When their services were required by the Home Office, Nepean would engage and employ them on an ad hoc basis, sometimes for considerable periods. Phillip, for example, was engaged by Nepean and remunerated by the Home Office for twelve months from 14 October 1784 and for another twelve months from 1 December 1785. From Toulon in January 1785, and again on 21 March of that year, he sent reports to Nepean setting out his observations and confirming the administration's apprehensions about French re-arming. Ominously, Phillip said that the French arsenal at Toulon was very superior to that which he had seen 'before the War' – referring to the early 1770s before the American Revolutionary Wars (1775–83) or the Third Colónia War (1774–78). Phillip's second surviving report is numbered 'No 5' so it is evident that there were others, quite possibly from other ports. The two Toulon reports contain information about the escalation in French shipbuilding, including the importing of timber from Albania; the recruiting of shipwrights from neighbouring ports and the state of refitting of line-of-battle ships and frigates in the basin at Toulon. In one of those reports, Phillip observed that at Toulon harbour there were twelve men-of-war with their lower masts in and rigging up and nine frigates and store ships with their lower masts stepped.

Spying on each other's navies was the 'great game' of the late eighteenth century. The French and English were constantly engaged in mutual espionage activities to assess the naval capacity of the other or to ascertain and emulate the latest advances in shipbuilding techniques. Each despatched clandestine missions to the ports of the other to gather information. After the end of the American Revolutionary Wars, Britain's primary concern was with any increase in the French navy's size and capacity and its possible deployment for global political and commercial advancement. France's objective was to learn about the latest innovations in shipbuilding techniques in order to be able to match the Royal Navy's prowess. While Phillip went about his work in Toulon, French spies reported from the Thames dockyards, and no doubt also from Portsmouth and Plymouth. They had been doing so throughout the century. Few reports survive but one of the most comprehensive was written by the French naval officer Daniel Lescallier in 1789, only a few years after Phillip was sent to the ports of France to investigate its naval force. Another earlier surviving report was written by Blaise Ollivier, a master shipwright from Brest. And among other examples, we know that one French officer visited Britain to examine the construction of naval vessels at the dockyards at Deptford, Woolwich and Chatham under the disguise of a *débonnaire bourgeois commerçant*' – an easygoing, middle-class businessman.

The work of such agents was dangerous and required discretion, but at least in England it was not as difficult as might have been thought. Although foreigners were forbidden to enter the Royal Navy's arsenals and dockyards, it was easy enough to assess armed warships at close quarters on the river and in the ports. And the banks of the Thames were covered by a huge jumble of docks and dry-docks owned by large private shipyards that did not present the difficulties of access surrounding naval establishments. There the latest techniques could be readily observed – on which Lescallier reported in impressive detail. He described improvements in the cultivation and use of timber for ship-building and new techniques and developments in construction, copper sheathing, launching, tarring, pulleys, pumps and cordage. He even went so far as to include a summary of British naval administration and information on the salaries paid to the Lords of the Admiralty.

British intelligence was thought to be 'prodigiously efficient'. In 1778, for example, less than 48 hours after the signing of the treaty of alliance between France and the American colonies, the terms of the treaty were passed on to London. But intelligence gathering operated at many levels and its quality was inevitably variable. Naval intelligence was a specialised area, but half pay officers such as Phillip, who were under orders to collect specified intelligence in closed areas, were not Nepean's only sources of information. Sometimes intelligence was haphazardly obtained from enthusiastic informants who volunteered information of variable quality and invariably requested a fee for their trouble. Another regular conduit of information to Nepean on shipping news and naval affairs was Thomas Taylor, the Master of Lloyd's Coffee House – an institution in eighteenth-century London and the pre-eminent coffee house for those with shipping and maritime connections. Thomas Taylor managed the operations of Lloyds for the whole of the period from 1774 to 1796. He knew all that there was to know about the arrivals, departures and losses of ships, of all European countries. As a source of naval intelligence, Taylor was so valuable that, as he did with Phillip, Nepean fostered a connection with him.

The rapid expansion of French naval shipping at Toulon was not the only cause for British concern in the mid 1780s and not the only subject of rumour and gossip in the coffee houses and taverns of London. During early 1785 Brest was the centre of much frenetic activity of a different kind. The expedition of the Comte de Lapérouse was planned in conscious emulation of the voyages of Captain Cook and designed to advance France's reach of empire. Although it was promoted as having scientific and geographic objectives, it also had a political and commercial dimension. Louis XVI's instructions, separate from those setting out Lapérouse's scientific and geographic mandate, required him to consider and report upon the political conditions, the possibilities of commerce and the suitability for settlement of the lands visited by him. He was to note likely places for French settlement and report on all European commerce and possessions 'which may be interesting ... in a military point of view'. Among other things, he was directed to the South Pacific and specifically requested to ascertain whether the English had formed a settlement on the islands of New Zealand. If so, he was directed to report on the 'condition, strength and object of the [English] settlement'.

The French curiosity as to whether the English had actually settled any of the newly discovered lands in the South Pacific was matched by an equivalent British concern that the French might themselves do so before they did. Thus Dorset, the British ambassador in Paris, demonstrated his anxiety when he reported in May 1785 that he had heard that Lapérouse had orders to visit New Zealand and that 'the French have a design of establishing some kind of settlement there'. The following month, both Dorset and his friend Lord Dalrymple passed on intelligence, which each of them had separately received, that there was little room to doubt that the French had a desire to make a settlement in New Zealand by landing convicts there. In particular, the intelligence included the alarming but erroneous information that 'sixty criminals from the prison at Bicêtre were last Monday conveyed under strong guard and with great secrecy to Brest, where they are to be embarked on board Monsieur de Lapérouse's ships, and it is imagined that they are to be left to take possession of that lately discovered country'.

The British assumption that France might be engaged in a race for territory in New Zealand or New South Wales or both was more paranoid than real but it had a sound historical basis. There was widespread belief in France during the eighteenth century of the existence of a vast southern land. It was called 'Gonneville land' after the French explorer of the same name. And there was tremendous enthusiasm for the tales of the English pirate and explorer William Dampier, who had landed on the west coast of Australia in 1688. The first French translation of Dampier's story appeared only a year after the original English publication, which was soon followed by seven more editions. Equally popular were Daniel Defoe's *Robinson Crusoe* and Jonathan Swift's *Gulliver's Travels,* both of which were immediately translated into French. Two of Gulliver's voyages were set in or off the Australian coast. By the middle of the century, French appetites for new discoveries in the southern seas were stimulated even more by the publication of Charles de Brosses' popular two-volume *Histoire des Navigationes aux Terres Australes* (1756). It summarised the explorations of Abel Tasman and William Dampier and all that had so far been discovered about the southern seas. De Brosses was convinced that France had a unique opportunity to win wealth and glory by discovering and exploring these unknown lands. He urged Louis XV to 'turn his gaze entirely to his navies … at a time like the present when a neighbouring power … has the manifest ambition of being ruler of the seas'. He was referring to Great Britain.

De Brosses' encouragement may have had some effect, at least after the Seven Years War. Enlightenment aspirations and the confidence that came with the end of the war coincided with a surge in maritime and scientific exploration. The British moved first but France was not far behind. Commencing in 1764, ships of the Royal Navy carrying botanists, naturalists and astronomers undertook history-making scientific voyages to distant parts of the world. The first voyages were by the *Dolphin* and the *Swallow,* commanded by captains Samuel Wallis and Philip Carteret. They were followed in 1766 when the French commander Louis Antoine de Bougainville set off on his voyage around the world (1766–69). In very the same year, the Admiralty commissioned Lieutenant James Cook to undertake the first of his three famous voyages (1768–70). When Cook returned without solving the puzzle of the unknown southern continent, Louis XV commissioned Yves-Joseph de Kerguelen to search for the fabled *Terres Australes* – in the hope of 'improving France's strategic position in the Indian Ocean'. De Kerguelen, like Phillip, had previous experience in espionage. Louis XV emphasised to him that finding the southern continent was one of the most important discoveries still to be made in the geography of the world. In March 1771, in a joint memorandum with his Minister of Marine, Louis XV commanded that de Kerguelen's mission remain '*secrète*'.

De Kerguelen was the first Frenchman to go in search of the southern continent with the backing of the state. He did not solve the mystery but on 30 March 1772, less than two years after Cook first claimed possession of the east coast of Australia, de Kerguelen's second in command, François de Saint-Aloüarn, landed on the west coast and claimed possession of it. The annexation ceremony took place on the cliffs above Turtle Bay on Dirk Hartog Island. Just as Cook had done, the French wandered inland and did not recognise any evidence of organised human occupation. They then raised the flag, read a formal proclamation claiming possession in the name of Louis XV, shouted 'Vive Le Roi' three times and fired three volleys of musket shot. Before leaving, they buried one of their seamen in the sand and left several bottles, a few French coins and a white ensign. Remarkably, Saint-Aloüarn's annexation was not the only French activity in this part of the world at the time. Almost simultaneously in Van Diemen's Land, another Frenchman, Marc-Joseph Marion Dufresne, was making the first European contact with the Aboriginal people of what is now Tasmania.

Louis XVI inherited his grandfather's enthusiasm, and more. After he ascended the throne in 1774, it soon became apparent that he was a keen geographer, an avid reader of the accounts of Captain Cook's voyages and determined that France should rival Britain's naval supremacy. His exploratory zeal was motivated by the impact of the Enlightenment and a desire for new knowledge of the geographical and scientific dimensions of the world. The flora and fauna brought back from past expeditions had stimulated advances in natural history, science, anthropology, medicine and geography and contributed to the sense of 'improvement' that characterised the age. The expedition of the Comte de Lapérouse was one of Louis XVI's proudest achievements. The young King actively participated in drawing up the instructions for his commander and enthusiastically supported the expedition's objects. Even on his way to the guillotine in 1793, he is supposed to have enquired, 'What news of Lapérouse?'

Phillip could not have failed to be aware of Lapérouse's expedition or of its significance while he was undercover in France between 1784 and 1786, especially after May 1785 when it began to be reported in newspapers. As it turned out, Lapérouse sailed from Brest on 1 August 1785 without convicts and had no plans to establish a colony – despite British apprehensions to the contrary. But this did not prevent the continuation of British suspicion and anxiety about the French naval build-up. On 1 December 1785 Phillip sought and obtained from the Admiralty an extension of his leave of absence, this time to go 'on his private affairs' to Hyères for a further twelve months. This was another implausible mask. For although Hyères was fast becoming a popular location for British visitors and expatriates, it was only ten miles east of Toulon. At the beginning of November Nepean confirmed the true purpose of Phillip's leave by paying him another £160 of

Secret Service money – once again recorded in his own hand in the Secret Service ledger.

Phillip's instructions from Nepean were not confined to Toulon. They included 'other ports of France', of which Brest in western Brittany – France's major naval base on the Atlantic – was the most significant. There were also Rochefort, Le Havre and Dunkirk. And by 1784, in the harbour at Cherbourg, the construction of several massive jetties had commenced. During the two-year period of his assignment, Phillip probably visited and investigated all of these ports. However, other than the two reports sent from Toulon in January and March 1785, nothing survives to indicate where Phillip lived and travelled in France; whether he adopted a disguise; what name he used; who he met; the circles in which he moved; or just how he carried out his responsibilities. But as the showpiece of the French naval machine, Toulon clearly featured in his peregrinations. Its old town was a place of narrow streets, small squares, white stone houses and many fountains. The town was secured by a formidable gate and drawbridge. And its harbour was one of the best natural anchorages on the Mediterranean and one of the largest in Europe. A naval arsenal and shipyard dominated the township and had done so since 1599. The waterfront was a hive of activity where thousands of tradesmen and workers were employed in the service of the French marine administration. Every trade and service associated with wooden ships could be found there – rope-makers and sail-makers, caulkers and coopers, timber merchants, providores, suppliers of pitch and tar and blacksmiths with their iron forges. The smell of paint, varnish, vinegar, timber and hemp was everywhere. Hemp was turned into rope in a long narrow building known as the 'Corderie', which was 21 yards wide by 350 yards long. This unique configuration was designed to enable ropes to be twisted and stretched along the entire length of the building by convicts who worked in an enormous treadmill like plodding mules. They came from the nearby Bagne of Toulon, the notorious prison created in 1748 to house the convicts who, in an earlier era, had been sentenced to row the galley ships of the French Mediterranean fleet.

Some indication of the nature of the work that Phillip must have carried out is revealed by a report sent to Nepean two years later by another agent, Lieutenant Monke, a naval colleague of Phillip. Just as Phillip had done when going to Flanders in the early 1770s, Monke used the pretence of travelling to Nice for the benefit of his health. In reality he proceeded to Marseilles and then to the French naval dockyard at Toulon. In Marseilles he learned that 'all the shipwrights and carpenters, joiners, blacksmiths, locksmiths, rope makers, caulkers, bakers etc etc were gone to Toulon to assist in fitting out a squadron'. Then, in the darkness of night, he followed the postman carrying the mail to Toulon, knowing that the town gates were opened to him at four o'clock in the morning, and that 'any carriage following very closely might, by a small bribe, take that opportunity of entering the Town'. Once in Toulon, he confined himself to a hotel room all day until he thought the French officers were at dinner.

He then 'slipp'd downstairs unobserved by the people of the house and went out at a back door which open'd into a very private street that led directly to a spot ...' which was 'the most advantageous for viewing the shipping in the harbour'. He explained that to reach the viewing point 'I had to pass six or seven centinels [sic] to arrive at this spot, which all strangers were expressly forbid to approach. But having taken the precaution of frenchifying my person as much as possible, I deceived them by my appearance and gained my point'. Now in position to make strategic observations concerning the number of ships of the line, frigates and corvettes in the harbour, as well as their state of readiness for sail and the numbers of guns which they carried, he retired to a coffee house to consider his next move. Later in the afternoon, when he saw a number of people going into the shipyard, he 'got into the midst of them and passed the two outside centinels [sic] and the Corps de Garde without being challenged as a foreigner, so much did my appearance favour my design'. But caution prevailed and he soon retreated when he encountered a sergeant's guard conveying to prison several unauthorised entrants and the bribed or negligent sentinels who had permitted them to pass.

In the evening, Monke excelled himself. He resolved to get himself in a position to overhear the conversations of some of the captains of the French men-of-war. He knew there was to be a play that evening and 'knew the custom of their provincial theatres was not to light up the house till a few minutes before the drawing of the curtain'. Loitering in the lobby, he observed four or five naval captains, followed them with as little noise as possible, seated himself unperceived behind their box and commenced to eavesdrop. To his satisfaction, the French captains engaged in careless and confidential conversation about naval and military movements, which he managed to record in lengthy and impressive detail. He then had supper in a coffee house and obtained yet more information, including about improvements to the pumps on French men-of-war.

In the morning, Monke must have thought the game was up when he was visited by two 'sergens de ville' and asked to state his business – to which he replied that he had come from Marseilles and was travelling to Nice for his health. He quickly resolved to leave Toulon, concluding that 'a longer stay would be attended with very dangerous consequences to myself'. In England a convicted spy could still be hanged, drawn and quartered. This was the sentence given to the French spy Francois Henri de la Motte in 1781 and the Portsmouth naval clerk David Tyrie in 1782. Monke wisely departed, taking the road to Nice and turning off onto the Aix Road after 50 miles. From this point, he 'never stopp'd till I reached Paris', from where it seems, he returned in safety to England.

As a record of Phillip's clandestine activities, we have nothing quite so vivid. Indeed, such a full account was neither usual nor necessary. Whitehall was interested in the objective information rather than the means by which it was obtained, however colourful those means may have been. Judging by Phillip's two surviving reports, he was more circumspect in his despatches. But Lieutenant Monke's frank account reflects the activities of spies of both countries in the late eighteenth century.

CHAPTER 8

PIONEER

The reasons for Great Britain's decision to establish a settlement in New South Wales and the terms of Phillip's appointment as commander and governor

Phillip returned from his covert service in France in August or September 1786. He had not served the full twelve months for which Nepean had paid him, but his return must have been at Nepean's instigation. At the time, a number of issues of national importance were swirling through the corridors of Whitehall that would determine Phillip's immediate future. Not all of them were generally known or fully understood, but collectively they led to a decision by the administration to establish a settlement in New South Wales. One of those issues was the subject of much press and public agitation. It was well known that Pitt was searching for a solution to the problem of overcrowded jails and overflowing hulks. The way had been prepared after the conclusion of the American Revolutionary Wars when Parliament passed a new act for the resumption of transportation. From August 1784 transportation beyond the seas was permitted anywhere in the world and was no longer confined to places within the existing, and recently diminished, British Empire. But no convenient place could be found, whether within or without the empire. It was not until August 1786 that a decision was finally reached on a suitable location.

That was the domestic problem, but there were also international concerns. Pitt aspired to create a global commercial network, the Admiralty needed secure supplies of naval materials in the East and the South Pacific and there was apprehension about France's territorial and strategic ambitions in the Indian and Pacific oceans. These were threads in a tapestry that rendered the establishment of a British settlement in New South Wales not merely advantageous, but urgent and necessary. The convicts would facilitate the proposed settlement, but they were not the sole reason for it. They were instead the means by which it would be established. As one historian has observed, 'The convicts were what they had always been – the servants of mercantilist interests.'

France's naval build-up had been a concern for some years. It was the very reason for Phillip's despatch to France in October 1784. By the time he returned to England in mid 1786, the political situation had deteriorated. Among other things, the treaty between the Dutch and the French, which Britain had struggled to prevent by diplomatic means, had finally come into existence in December 1785. Castries, the French Minister of Marine, saw the treaty as enabling French forces, assisted and fortified by Dutch ships and Dutch bases, to overwhelm the British settlements at Bombay, Madras and Calcutta and threaten

British wealth and power in India. For Pitt and his Cabinet, there was really no doubt about the French intentions. In February 1786, Harris, still the British ambassador at The Hague, warned that the 'intentions of France in forming a connection with [the Dutch republic] are too evident to admit of doubt'. Then, over the next few months, the French engaged in transparently provocative actions in Bengal, asserting that their ships could sail up the Ganges River without paying customs duties or submitting to British inspections.

These were the first drumbeats of war. They were followed by alarming news. On 1 August, Harris wrote that there would soon be a major development and that France intended to send troops to the Dutch bases in India. On 8 August, he reported that the crisis 'is drawing nearer and nearer every hour'. On 16 August, Sydney sent an account of the French naval capacity in the East to George III. Within hours the King acknowledged what Pitt, Sydney and their colleagues knew all too well: 'France certainly under the name of *flûtes* can soon collect a considerable naval force in the East Indies'. Three days later Pitt's Cabinet decided to establish a settlement in New South Wales.

In the background was another issue. Both the British and French claims to possession, on the east and west of the Australian continent, were only conditional. When it came to the annexation of new lands, the international law of nations had two principal tenets. The first was an assumption that a country could be effectively without an owner, and therefore *terra nullius*, even when it was inhabited, as long as the occupants consisted of no more than an indefinite population of itinerant hunter-gatherers. Since the time of the philosopher John

Locke, Enlightenment thinkers had maintained that ownership of land through habitation could only be established when labour was mixed with the land through agricultural activity and construction. Cultivation was therefore necessary to ownership. The rights of an indigenous population with no permanent settlements, whose members lived by hunting, gathering and fishing, could therefore be ignored.

The second tenet was that a nation's claim to 'uninhabited' land required more than a bare proclamation. Hoisting a flag was insufficient by itself. Any claim would remain conditional unless and until it was followed by occupation and settlement. The principles were set out by the legal philosopher Emerich de Vattel in his influential 1758 text *The Law of Nations or the Principles of Natural Law*. In it he explained that title to unoccupied land necessitated the formation of settlements and actual use of the land:

> But it is questionable whether a nation can, by the bare act of taking possession, appropriate to itself countries which it does not really occupy, and thus engross a much greater extent of territory than it is able to people and cultivate ...
>
> The law of nations will, therefore, not acknowledge the property and sovereignty of a nation over any uninhabited countries, except those of which it has really taken actual possession, in which it has formed settlements, or of which it has made actual use.

Cook was therefore just 'a passing bird', as was Saint-Aloüarn when he claimed the west coast of the continent two years later. Since neither had established any settlement, nor made actual use of the land, the way remained legally open for other nations to claim sovereignty.

This is what makes explicable the British apprehensions in 1785 that Lapérouse might establish a settlement in the South Pacific at New Zealand with French convicts. The intelligence on which these apprehensions was based turned out to be wrong, but it revealed British sensitivities and acted as a reminder, if one were needed, that until a British settlement were established in New South Wales, the French might still win the territorial race. As is well known, the crucial task of establishing a settlement in New South Wales was entrusted to Phillip. He was wary of the French, to which his period undercover in France in 1784–86 no doubt contributed. Tellingly, before his departure for New South Wales, he specifically queried how he should act 'in case of being opposed by any European ships when I arrive on the coast'. He presumably had Lapérouse most immediately in mind.

Britain's broader strategic and commercial objectives were a pervasive influence on the whole process of decision. Pitt, who was a Chancellor of the Exchequer before he was Prime Minister, and who professed himself to be a disciple of Adam Smith, envisaged an international trading network to advance British commercial interests in the Indian and Pacific oceans. Like his father before him, he was an avowed commercial imperialist for whom the expansion of British trade was of paramount importance. And he was certainly not a lone voice. To give effect to his aspirations, he needed secure shipping routes, strategic bases and accessible naval supplies. Between Europe and India, Britain was particularly poorly served south of the Equator, where it possessed only St Helena in the South Atlantic, with its unsatisfactory harbour at Jamestown.

The weakness in Britain's position was highlighted by the problems that beset its India Squadron in the mid 1780s. At a time of enhanced threat from the French and Dutch, the squadron was in dire need of naval materials but was forced to rely on shipments from Europe. Not only was the lead time lengthy and the journey uncertain, but supplies of European timber, hemp and flax were rapidly diminishing. Each 74-gun ship-of-the-line, the navy's workhorse, used about 40 miles of rope and more than an acre of sails. The manufacture of the rope, rigging and cordage required approximately 168,000 pounds of hemp. And the timber for the ship's construction had to come from approximately 3400 trees representing about 75 acres of forest. What is more, the vast majority of these trees had to be 'shipbuilding' oak trees 80 to 150 years old. And at least a third of the oak timber had to be curved for the knees and breast hooks on which the ship's integral strength depended.

The necessity of finding new sources of supply explains why, for several years prior to August 1786, there was much speculation within the administration about the potential commercial and naval advantages of establishing a settlement in New South Wales. The proposals of Matra (1783), Young (1784) and Call (1784) all promoted the advantages of navigation, trade and military influence. Specific mention was made of timber for masts from Norfolk Island, New Zealand and New Caledonia and of the flax from which canvas and cordage could be made. When the Beauchamp Committee reported in July 1785, it also noted the need for a strategic and commercial return, stating that a convict colony in the southern hemisphere should 'promote the interests of future commerce or future hostility in the south seas'. Nepean had no doubt about the strategic and commercial objectives of a settlement in New South Wales. A few months after the decision was made, he mused in a draft letter to an Irish colleague that 'above all, the cultivation of the flax plant seems to be the most considerable object'. The fact that he annotated the official copy by stating that he had removed this paragraph from the original only reinforces its significance. He clearly thought better of advertising the expedition's commercial objectives. Sydney also revealed his true feelings. In a communication with the East India Company, he said that the proposed settlement in New South Wales was 'a means of preventing the emigration of our European neighbours to that quarter'.

These strategic and commercial objectives were not merely contextual; they constituted part of Phillip's core instructions. Among other things, he was directed to secure Norfolk Island as quickly as possible 'to prevent its being occupied by the subjects of any other European power'. And he was ordered to attend to the cultivation of the flax plant because it was perceived to have 'superior excellence for a variety of maritime purposes'. To this end, the fleet was supplied with the necessary equipment for dressing flax and an adventurous master weaver named Roger Murley was induced to join the expedition as a free man. No one connected with the expedition was really under any illusion about the reason for these instructions and their strategic and commercial objective. When the hopes for Norfolk Island flax subsequently failed to materialise, Watkin Tench, an alert junior marine officer, made the uncomplicated observation that 'the scheme of being able to assist the East Indies with naval stores in case of war, must fall to the ground'.

An additional consideration, tantalising but difficult to verify, appears to have been the proximity of New South Wales to the Spanish Pacific empire, stretching from the Philippines to Acapulco, not to mention the Dutch settlements in Java. As James Matra had pointed out in his 1783 proposal, a settlement at New South Wales could give

England a 'commanding influence in the policy of Europe'. That was because, he said, if England should be at war with the Dutch or Spanish 'we might very powerfully annoy either State from the new settlement, and with equal safety and expedition, make naval incursions into Java, and the other Dutch settlements, or invade the coast of Spanish America, and intercept the Manilla ships'. These statements, although for obvious reasons not official government policy, received widespread and worldwide circulation, repeated in newspapers in Europe and America.

Notwithstanding the importance and secrecy of all of these issues, the more visible and troublesome question was the domestic convict furore. For ordinary members of the English public, it was effectively the only known reason for Phillip's expedition to New South Wales. Offshore detention then as now had popular support. But the government needed to find a place to which felons sentenced to transportation across the seas could actually be sent. Since mid 1783, government ministers had been receiving a barrage of complaints from municipal authorities about their overflowing jails. The Lord Mayor of London was understandably vocal. Although English judges continued to hand down sentences of transportation, no clear alternative had emerged to Virginia and Maryland, where transportees had usually been sent in the past. Convicted felons simply multiplied in typhus-ridden jails in London and the counties. Not surprisingly, the problem had a very public airing and soon became a source of embarrassment. And it took the government three agonising years to settle on a solution. In the process, some desperate options were canvassed. The major initial focus was on West Africa and the southwest coast of Africa – first at

Lemane, an island on the River Gambia in the slave trading region, and second at Das Voltas Bay, near the present-day border between Namibia and South Africa.

But before the schemes for Lemane and Das Voltas Bay were entertained, another option was more than once canvassed which would be comic if it were not so callous. In August 1784 Nepean optimistically enquired of the Portuguese ambassador whether Portugal might be interested in taking malefactors off Britain's hands. He suggested that the Queen of Portugal might be able to put British convicts to good use as galley slaves; or in the settling of remote parts of her vast dominions; or in the cultivation of land, in mining or in any other forced labour, no matter how difficult or arduous. He even added that they could be transported to the East as soldiers, just as Portuguese nationals or *degredados* were. But Queen Maria I of Portugal, known as 'Maria the Pious', politely declined the offer.

The schemes for Lemane and Das Voltas Bay were only marginally more realistic than the Portuguese slave option. The idea of a convict colony at Lemane died under the withering parliamentary rhetoric of that conservative hero Edmund Burke, who described Gambia as 'the capital seat of plague, pestilence and famine'. It was, he said, quoting the poet John Milton, a place where 'all life dies and all death lives'. If convicts were just sent away to die, as they assuredly would in such a place, a serious question would arise as to the humanity, and possibly validity, of a sentence of transportation. Then the scheme for Das Voltas Bay, which had been recommended by the Beauchamp Committee in place of Lemane, simply disappeared when the sloop Nautilis returned from a survey of the region in late July 1786 and her captain reported that any proposed settlement there would be utterly hopeless. He had never seen 'so dreary a coast, along which we had sailed nearly 1,200 miles in a direct line, without seeing a tree, or procuring a drop of fresh water'. He was referring to what we now know as the Skeleton Coast of Namibia.

Within a few weeks of the dispiriting report from the captain of the Nautilis, the Cabinet settled on New South Wales. The decision was made on Saturday, 19 August 1786 at the beginning of the summer recess. Cabinet meetings were normally held on Tuesdays and Fridays but a royal levee had delayed the meeting. There were no minutes, and on the following Monday, Sydney's Under-Secretary, Nepean, drafted the letter announcing the decision. The resolution to found a settlement in New South Wales was effectively an executive decision of Pitt, Sydney and Nepean. Some others outside Cabinet were probably influential. On many questions, Pitt tended to operate through an inner circle of advisors, not all of whom were necessarily within Cabinet. The extent to which Pitt sometimes bypassed his ministers explains why historians have described him in the early years of his administration as 'essentially the government in all its departments'. Henry Dundas, WW Grenville, Lord Mulgrave and Lord Hawkesbury were part of Pitt's circle. There was no transparency in the dealings of these confident and imperious men. Much of the planning and policy making of government was conducted between them in conversation without formal agenda or memoranda. Their practice was explained by Dundas, reminiscing after Pitt had died. He said they sometimes lived almost unremittingly together, occupied in discussions of a public concern, and that there were no written documents recording their discussions and decisions, merely memory and recollection.

Helpfully for Phillip, the implementation of the decision to settle New South Wales was underpinned by sage and experienced departmental secretaries – particularly Evan Nepean at the Home Office, Philip Stephens at the Admiralty and George Rose at the Treasury. Phillip was well known to these mandarins of the public service. Stephens had been First Secretary of the Admiralty for over twenty years. Phillip had been in contact with him since at least 1778, when he commenced his consultations with Lord Sandwich concerning raids on Spanish settlements in South America. His familiarity with Nepean may have commenced in late 1779 when he sought permission from Sandwich 'to Cruise as a Volunteer in the *Victory*', on which Nepean may have been the purser. Their relationship was cemented after 1782 when Nepean became Under-Secretary of the Home Office – and by 1787 they were firm friends. This could be seen occasionally when Phillip abandoned formality in his private letters. Writing to Nepean from Rio de Janeiro en route to New South Wales, he concluded affectionately, 'Adieu, my dear friend; health and happiness attend you and your good little woman and child.' Rose, with whom Phillip would need to deal frequently in the funding and fitting out of the expedition to New South Wales, owned a grand home called 'Cuffnells' at Lyndhurst. But despite occasional references to the supposed connection between Phillip and Rose through neighbouring farming interests, there was none. Rose did not acquire Cuffnells until 1784 and his relationship with Phillip was professional, not personal. We may never know whether Phillip also dealt with William Pitt. Pitt was directly and personally involved in the decision to establish a settlement at New South Wales, but Sydney as Home Secretary and Nepean as his Under-Secretary were responsible for its implementation and Phillip was mostly engaged with them.

When the decision was finally made, the wheels of the bureaucracy cranked quickly into motion. On 21 August Treasury was informed and funds were requested. On 31 August the Admiralty was informed and ships were requested. And on 15 September the East India Company was informed and its approval requested, something that was necessary because its Royal Charter gave it the exclusive monopoly of all British trade in the vast region from the Cape of Good Hope to the Americas. As to a leader for the expedition, Nepean and Sydney seem to have had Phillip firmly in mind. In late August Sydney made known to Howe, the then First Lord of the Admiralty, his intention to appoint Phillip to lead the convoy and to establish the settlement. Howe, an 'austere, morose and inaccessible' man, was not enthusiastic about Phillip, and doubted his suitability 'for a service of this complicated nature'. But Howe's views did not seem to matter. Phillip was Nepean's man and the expedition was a Home Office responsibility.

History and circumstance combined to make Phillip an astute choice. He knew the South Atlantic and was familiar with the Canaries, Rio de Janeiro and Cape Town. He had doubled the Cape of Good Hope and crossed the Indian Ocean to the Bay of Bengal. He had served as a covert agent in France and understood its naval threat and probably also its territorial aspirations. He had experience as a farmer at Lyndhurst. He was cerebral and his natural disposition was thoughtful. He had impressed the Portuguese Viceroy in Brazil and gained the confidence of the British administration in Whitehall. And if there is any substance in the legend about him, he had already transported a shipload of convicts from Lisbon to Brazil. Phillip's credentials for the assignment were no better pinpointed than by Captain John Faithful Fortescue, who commanded the 50-gun *Trusty* from 1783 to 1785. He is reputed to have said that:

> I do think God Almighty made Phillip on purpose for the place, for never did man better know what to do, or with more determination to see it done; and yet, if they'll let him, he will make them all very happy.

His words were echoed in a letter written by a midshipman who accompanied Phillip to New South Wales on the *Sirius*. The young correspondent informed his uncle from Rio de Janeiro that Phillip had 'seen much of the service, and much of the World; and studied it'; that he was 'possess'd of g^t good sence, well inform'd, indefatigable upon service'; that he was 'humane and at the same time spirited and resolute'; and that he was 'made on purpose for such a Trial of Abilities'. And looking back from the mid-nineteenth century, George Landmann, whose biography of his father described Phillip as Isaac Landmann's oldest and most intimate friend, colourfully stated that 'the Commodore ... had doubled every cape, had navigated every sea, had been tossed by the severest hurricanes, and ... been longer on the seas than on the land'.

Phillip received his commission as Governor of New South Wales on 12 October 1786. In one relatively undisguised respect, its terms revealed the expedition's international political context. Phillip was given authority over the whole of the land of New South Wales from Cape York in the north to Van Diemen's Land in the south and as far west as longitude 135°E. Curiously, the western boundary was seven degrees further west than even Cook had claimed in 1770. The willingness to extend British sovereignty this far but not to claim the whole of the continent had its source in Dutch political sensitivities – which Pitt's administration did not wish to offend at a time of delicate political relations. The reason was the 1777 Treaty of Santo Ildefonso, which had concluded the war in South America between Spain and Portugal. Phillip knew all about it, perhaps more than anyone else in Whitehall.

The text of the Treaty of Santo Ildefonso reached Rio de Janeiro in January 1778 and was a prime subject of interest and conversation. Phillip had been at leisure in Rio de Janeiro until May of that year and would no doubt have considered the treaty's effect. He would certainly have discussed it with Nepean in the process of drawing up his commission. Article 21 of the treaty recognised that the 'Ancient Line of Separation' was still operative. This was a reference to the line of demarcation laid down in the 1494 Treaty of Tordesillas – the line that divided the then known world between Spain and Portugal. Significantly, the 1777 treaty made clear that what had originally been a line of demarcation through the Atlantic was regarded as continuing through the corresponding meridian on the other side of the globe – in the eastern hemisphere.

As the Dutch republic had become Portugal's legatee in the Indian Ocean, it was now the country with the primary interest in the western half of what had been known for two centuries as 'New Holland'. Although there was uncertainty as to where precisely the ancient line ran in the eastern hemisphere, a contemporary map that was almost certainly available to Pitt's administration shows the line of demarcation along the 135th meridian. This was the boundary chosen to delineate the western extremity of the land over which Phillip's commission would extend. By adopting that boundary, the British government was seeking to respect the ancient line of demarcation and avoid offending the Dutch. The prospect of offending the Spanish did not seem to matter. That this was the true reason was later confirmed by Sir Joseph Banks in a preface he wrote for Matthew Flinders' 1811 book *A Voyage to Terra Australis*, in which he explained that the selection of the 135th meridian was intended to observe 'the Ancient Line of Separation' with which it was 'nearly corresponding'. The issue, however, was apparently so sensitive that Sir Robert Peel, then the Prime Minister, wrote to Banks requesting that he 'omit any notice of the reasons which are supposed to have informed His Majesty's Government in placing the western boundary of New South Wales'. Banks withdrew his preface, which was never published.

In April 1787 Phillip's commission was expanded. His powers were broadened but the extent of the land over which he would govern was unchanged. The first commission had assumed a military form of government but the administration soon recognised that convicts sentenced under civil law could not be made amenable to military justice. And martial law was not consistent with the lofty ideal of 'improvement' that Sydney increasingly hoped to achieve in the proposed settlement. Phillip's second commission, based on the commission given the year before to Lord Dorchester, the Governor-General of Canada, was more detailed and extensive than the first. Its principal distinguishing feature was that, unlike the Canadian commission, Phillip was authorised to govern alone and without a council. A council would be impracticable in New South Wales where, for the time being, there would not be a sufficient number of free men to make up such a body. In theory, however, Phillip's power was not completely untrammelled. He was subject to the rule of law and a system for the administration of justice through a court structure was contemplated from the outset. There was to be a civil court and a court of criminal jurisdiction. An appeal from the civil court lay to the Governor, unless the amount in question was more than £300. And the criminal court could not issue a capital sentence unless five of its members agreed.

In reality, the embryonic society under Phillip's governorship would be patriarchal, his authority effectively total. It would extend over half a continent and he would be almost as much a 'viceroy' as his friend Vasconselos in Brazil. He received all the powers that he thought a founding Governor should have. And his commission was arguably 'a more unlimited one than was ever before granted to any Governor under the British Crown'. He could raise an army, erect forts, castles and fortifications, grant pardons absolutely or conditionally, remit the sentences of convicts and of course make grants of land to those convicts whom he emancipated. And whenever he thought it appropriate, he could also make grants of land to marines and sailors who wished to settle in the colony.

Associated with Phillip's appointment as Governor was the question of his naval rank. He had been a post captain since 30 November 1781. Admirals were chosen by seniority from the top of the captains list. Phillip was still relatively junior, the list was long and promotion to admiral was only a distant future prospect. But captains were sometimes appointed as commodores when they were in command of a detached squadron. 'Commodore' was a temporary rank that lasted only for the duration of the command. It carried with it the right to fly a broad red pendant from the masthead and most of the status of a rear admiral. It also entitled the recipient to additional remuneration. Phillip duly requested permission from the Admiralty to fly the broad pendant — in effect that the rank of commodore be given to him — but without the increased remuneration. There was clearly some justification for Phillip's request as he would command eleven ships and John Hunter would be his second captain on the flagship *Sirius*. But once the transport ships were safely delivered to New South Wales, Phillip would be exercising a civil command and would direct the colony on behalf of the Home Office, to which alone he would be answerable. The Home Office and not the Admiralty would pay his salary and emoluments in New South Wales. In these circumstances the naval promotion that Phillip sought was complicated. Howe disliked innovation in naval protocol and refused the request.

Phillip, however, persisted. He took the issue up with Sydney, emphasising that however flattering he found the offer of the governorship, the task was not without its *désagrémens* for which the broad pendant would compensate. He even went so far as to say that the granting of it would be of small consequence to the nation but of considerable consequence to him. Sydney, however, had no authority on matters of naval rank and protocol and could do no more than ensure that Phillip was adequately recompensed by the Home Office. He fixed Phillip's remuneration as Governor at £1000 a year. This was a substantial sum and several times the rate of pay for naval captains. Even after the increases that occurred during the Napoleonic Wars, a captain of a typical sixth-rate vessel received no more than £200 a year; a captain of a first-rate vessel less than £400 a year. Phillip's senior civil officers, John White the principal surgeon and David Collins the judge-advocate, only received £182 a year. And in London, Evan Nepean received only £500 a year as Under-Secretary of one of the most important state departments in the most powerful country in the world. In fact, Phillip's remuneration put him on the same level as six of the seven Lords of the Admiralty. The amount was such that the authors of a nineteenth-century biography of Phillip referred to 'the outstanding generosity of the Government'.

Ultimately, Phillip sailed for New South Wales as a captain and not as a commodore. He was probably unfortunate and may have been hard done by. The sensitivity he displayed, although perhaps precious from a contemporary perspective, was probably no more or no worse than could have been expected from most senior naval officers of the era. Rank and title were matters of some moment. Phillip's strong feelings even continued after he reached New South Wales. In July 1790 he wrote privately to Sydney, taking up the subject again. Sydney's son-in-law had by then succeeded Howe as First Lord of the Admiralty. Phillip requested Sydney 'to submit to the consideration of Lord Chatham, whether employing an Officer on a Service which renders the appointing of a Second Captain to that Ship necessary, and refusing at the same time to give the Commanding Officer a distinguishing Pendant, as is the established custom of the Service on which he is employed ... tend[s] to any real advantage to His Majesty's Service'. His plea was to no avail.

CHAPTER 9

PHILOSOPHER

Administrative, practical and philosophical preparations for the settlement in New South Wales including the symbolism of 'Albion' and the Wheatley portraits

From October 1786 to May 1787 Phillip was constantly engaged in the preparation of the expedition for New South Wales. His immediate concern was the conversion and fitting out of the ships and the procuring of food, medicine, clothing and building supplies for the voyage and first years of the settlement. But there were many other issues that engaged his pragmatic and contemplative sides. It was necessary to consult with Admiralty officials in determining the route that the convoy would take. And hundreds of hours were required to be spent with Home Office officials discussing and resolving the detail of his instructions, the terms of his commission, the nature of government that should apply and the system of laws that should be administered. Phillip, Nepean, Sydney and their officials were in truth deliberating over the creation of a new society, one where there would be no currency and no slavery, and where the labour of convicts would be used to build the settlement and cultivate the land. There was no precedent for what they were seeking to achieve.

The first practical issue, the fitting out of the ships and the procuring of supplies, was a complex, disagreeable and troublesome business that required Phillip to call on all of his experience of the naval administration. He knew that his expedition would be longer, more difficult and qualitatively different from any previous undertaking in the navy's history. But the officials with whom he dealt at the Navy Board and its related departments could not always see it. These men, perhaps lacking imagination, inevitably hidebound by precedent, were the bureaucrats who pursued their careers in the multiple bodies and related departments with which it was necessary for Phillip to deal. Men such as these were not disposed by nature or training to make exceptions to longstanding practices. For eight months Phillip engaged in tedious and interminable negotiations. Approximately 800 letters were written and there were many hundreds of personal attendances.

Logistically, the proposed expedition was inherently different from the transport of soldiers or marines for the purposes of a military campaign. Phillip's expeditioners were settlers not fighting forces, and they were mostly unwilling at that. And they would have to endure a voyage whose length and duration would be greater than that of any previous undertaking, whether of convicts, soldiers or settlers. When they arrived at their destination, there would be no receiving station. And they would need to be sustained and provisioned for some years before they could expect to be self-sufficient. All of these features of the expedition and many more necessitated planning and foresight of a wider dimension than had previously been required.

The principal body with which Phillip dealt was the Navy Board but the organisational structure that constituted the Georgian navy was like a multi-headed hydra. The Navy Board was actually larger and older than the Admiralty itself. It was the body responsible for the acquisition, design and re-fitting of ships as well as the supply of all sorts of naval stores. It carried out the conversion of the merchant ships assigned to Phillip at Deptford, the oldest of the Royal dockyards on the Thames. The Victualling Board, second only to the Navy Board in size and complexity, was another with which Phillip was required to deal. It maintained victualling yards and stores at all of the dockyard ports on the Thames and at Portsmouth and Plymouth. Equally important was the Sick and Hurt Board. It was constituted by commissioners who were responsible for the appointment of surgeons and the provision of medical supplies to the navy, including anti-scorbutics. Then there was the Board of Ordnance, which was responsible for the supply of armaments and munitions to the Royal Navy and the British Army. Finally there was the Board of Longitude, of which the Reverend Dr Nevil Maskelyne, the Astronomer Royal, was the most influential member.

Throughout the long process of preparation, Phillip's abiding concern was the maintenance of the health of the convicts and marines during the voyage. This was a matter of professional pride but there was more to it than that. Phillip's resolve on this issue owed much to his humanity but even more to his realistic understanding of the magnitude of the task ahead. In March 1787 after many months of frustrations, Phillip took his anxieties directly to the Home Secretary, imploring Sydney for assistance. He wrote, he said, to prevent his character as an officer from being called into question should the consequences that he feared be realised. He pointedly explained that 'the garrison and the convicts are [being] sent to the extremity of the globe as [if] they would be sent to America – a six weeks passage'. He stressed that he had repeatedly pointed out the consequences that must be expected from the men and women being crowded on board such small ships for such a long voyage. He was anxious, he told Sydney, to avoid the possibility 'that it may be said hereafter the officer who took charge of the expedition should have known that it was more than probable he lost half the garrison and convicts crowded and victualled in such a manner for so long a voyage'.

Experience had given Phillip a keen appreciation of the problems of sickness and disease. As a naval officer, he had seen much of it, especially at Havana in 1762. His real fear was scurvy, a disease which on long voyages was the Royal Navy's greatest threat. In 1783 on the *Europe*, Phillip was part of a convoy that saw approximately 1800 seamen affected on the return journey from Madras to Cape Town. And all sailors knew of the appalling loss suffered by Commodore George Anson in 1740–44 during his voyage around the world, when more than 1000 seamen died from scurvy and only four were killed by enemy action. Although the threat to seamen was great, Phillip knew that the threat to convicts who were confined, undernourished and ill-treated would be even greater – and never more so than on a sea voyage of unprecedented length. His persistent demands exasperated Navy Board officials, some of whom complained that each day and each week he was continuing to increase the orders for stores, implements, medicines and supplies. One senior official, Captain George Teer, expostulated to the Board that Phillip's constant additions were so frequent that he felt 'obliged to put a stop to his wishes still to add'.

Scurvy was both a worry and a mystery to the navy. Although its diabolical consequences were well known, its causes were not, and by the 1780s there was still no consensus about how to treat it. The disease usually commenced with listlessness and swelling gums. Without effective treatment it then progressed to rotting teeth and pain in all external and internal parts of the body. In its final stages, the gums grew putrid with a cadaverous smell, the teeth became successively yellow, black and rotten, and gangrene ensued. Contagion then spread rapidly and death soon followed, usually preceded by one or all of diarrhoea, dysentery, consumption, convulsion, trembling, voiding of blood 'upwards and downwards' and putrefaction of the liver, spleen and pancreas. By 1747, the Scottish physician James Lind had established, without knowing why, that oranges and lemons were the most effective antidote for scurvy. But although he published several papers on the subject, the naval medical establishment – effectively the Sick and Hurt Board – dismissed his evidence as unproven and anecdotal. It adhered to malt, wort, sauerkraut and elixir of vitriol – the first having no anti-scorbutic effect whatsoever, the last being no more than a diluted solution of sulphuric acid tempered with alcohol and spices and the others having only limited value. It was not until 1795 that the Admiralty finally acted on Lind's findings and ordered the general issue of lime juice.

In the meantime, astute captains such as Phillip adopted an instinctive approach based on their own broad and empirical experience. Phillip had seen the benefits of oranges without knowing the medical pathology. In this respect he was ahead of his time and followed Lind rather than Cook, who had placed his faith in malt. Cook, to be fair, also adopted a regimen of fresh meats, vegetables and salad greens, as well as the drinking of water, the taking of exercise and the ventilation of bedding and sleeping quarters. Cook was remarkably successful but he did not have the added burden of carrying almost 800 convicts on six separate transport ships for whom the provision of fresh air and exercise presented practical problems. Phillip was prepared to follow Cook's measures scrupulously, but wanted an effective anti-scorbutic. The authorities had not yet accepted Lind's recommendations and continued to recommend malt and wort. There was nothing Phillip could do, at least while he was in England. He knew, however, that he could obtain fresh provisions including citrus fruits in Tenerife, Rio de Janeiro and Cape Town. And he was furnished with Treasury bills to enable him to do so.

Eleven vessels were entrusted to Phillip's overall command. Two of them – the *Sirius* and the *Supply* – were minor armed naval ships that were trifling in size when compared to large ships of the line such as the *Europe*, Phillip's last command. The *Sirius* was nominally a sixth-rate vessel because she was the flagship of the fleet and was commanded by a post captain. But at just 512 tons and carrying only ten guns and 136 men, she would not otherwise have been rated. The *Supply* was smaller still at 170 tons and carried just eight guns and 50 men. In her previous role, she had done little more than ferry naval stores between the Thames and the Channel ports.

Neither the *Sirius* nor the *Supply* had ever undertaken a voyage of the scale now proposed, or anything like it. Nor had any of the nine transports and store ships, which were simple ocean-going merchant vessels chartered by the navy – modest in size but comparatively newly built and seaworthy. The largest was the *Alexander*, which was the same length as the *Sirius* – just over 100 feet. Each of the transports had been inspected, surveyed and selected by naval officials following a competitive tender process. Although they were blunt-nosed, round-bodied and sailed poorly, speed was not an essential consideration and they were regarded as the best qualified to undertake the hazardous voyage. The six transports required considerable physical alteration by the shipwrights to transform them from merchant vessels built for commerce to prison ships suitable for carrying hundreds of convict men and women.

Phillip approved the introduction of three principal security measures on the transports. Thick bulkheads were constructed from side to side between decks. These were effectively walls behind which the convicts were confined. They were studded with nails. Holes known as loop holes were built into the bulkheads to enable the marines to fire at the convicts in case of unrest. There were no portholes. The hatches were also secured. This was achieved above decks by cross-bars, bolts and locks. Between decks, the hatchways were 'rail'd around from deck to deck with oak stanchions' to prevent access. Finally, an exercise area above decks in front of the mainmast was rendered secure on each transport. It was separated from the quarterdeck by a vertical wooden wall surmounted by iron spikes and constructed horizontally across the deck. At the base of this barricade, two small cannon were fixed in position, facing the exercise area.

Gidley King said that the transports were fitted up for the convicts the same as for carrying troops, except for the security arrangements. A letter to *The Gentleman's Magazine* marvelled at the administration's minute attention to detail, citing as one instance, 'They now have comfortable beds. Formerly when the convicts were transported by contract to America, there were no beds.' However, these were not beds as we know them. They were a sort of bunk each about six foot square, constructed in rows against the walls of the section of lower deck where the convicts were held. Multiple convicts occupied each of these communal sleeping spaces. As for the stowage of goods, the standard form of container was the wooden barrel, varying in size but not in proportion. Thousands of firkins, casks, puncheons, pipes, butts and hogsheads were laden on the ships. Their maintenance and repair were the responsibility of the 'cooper' and they were secured among the ballast deep in the ship's holds beneath the lowest deck.

Not everything could be stored in barrels, however. Wood and coal had to be conveyed, as well as livestock, plants and seeds, tools and agricultural equipment. Ten thousand bricks were included, as well as Surgeon Worgan's piano and 4200 bibles, prayer books, testaments, psalters and catechisms. Dogs, including greyhounds belonging to Phillip, and cats belonging to the chaplain, were also accommodated. The inclusion of greyhounds is not altogether surprising, although the number attributed to Phillip by one officer seems dubious. They were fashionable eighteenth-century accoutrements, often depicted in portraits by Thomas Gainsborough, Joshua Reynolds and their imitators, sitting loyally beside their masters or peeking out from behind billowing skirts. Lieutenant Ralph Clark complained that at Portsmouth, Phillip ordered that all dogs belonging to the officers and marines should be sent ashore although 'he himself carrys out between thirty and forty'.

Planning the voyage's route required much consultation. Phillip studied Cook's charts, especially those of his second voyage, and had access to charts in the Admiralty's possession recording voyages in the Indian Ocean by English and Dutch East India Company vessels. It is a measure of the importance of the expedition, and the uncertainty of navigation beyond the Cape of Good Hope, that the Board of Longitude also provided Phillip with a chronometer. Although the sailing routes in the Atlantic Ocean were well established, and the trade winds and currents were well known, every assistance would be needed in the waters of the Southern Ocean and the far reaches of the southern Indian Ocean. In the 1780s the use of a chronometer to determine longitude was not at all widespread. Only in the 1790s did the Royal Navy begin to supply them to ships in distant waters. Even by 1802 only seven per cent of British warships had a chronometer. And they did not become standard issue until the 1840s. The chronometer given to Phillip was 'K1', named after Mr Kendall – the same one taken by Cook on his second and third voyages.

This rare jewel of timekeeping was one of the Admiralty's most valuable possessions. The principle by which it determined longitude was deceptively simple, depending only on knowing the time at a place of known longitude, such as Greenwich. On a rolling deck at sea, a mechanical clock set at Greenwich time would behave aberrantly – slowing down, speeding up or stopping altogether. And en route from a cold country to a tropical zone, the clock's parts were affected not only by changes in temperature, humidity and barometric pressure but also by subtle variations in the earth's gravity from one latitude to another. The chronometer, however, could reliably report the time at Greenwich regardless of the ship's location or the sea conditions or the prevailing weather and humidity. Longitude could then be established by comparing Greenwich time with the time at sea – itself determined by using a sextant to observe the altitude of the sun. Each hour's difference between the time at Greenwich and that of the ship marked a progress of fifteen degrees to the east or west. Hence the saying 'time is longitude and longitude time'.

Although Cook called K1 'our trusty friend' and 'never-failing guide', it was not yet a commonly accepted substitute for celestial navigation by the lunar distance method, to which most captains still faithfully adhered. This method depended on the use of lunar distance tables published in the Nautical Almanac and updated annually. The process was not straightforward, however, and required celestial observation and trigonometrical calculation in conjunction with the use of the tables. Cook's legendary biographer JC Beaglehole said that the 'ordinary sea captain would take about four hours to work out the result' using the lunar tables. Calculation was piled on calculation and adjustment upon adjustment – something that the writer Simon Winchester once described as 'ever-more entangled filigrees of arithmetic'. Among other complications, allowance had to be made for the nearness to the horizon of the celestial object from which a reading was being taken. And further adjustments were required to counter the phenomenon of lunar parallax.

Phillip was characteristically cautious in his approach to the chronometer. He knew that, like any mechanical timepiece, it was only as good as the care taken to ensure that it was wound regularly. As soon as he received the chronometer from the Board of Longitude, he had it immediately checked by the headmaster of the Royal Naval Academy at Portsmouth. Then before setting sail, he specified a rigid routine for the noonday winding at sea. William Bradley, the first lieutenant on the *Sirius*, described the procedure as if his life depended on it:

Capt. Phillip, who with Capt. Hunter or Mr Dawes were always to be present at the winding of it at noon, and it was ordered to be the duty of the Lieutenant who brought 12 o'clock to see it done, and the officer who relieved him was not to take charge of the deck 'til he was informed that it was done, the sentinel at the cabin door was also ordered to plant himself inside the cabin on hearing the bell ring at noon, and was not to go out to be relieved until he was told or saw that the timekeeper was wound up.

In addition, Phillip intended that while at sea, constant cross-checks of the chronometer's results should be carried out against the readings obtained by the lunar distance method. This was to be the responsibility of Lieutenant Dawes, the unofficial astronomer to the expedition. He was not one of Phillip's chosen naval officers but a volunteer and marine lieutenant whose credentials had been promoted by Astronomer Royal Nevil Maskelyne. During the voyage Dawes would be assisted by Bradley and the midshipmen. The notes and comparative calculations of one of the midshipmen, George Raper, remain in existence. Alarmingly, they show frequent variations and differing results, which were naturally assumed to be the fault of the chronometer rather than any human error in the arithmetic of the young gentlemen who carried out the calculations.

In his preparation for the expedition Phillip clearly contemplated the proposed settlement's strategic and commercial potential. He expected that the colony would in time become 'the Empire of the East' and a future 'seat of Empire'. More than once he expressed the opinion that it would be 'of the greatest consequence to Britain'. In his early months at Port Jackson he wrote a lengthy report to Sydney expressing 'no doubt but that this country will prove the most valuable acquisition Great Britain ever made'. But there are indications that he may also have had in mind the colony's capacity for the improvement of the human condition. A gulag, where men and women simply worked and withered in useless and remote isolation, was not intended – not by the administration and certainly not by Phillip. In a private despatch to Sydney from Port Jackson he described himself as 'serving my country and serving the cause of humanity'.

The nature of transportation to New South Wales, and its difference from the previous system, partly explains why Phillip saw himself as serving the cause of humanity. The convicts sent to New South Wales were to be used to build a settlement and establish a self-supporting community that would serve their own as well as British interests. They were a public investment underpinned by the prospect of their intended future emancipation. In contrast, the convicts transported to Virginia and Maryland had been components in a system that was essentially a private commercial business. The only public concern was in their removal from Britain. Once the merchants had taken custody of the convicts and signed the requisite certificates and bonds, the convicts ceased to be a government responsibility and were forgotten. They were on-sold in bondage to serve the balance of their prison terms in local plantations and households, effectively as white slaves, beyond the government's control and without its supervision.

Under the New South Wales experiment, Phillip was empowered to release the convicts whenever their good conduct and disposition to industry were deserving of favour. In each case, he was to grant them land 'with all convenient speed'. Even the precise acreage was stipulated. Single men were to receive 30 acres and married men 50 acres. A surveyor of lands, Augustus Alt, was appointed to administer land grants. It was hoped that the convicts would be improved and reformed; that the men would become peasant farmers, the women would raise children, and the land would be settled. These goals were infused by a utopian idea of a simple rural society, without money, where convict men and women would become reborn through hard physical labour and subsistence farming.

The central pillars of this scheme of 'improvement' were the cultivation of the land and the issuing of land grants. James Matra, who inspired some of the thinking about the establishment of the colony, had earlier expressed his own view to the administration with robust certainty: 'Give them a few acres of ground as soon as they arrive ... with what assistance they want to till them'. If that were done he said, then 'it is very probable that they will [become] moral subjects of society.' The same point, rather more quaintly stated, was explained by another: 'It is sufficiently proved by ancient and modern history that [even thieves] ... cease to be enemies of society whenever they have regained their full human rights and become proprietors and cultivators of the land.' These were truisms of the time. It is no coincidence that at the very same time in North America, Thomas Jefferson was describing the cultivators of the land as heroes of society.

Progressively, as Phillip's instructions were discussed and negotiated within the Home Office, this theme of improvement achieved more and more prominence. When Phillip's instructions were eventually finalised in April 1787, it was made abundantly clear that every incentive and much generous practical assistance should be given to assist and encourage the convicts to undertake independent agricultural development. Not only was Phillip directed to emancipate deserving convicts and give them land, but he was now also instructed to provide each emancipated convict with twelve months' supply of start-up provisions 'together with an assortment of tools and utensils, and such proportion of seed-grain, cattle, sheep and hogs as may be proper, and can be spared from the general stock of the settlement'.

Phillip's opinions as the Governor-elect were naturally sought and the whole process was necessarily consultative. He commented on drafts of his instructions and provided the administration with a detailed statement of his hopes, expectations and proposals for both the voyage and the establishment of the colony. In doing so, he revealed his own developing thoughts on matters that would affect the conduct of society in the new settlement. His approach was humanitarian and pragmatic. He made no mention of religion or church, of which there is no evidence of personal interest, but expressed preliminary views on more worldly topics such as relations with the Aborigines, convict prostitution, capital offences and slavery.

Phillip rightly thought that the Aborigines might be more numerous than Cook had observed. It would be a great gain, he wrote, if he could proceed 'without having any dispute with the Natives'. His approach was philanthropic, characterised by an Enlightenment benevolence. He assumed the best, not the worst. He said he would endeavour to persuade a few of the Aborigines to settle near us so that he could 'furnish [them] with everything that can tend to civilize them'. He hoped to impress them and 'to give them a High Opinion of their New Guests.' However, he did not expect that the Aborigines would be impressed by the crews of the transport ships or the convicts. Indeed, he thought it would be 'necessary to prevent the Transports Crews having any intercourse with the Natives if possible'. The convicts, he said, 'must have none'. Significantly, when it came to homicide, Phillip regarded the life of an Aboriginal man as the equal of any Englishman, recording memorably, 'Any man who takes the life of a Native, will be put on his trial as if he had kill'd one of the Garrison. This appears to me not only just, but good policy.'

The gender imbalance was an important issue. Only a quarter of the convicts were female and some commentators predicted that there would be 'odious consequences'. Phillip's instructions therefore required him to 'procure' women from the Pacific Islands – an instruction that he studiously ignored, later observing to Sydney that it would only be bringing them 'to pine away a few years in misery'. He suggested that it may be best if 'the most abandoned of the female convicts might be permitted to receive the visits of the (male) convicts in the limits allotted them at certain hours and under certain restrictions'. He added that 'At Mill Bank [jail in London] something of this kind had been permitted'. But nothing ever came of this pragmatic proposal.

While tolerant of prostitution, Phillip took a harsh view of murder. And like most eighteenth-century naval officers, he lumped sodomy into the same category. In fact, sodomy was almost the only crime in the navy for which the death penalty was often awarded. During the Seven Years War there were eleven courts martial for sodomy, although the convictions were few. It was an offence that would bring disgrace on a ship. In Phillip's New South Wales, two crimes would merit death: murder and sodomy. In either case he said he would wish to confine the criminal till an opportunity offered of delivering him as a prisoner to the natives of New Zealand – 'and let them eat him'.

Wryly, he observed that the dread of this 'will operate much stronger than the fear of death'. In fact, Phillip never despatched anyone to be feasted on by Maori cannibals.

On slavery, Phillip was firmly opposed. He had seen the worst of the Portuguese and Dutch slaving practices in Brazil and at Cape Town and set his face against the introduction of slavery to the new colony. He wrote, 'There can be no slavery in a free land and consequently no slaves'. On this issue, he supported the anti-slaving views of William Wilberforce and his friend, the Prime Minister William Pitt. Pitt must have clearly sanctioned Phillip's stated opposition to the introduction of slavery in New South Wales, for he had spoken in favour of the immediate abolition of slavery on a number of occasions during the years 1785 to 1787. The issue was not a party or factional matter and Pitt's conviction was personal and based on humanitarian principles. A few years later in the House of Commons, he declaimed to the members of parliament gathered in the chamber that: 'No nation in Europe ... has ... plunged so deeply into this guilt as Great Britain.'

As the long months of preparation progressed, some began to see the expedition to New South Wales as a social experiment, an undertaking of humanity that was essentially hopeful and a force for good. From their perspective, the expedition was a manifestation of the optimism that marked the Enlightenment – an age that was energised by the possibilities of improvement, not just of land but of the human condition. One thoughtful correspondent to the *St James Chronicle* wrote in January 1787: 'The Expedition to Botany Bay comprehends in it more than the mere Banishment of our Felons; it is an Undertaking of Humanity ...

[by which] a capital Improvement will be made in the southern part of the New World.' Within a few short years, Erasmus Darwin, one of the great thinkers of the age and a grandfather of Charles Darwin, would burst into rapturous poetic optimism about the colony's future. His poem *The Voyage of Hope to Sydney Cove* prophesied a peaceful and joyful transformation of the wild landscape through commerce, agriculture and public works. And Josiah Wedgwood – Charles Darwin's other grandfather – would create a commemorative medallion made from clay found at Sydney Cove that Phillip sent to him via Sir Joseph Banks. Its classical symbolism was prophetic, auspicious and imbued with hope.

Phillip had his own grand designs. He conceived for the settlement the name of 'Albion', the ancient synonym for Britain. His selection put him in good company. When Sir Francis Drake claimed the northern coast of California for Elizabeth I in 1579, he adopted the same symbolism, naming it 'New Albion'. The story of Albion is Britain's foundation myth. In *The Faerie Queene* (1596), the poet Edmund Spenser said that the name Albion was bestowed in honour of an ancestral giant who conquered the British Isles. According to legend, Albion founded the island country that became Britain and ruled there until he was killed by Heracles. Albion's giant descendants continued to inhabit the island until Brutus of Troy vanquished them more than a thousand years before the Roman invasion. The huge white horses inscribed on the chalk hills of southern England are said to be traces of that era. In 1820 William Blake took the legend of Albion to new heights in his poem *Jerusalem*, which was subtitled *The Emanation of the Giant Albion*. But in 1787 the patriotic significance of Albion was already firmly imbedded in Phillip's thinking as he pondered over the significance of his mission.

Soon Phillip came to be spoken of as someone from whom great things were expected. Among his influential patrons, Sydney was the one to whom he owed the most. It is clear that if he had not already done so, Phillip acquired Sydney's entire confidence as they worked together through the winter and early spring months. And their relationship was personal as well as professional. Phillip was introduced to Lady Sydney; he befriended their son, John Townshend; and he became acquainted with their daughter, Mary, not to mention her mother-in-law, Lady Chatham, the mother of Prime Minister William Pitt. Lord Lansdowne was another who was enthused by Phillip's expedition. He and Phillip first became acquainted in 1782 while poring over Phillip's South American naval charts together with Nepean and Sydney. Lansdowne, then known as Shelburne, was Home Secretary at the time, before becoming Prime Minister. Upon retirement, he became a major figure of the Enlightenment who gathered around him a vibrant intellectual circle at his sumptuous home at Bowood House in Wiltshire. Another patron from whom Phillip received much polite attention was Sir Joseph Banks, an original progenitor of settlement in New South Wales. Banks threw himself into many aspects of the expedition and in the months before the fleet sailed, Phillip frequently attended his home in Soho Square, London. It was a perfect museum, full of treasures and curiosities. When Phillip reached New South Wales, he corresponded, privately and at length, with each of these men – Sydney, Lansdowne and Banks.

There was another aspect to Banks' patronage. He was, as was well known, a trusted friend and confidant of George III and had been the King's botanical advisor since 1773. In the gardens of the Royal Palace at Kew, George III would walk with Banks on Saturdays, examining plants and inspecting the glass houses. He responded enthusiastically to Banks' ideas, supporting plant-collecting expeditions, exhibiting an interest in agricultural and horticultural developments, and in due course sharing his enthusiasm for the agricultural advances and benefits to be derived from New South Wales. In early January 1787 George III interviewed Phillip at St James' Palace. It was Phillip's second royal audience. The first had been with the King of Portugal twelve years earlier. In both cases his destination in the first instance was Rio de Janeiro. The timing of Phillip's audience with George III was significant. The ambit of his official instructions had not yet been finalised and the King was soon to address the opening session of parliament to publicly announce the expedition. History does not record the content of their discussion, but it is clear that Phillip understood his paramount responsibility for the cultivation of the land and the agricultural development of the colony. One may surmise that this was also a matter of interest to the King who was known, not necessarily always with affection, as 'Farmer George'.

As the idea and significance of Phillip's expedition took root, it was fitting that the painter Francis Wheatley, who had recently returned to London, should be commissioned to record his image for posterity. History records Wheatley as one of the leading artists of the late eighteenth century. He is often mentioned in the same breath as Gainsborough and Reynolds and frequently exhibited with them. But he did not quite have their genius for producing grand and flattering visionary portraits for illustrious patrons. Nor did he have their business skills. For Wheatley liked the ladies and lived excessively. But he was a member of the Royal Academy, had many wealthy clients and achieved fame, if not ultimately fortune. He also spread his redoubtable talents across landscape as well as portraiture. In the latter category his clients included Christian VII of Denmark and many dozens of notable and well-to-do families. Wheatley is said to have 'mirrored to perfection the taste, the manners and that confident grace which so characterized the elegant society of his day'. Although his pictures were much in demand, and frequently engraved, history now remembers him best for his *Cries of London* series, poignantly depicting everyday scenes of London life among the urban poor.

Wheatley was commissioned by Elizabeth Everitt and painted Phillip twice in 1786. He was a logical choice, not just because of his high standing, but because he had been a pupil of Richard Wilson, one of the original members of the Royal Academy. In 1747, Wilson had painted Elizabeth Everitt's late husband Michael, Phillip's first patron. And family connections such as these are often preserved. Wheatley's major picture of Phillip remained in the extended family until the twentieth century. The subsequent history of Wheatley's smaller picture of Phillip is less clear. It is oval shaped and portrays Phillip looking mildly bookish, a touch diffident, indoors, against a dark interior, holding a plan of New South Wales. It was quickly engraved and in 1789 appeared on the front cover of Stockdale's publication of the voyage.

The composition of the larger picture is grand and sweeping. Phillip is portrayed on the shore of a distant land. In the far background is a man-of-war with red ensign aflutter at the stern. Nearby are two sailors in a small boat. One has a grappling hook. Phillip is at the water's edge and appears to be taking his first steps. The sky is threatening and dark clouds move across the skyline. Phillip appears cautious, alert and curious, not imperious. He is wearing a grey powdered wig, a captain's undress uniform of the period, and a black bicorne hat in the transverse style with black cockade. The number and arrangement of buttons signify his seniority and indicate his rank – twelve buttons on each blue lapel arranged in groups of three. His legs are in white breeches and stockings; the upper body and shoulders are small. A dress sword or smallsword hangs from his left hip. Despite the magisterial pretensions, the overall imagery is dignified, calm and ordered. Phillip is portrayed as a symbol of authority but with an appearance and bearing that suggest sensibility – a key feature of the Enlightenment period. It was an attitude reflected in moderation and rationality. Discussion was preferred to disputation, conversation to controversy and politeness to pedantry. In polite society at least, machismo was vulgar and unfashionable. It was certainly not Phillip's style.

CHAPTER 10

COMMANDER

The Journey to New South Wales – Tenerife, Rio de Janeiro, Cape Town and the Southern Ocean

In the early light of dawn on Sunday 13 May 1787 Phillip gave the signal to the captains to weigh anchor. Some of the women's clothing, a sufficient quantity of musket balls and sundry other items were outstanding, but they could be obtained in Rio de Janeiro or Cape Town. The sails of the eleven ships soon bellied and stiffened in the breeze and, as the sun rose higher, the convoy emerged from the Solent, passed the three distinctive stacks of chalk known as the Needles at the western end of the Isle of Wight and entered the English Channel. They were headed for the Atlantic Ocean. For many there would be no return. Phillip's term was not fixed and he could not know when he might see England again. His farewell note to Nepean revealed his optimism – 'At a future period when this country feels the advantages that are to be drawn from our intended settlement, you will enjoy a satisfaction that will, I am sure, make you ample amends'. He was leading his band of naval and civilian officers, seamen, marines and a smattering of wives, together with their cargo of almost 800 convicts and about 30 babies, toddlers and young children, to the far end of the world to build a new society in an alien land, on virgin terrain. It was absurdly ambitious – 'the largest forced exile of citizens by a European government in pre-modern history'.

Until they reached their destination, the men, women and children under Phillip's command would inhabit a floating world constantly at the mercy of the sea, exposed each day to the vagaries of wind and current. Except for ballast, the ships were wholly made from materials derived from trees and grass. The hull, masts and spars were of wood; the rigging, rope and cordage of hemp; and the sails of flax. At sea, the ships would pitch and roll and scend, searching for equilibrium. The movement of timbers and the chafe of rigging created a discordant symphony of sounds – creaks, groans, shrieks, wails and vibrations that never ceased. Experienced sailors like Phillip knew to work with the winds and the currents, to go with the flow, to harness the forces of nature. They were ever sensitive without even knowing it; attuned to the natural forces that controlled their destiny; alert to the complex relations and reactions between ship and sea and wind. So much was intuitive and ingrained – deducible simply from the tension on a rope, the spring of a spar, the creak of a block or the tune in the rigging. Out on the open ocean, the sea was wide and featureless, unmarked and largely unknowable. The ship's master would peer into the distance, his gaze fixed on the endless approaching swell lifting and running under the vessel. In big seas, waves would crash on board, occasionally flooding below decks. At other times, the ocean would glisten and sparkle like hammered silver. Often it was grey-green, heaving, leaden and dull. Whatever the conditions, they would never last. The barometric pressure would invariably drop and the winds would always freshen. Then all eyes would watch the horizon as a wall of cloud or rain or hail or snow rolled inexorably towards them.

For the seamen, their day-to-day work at sea was intensely physical. Pulling and hauling was their staple activity, in all weathers. And whenever sail had to be made or handed, the 'topmen' as they were called had to go aloft, out on the yards. Night and day, men were posted high in the lookouts. And for some tasks all seamen were needed. When weighing anchor or hoisting in the longboat, scores of men would strain around the capstan for hours to bring in the huge anchors and the cumbersome hemp cables. Daily life was governed by the watches. On naval ships such as the *Sirius* and the *Supply*, the seamen never had more than four hours' sleep. The master and the lieutenants took it in turns to be officer of the watch. Each watch was of four hours, and time aboard ship was measured by the changing of the watches. A petty officer kept a half-hour sandglass and when he turned the sandglass, he rang the ship's bell – once at the first half-hour, twice at the second, and so on. After four hours, he rang eight bells and the watch changed. Lights out was at eight o'clock in the evening when the watch coming off duty went to sleep until midnight.

On a merchant vessel, life was even more arduous. Transport vessels were always cramped. In fact, owners generally only tendered small vessels for transport service as larger vessels were more profitably employed elsewhere, on routes where lucrative return cargoes could be collected. Often they were under-manned so that the ratio of ship tons to men was frequently higher than on naval vessels. And on a merchant ship which had been converted for carrying convicts, there were additional difficulties. Marines had to be accommodated to guard the convicts and surgeons to supervise their medical care. To add to the difficulties, the seamen who worked the merchant vessels were inevitably drawn from the dregs of society.

When Phillip's fleet emerged from the English Channel in high seas and fine weather 300 miles west of Portsmouth, the ships charted a course to take advantage of the trade winds and elemental currents of the Atlantic Ocean. They sailed for Santa Cruz on the island of Tenerife in the Canaries. For centuries, when European sailing ships headed south out of the North Atlantic, they made their first port of call at the Canary Islands, perhaps at Madeira, occasionally at the Cape Verde Islands. The route to the Canaries was second nature to European navigators. It was facilitated by the northeast trade winds and the surface currents of the North Atlantic. In Stockdale's publication of Phillip's voyage, it was said that the Canary Islands 'seem as if expressly placed to facilitate the navigation to and from the Cape of Good Hope'.

It may seem curious then that the fleet should next make for Rio de Janeiro on the South American coast. But a broad westerly loop, with or without a stop at Rio de Janeiro, was the second leg of a time-honoured route to the Cape of Good Hope. It was dictated by the trade winds and the currents and designed to avoid the Doldrums – or the Intertropical Convergence Zone as the meteorologists call it. In the eighteenth century, the sailing rituals of old were fundamentally unchanged – follow the currents, sail before the winds and follow the paths of seabirds. Thus nature laid an indirect path to the Cape of Good

Hope. Off the North African coast, the Canary Current merges with the North Equatorial Current. Fuelled by the southeast trade winds, the latter sweeps across the Atlantic towards the Antilles and the South American coast. There it divides, the greater part being deflected north through the Caribbean and the Gulf of Mexico, eventually becoming the Gulf Stream and completing the clockwise circle of the North Atlantic gyre. The smaller part forms the Brazil Current flowing south along the South American coast before being deflected eastwards across the South Atlantic to the Cape of Good Hope. This deflection is known as the Southern Connecting Current and it provides a red carpet ride to Cape Town. When it meets the South African coast it joins forces with the Benguela Current thundering up from the Antarctic. This is the eastern boundary of the South Atlantic gyre, moving in a circular anti-clockwise direction in perfect countervailing symmetry with the northern gyre.

For these reasons, there was no established sailing route directly south from the Canaries to the Cape of Good Hope. There were too many natural obstacles of wind and current. And if any sailing ship attempted such a course, it would first have to pass through the worst of the Doldrums in the Equatorial zone near the West African coast. In this region, the violent thunderstorms and stagnant calms that are a feature of the whole of the Equatorial waters are more frequent. Often there is no wind, not the slightest breeze. And a ship becalmed in extreme heat is a danger to the health of its crew, let alone to any human cargo below decks without adequate ventilation. Here the trade winds of the North and South Atlantic cancel each other out. This convergence, combined with the intense sun and perpetually warm water, contribute to increased atmospheric moisture, which is released in an ongoing series of thunderstorms and squalls. As was so neatly explained in Stockdale's account: 'The calms so frequent on the African side are of themselves a sufficient cause to induce a navigator to keep a very westerly course.' If a ship persisted in maintaining a southerly bearing, it would, when finally emerging from the Doldrums, be slowed by the South Atlantic gyre flowing in the opposite direction. And if it stayed close to the West African coast, it would encounter head-on the full force of the Benguela. Phillip therefore steered a south-westerly course from Tenerife.

There was a point however, before the fleet's arrival at Tenerife, when Phillip showed his steel and demonstrated his humanity. It was one of those flashes that sometimes reveals the measure of a man. The third lieutenant of the *Sirius* had engaged in the customary practice of striking some of the seamen with a cane or knotted rope to make them work harder. This was an unnecessary and brutal naval custom that was readily abused and too often connived at. It was known as 'starting' and was a delicate issue. Some captains contended that in moments of urgency, there was no alternative to herding seamen about the deck with blows or chasing up the lazy with a rattan. Phillip on the other hand would have none of it. When he heard of the incident, he ordered every officer 'even to a Boatswain's Mate' to the great cabin. There, he informed them that if any officer struck one of the crew, he would 'break' him immediately. Those men, he explained, 'are all we have to depend upon and if we abuse those men that we have to trust, the convicts will rise and massacre us all. These men are our support. We have a long and severe station to go through ... if [the crew] are ill-treated by their own officers, what support can you expect of them?'

One would have thought this was clear enough but the incident was quickly followed by two more. In the first, a midshipman ordered the armourer's mate to carry his hammock on deck for airing, to which the sailor apparently responded by saying that he could not do so immediately as he had a job for the captain. The midshipman, to his discredit, struck the sailor, knocking out one of his teeth. Not surprisingly Phillip was furious. This time he ordered all hands to be turned out on the quarterdeck. To the midshipmen of the *Sirius*, he explained some home truths, telling them that when he was a midshipman, he had to carry his own hammock on deck and that they 'were no better than he was'. Turning to the seamen, he said that if he found any man carrying a midshipman's hammock or a cot, he would immediately flog him. To Phillip's astonishment, a few days later, a seaman was found carrying a midshipman's hammock. Determined to see his orders enforced, Phillip ordered the man tied up and directed the Boatswain to have all hands turned out to witness the punishment. Only the entreaties of Captain Hunter and Lieutenant Bradley, together with the fact that it was a first offence, saved the man from a flogging. But Phillip had made his point.

The second leg of the voyage, from Tenerife to Rio de Janeiro through the equatorial waters of the mid Atlantic, involved considerable hardship for everyone – especially the convicts. Food and water had to be restricted. And the high temperatures and heavy tropical rain caused distress and anxiety. In the enervating heat and debilitating humidity of the equatorial region, the convicts suffered. None of them could have been familiar with the ambient temperatures to which they were exposed above decks, let alone the state of incalescence they must have suffered in their cramped quarters below decks. Phillip required the captains of the transports to allow the convicts on deck as often as possible without their leg irons – day and night. However, the use of the exercise area above decks depended on the captain's discretion and his goodwill, which could not always be assumed. For the merchant captains in command of the transports were drawn from a rougher caste than Phillip, and humanity towards the convicts was often the least of their concerns. They were mostly men of little education or refinement; hard-drinking, hard-swearing and occasionally brutal. Concern for the health of the convicts was often secondary to real or imagined anxieties that the safety of the ship would be imperilled or the security of the convicts compromised. And there was ample room for legitimate disagreement.

There were further complications. The principal surgeon, John White, adhered firmly to prevailing naval medical views about the dangers of dampness to human health. He felt it essential that the convicts be kept out of the torrential rains, no matter how warm the rain or how rapidly the convict clothing might dry in the fierce sun. Thus the practical effect of the regular tropical storms and squalls was to limit the opportunities for the convicts to be brought on deck. Whenever the periodic rains lashed the convoy, the convicts were kept below while rain pounded on the hatches and washed across the deck. The position of the women convicts was even worse. During the suffocating sultry nights they were battened down as a matter of course, whether or not there was rain, to avoid what some officers primly described as 'a promiscuous intercourse' with the seamen and marines that was 'uncontrollable'.

On the *Alexander* the suffering of the all-male convict contingent was dangerously aggravated for yet another reason. At one stage en route, the ship's bilge water, from the lowest part of the ship beneath the hold, inexplicably rose to such a level that many became sickly. The noxious effluvia was so powerful that cabin panels and buttons on officers' jackets turned black. When the hatches were removed, the stench made it scarcely possible to stand over them. Beneath the hatches, in oppressive conditions, in semi-darkness and filth, without portholes, where rats, cockroaches, fleas and bedbugs ran free, the convict squalor was at its very worst. When complaint reached Phillip on the *Sirius*, he immediately ordered the *Alexander*'s master, Duncan Sinclair, to pump out and regularly replace the bilge water. Only Phillip's prompt reaction brought these convicts back from the brink. Sinclair had prior form on matters of health and hygiene, having been responsible for much avoidable sickness on the *Alexander* when it was moored at Portsmouth.

The heat and tropical squalls were not the only natural phenomena to which the bewildered convicts were exposed. Schools of flying fish abounded in these ocean waters. White recorded his astonishment at the behaviour of the streamlined torpedo-shaped fish, whose wondrous flight is an escape mechanism from predators. More confusing still was the changing celestial panorama of the night sky. At certain times of the year, and for a few hours each night, and only within about 20° north of the Equator, both the North Star (*Polaris*) and the Southern Cross (*Crux*) can be seen simultaneously – the former sitting low over the North Pole and the latter on the far southern horizon. If that were not strange enough, the uninitiated would have been startled to see stretching across the heavens the broad, blazing and unfamiliar band of the Milky Way. In the northern hemisphere, the axial tilt of the North Pole, away from the galactic centre of the Milky Way, renders its appearance indistinct and almost inconsequential – no more than a 'faint silvery vapour' according to the Scots writer Robert Louis Stevenson, observing from the mountains of the Cevennes in France.

Eventually, at the beginning of August, after a longer than expected two months' sailing from Tenerife, the fleet approached the capacious harbour at Rio de Janeiro. White recorded in his journal that 'Captain Phillip for the first time displayed his broad pendant'. This is somewhat surprising given Howe's refusal to appoint Phillip as commodore. Equally surprising is the midshipman George Raper's contemporary illustration of the fleet in Rio de Janeiro showing the broad red-forked commodore's pendant flying from the *Sirius'* mainmast. It would seem that like other captains before him, Phillip was prepared to take liberties when beyond the reach of the Admiralty – 'south of the line' as it was known.

For the convicts, the arrival of the fleet in Rio de Janeiro was a relief. They were rested and provided with fresh food. For Phillip, it was a homecoming to a port with which he was affectionately familiar. Although his friend and admirer Lavradio was no longer the Viceroy, Phillip knew his successor Vasconcelos, who had befriended him when he visited Rio de Janeiro in 1783 on the *Europe* and now treated him as someone to whom the Portuguese nation was indebted. Thus the fleet's arrival was greeted with pomp and ceremony. As the eleven ships entered past Sugarloaf and Santa Cruz, each flew an ensign from the stern and hoisted a pennant from the mainmast. And the *Sirius* saluted with a volley of thirteen cannon, conforming to a tradition designed to show that by firing and thereby partially disarming the ship, she had no hostile intent. In turn, the Portuguese fort returned the salute with an equal number of guns. When Phillip was ready to disembark, Vasconcelos sent the palace guard to formally receive him as he came ashore. The guard was directed to pay to Phillip the same honours as were paid to Vasconcelos as the representative of the Portuguese crown. This was high praise indeed. And at the ensuing vice-regal reception, Vasconcelos ordered that Phillip's senior officers – but not the merchant captains, the seamen or the marines – be permitted to move freely about the city and its environs unaccompanied by a military escort. This gesture was almost unheard of in security-conscious Rio de Janeiro, and Hunter described it as an extraordinary mark of civility and confidence. All took it for granted that it was due to the standing of Phillip in the Portuguese community.

Phillip knew what to expect of Rio de Janeiro but for his untravelled companions, especially the civilians, the city was a novel cultural experience. The vivacity of the religious processions and feast days that punctuated daily life was a revelation to them, as were the multitudinous convents, churches, chapels and seminaries, not to mention the altars on street corners dedicated to the Virgin Mary and the constant exhibitions of public veneration wherever they went. White the surgeon and Collins the judge-advocate were intrigued by the Portuguese women whose dark and lively eyes seemed to follow the English visitors from balconies and windows and even from behind convent gates. Collins notably lapsed into rhapsody when later recording his impressions. He described the women of Rio de Janeiro as 'daughters of the sun' and made other even more Delphic comments about them. But whatever he may have experienced, or possibly imagined, there was little time for attachments.

As usual during the voyage, Phillip's first concern was the health of the convicts and marines. The sick were taken off the ships, landed on an island in the harbour known as Ilha das Cobras and provided with generous allowances of fresh meat and vegetables. Phillip also procured prodigious quantities of citrus. At Tenerife, the only fresh fruits in season had been figs. And as the voyage progressed, scurvy had begun to make its presence felt. Fortunately, oranges were abundant in Rio de Janeiro. Baskets brimming with Brazilian citrus were brought to the ships and hauled up over the rails. Men on the Portuguese guard boats even amused themselves by throwing oranges onto the decks of the transports. Within a week of arrival, the marine private John Easty described an entirely new culinary experience on his ship – ten oranges a day prescribed for each of the convicts and marines. Soon every symptom of the scurvy receded.

All of the ships lowered their yards and topmasts and overhauled their rigging. An observatory was set up on Enxadas Island in the harbour where Dawes and two of the midshipmen took their instruments. Daily the convicts were served with a pound of rice and a pound and a quarter of fresh meat, together with vegetables and fruit. And Phillip attended to the business of obtaining the flora that would be suitable for the climate in New South Wales. He took on board as many of the seeds and plants recommended by Sir Joseph Banks as he could. They included coffee and cocoa, prickly pear with cochineal insects, tamarind, banana, orange, lime and lemon as well as guava, tobacco and rice. He also procured 115 pipes of poor-quality rum for the marines. It was inferior to rum from the West Indies and the marines said that they drank it 'only out of absolute necessity' … of course. Wine was important for medicinal purposes but its limited availability and high price led Phillip to purchase only fifteen of the 30 pipes proposed. One hundred sacks of the bread substitute casada were also purchased. Phillip thought that the sacks, made of strong

Russian flax, would serve the dual purpose of providing clothing for the convicts, 'many of whom are nearly naked'.

There was good-natured fraternisation by the senior officers at many levels, onshore and on board some of the ships. Dawes assisted Portuguese astronomers to establish the then still uncertain longitude of Rio de Janeiro. White assisted the Portuguese surgeon Ildefonso, teaching him the Allenson's method of leg amputation and performing it on one of his patients, to Ildefonso's consternation. Phillip and Vasconselos enjoyed each other's company as friends. And at the gates of the Ajuda Convent, three English gentlemen, including the principal surgeon White, basked in the charms of the young ladies who were confined in monastic isolation inside. White wistfully explained how 'We formed as tender an intercourse with them as the bolts and bars between us would admit of'.

Finally, in early September at the Viceregal Palace, the Portuguese colours were laid at Phillip's feet and Vasconcelos raised a toast to Phillip. In his private apartments, they farewelled each other as friends. At dawn on 3 September, almost a month after they had arrived, Phillip led the fleet out of the harbour at Rio de Janeiro. The fort at Santa Cruz performed a 21-gun salute, the highest national honour. And the *Sirius* duly responded gun for gun. Phillip then charted a course southeast across the South Atlantic Ocean. For the next five weeks, the conditions were robust and challenging. The weather was stormier than it had been during the first and second stages of the voyage and the convoy encountered strong gales and winds for the greater part of the passage to the Cape. The transports pitched and rolled, sometimes shipping large quantities of water, flooding between decks and causing misery to the convicts who were compelled to remain below, wet and seasick. Miraculously, only one life was lost, a convict from the *Charlotte* who fell overboard. The boisterous weather ensured that the convicts were generally subdued and well behaved, although those in charge of them were not. Surly tempers and bickering began to emerge with more than usual frequency. All yearned to reach Cape Town. When they arrived, 93 convicts and twenty marines were on the sick list.

Cape Town was the last outpost of European civilisation before the fleet would embark on the final leg to New South Wales. The little ships lay moored in Table Bay from mid-October until 12 November 1787. Phillip and his officers took lodgings in the town while the convicts remained on board, as did the merchant captains, some of whom held drinking parties and quarrelled excessively. It was a difficult, fractious time. Although there were some lighter moments, the period was marked by a sense of foreboding and a sense of urgency. English naval ships and East Indiamen had been calling at Cape Town since the seventeenth century to rest their sick and replenish their provisions en route to and from India. It was well known that Dutch hospitality was frequently grudging and rarely generous. And prices were invariably high. Phillip experienced this himself on the *Europe*'s return journey from India in 1783. And on this visit the Governor, Van de Graaf, used the excuse of a recent drought which he said had reduced the amount of grain that could be supplied to the fleet. Phillip sent Gidley King to the Governor for permission to purchase food and livestock. It took a week of repeated applications, explanations and judicious perseverance before the Governor and Council would accede to Phillip's request.

Although Van de Graaf complained of a shortage of grain, Phillip's own enquiries of local traders revealed a different picture, entitling him to be sceptical. He wrote to Stephens at the Admiralty to say that, contrary to what had been represented to him, he had 'found on enquiry that the last year's crops had been very good'. Ultimately the fleet was supplied with 80,000 pounds of flour, 60 bushels of wheat and 800 of barley, as well as 18,000 pounds of bread. As to livestock and wine, permission was freely given but Phillip and his senior officers were dismayed by the avarice of the Dutch merchants who charged double or treble their usual prices. There was nothing they could do.

Cape Town represented a very different civilisation from the one whose gaiety and charms had delighted Phillip's officers in Rio de Janeiro. There was little liveliness in this Dutch settlement and no exuberant festivals; the prevailing atmosphere seemed fearful; and unlike Rio de Janeiro there were very few churches – only one for the Lutherans and one for the Calvinists. The immense flat-topped pelmet of Table Mountain formed a bleak and forbidding backdrop to what appeared to be a neat and excessively ordered township that was much buffeted by winds; so windy in fact that Table Bay proved to be an unsatisfactory harbour. For Phillip's officers, Cape Town suffered by comparison with Rio de Janeiro. It did not seem at all picturesque and beautiful or 'abounding with the most luxurious flowers and aromatic shrubs'.

It was a cruel place as well. The thousands of slaves who constituted the economic foundation of the colony moved about the streets in fear. Their daily lives were governed by a Dutch 'Slave Code' that imposed a severe and unforgiving regimen. And in full view near the massive pentagonal fort that dominated the township was the site where punishments and executions were carried out each fortnight. Collins, who had a professional interest as the judge-advocate for New South Wales, viewed the instruments of execution with horror. There were wheels and crosses for 'breaking' criminals, a spiked pole for impalements and gallows for hanging. In Great Britain at that time the usual means by which the state took the life of a convicted felon was by hanging. The last person to be broken on the wheel was a Scot in 1604 and it was hardly ever practised before then. Impalement was unknown. The barbarism of the Dutch was unsettling. Its grim reality was evident when Phillip and his officers took lodgings. The mutilated body parts of a Malay slave who had run amok with a machete and been captured and broken alive on the wheel were still on display in the township, contributing to the prevailing sense of menace.

Once the supply of provisions was secured, the remaining time at Cape Town became a constant bustle. As one midshipman wrote home 'this is the last port … [and] it is right to take every advantage of it'. Phillip devoted himself to laying on as many provisions and as much livestock as could possibly be added. The ship's carpenters were kept busy refitting the ships' lower decks to accommodate more and more animals. Convicts were moved from one ship to another to allow more space for livestock and supplies. The ships had always been crowded but they now became thoroughly congested. Hundreds of animals were brought on board including large animals such as horses, cattle and pigs, as well as sheep, goats, geese, ducks and hens. And some officers found room for further livestock intended for their private use or consumption. On the decks of the *Sirius* alone, there were six cows, two bulls and sundry sheep, goats, pigs and hens.

The reluctant gardener Francis Masson, who had first come to Cape Town in 1772 and was part of Sir Joseph Banks' plans for the horticultural and agricultural development of New South Wales, was unwilling to join the expedition. But he at least assisted Phillip with the collection of flora. When the fleet departed, Masson wrote to Banks to say that 'Phillip's Cabbin was like a small Green House'. He informed Banks that as well as trees and plants from the Cape of Good Hope, Phillip was also taking many plants from Brazil including some rare medicinal species. They included 'Ipecacuana', presumably *Psychotria Ipececuanha*, whose dried root powder was highly regarded in Brazil as a treatment for dysentery and as an emetic, and 'Julapa', which must have been *Mirabilis Jalapa*, another medicinal plant whose powdered dried flowers were used by Brazilian Indians as snuff for headaches and as a root decoction to wash wounds and treat skin afflictions. Masson also referred to 'Cactus Tuna' on which cochineal insects were breeding. This must have been prickly pear (*Opuntia*), a genus in the cactus family, sometimes referred to by its Spanish name 'tuna'. Grape vines, about which Phillip was rightly optimistic, were also added. In time, the grape would turn out to be an outstanding success. Stockdale attributes to Phillip the percipient observation that 'In a climate so favourable, the cultivation of wine may doubtless be carried to any degree of perfection; and should not other articles of commerce divert the settlers from this point, the wines of New South Wales may, perhaps, hereafter be sought with avidity and become an indispensable part of the luxury of European tables.'

When all was finally done, Phillip took his ships to sea again on 12 November, heading north out of Table Bay, past Robben Island with its melancholy history and back into the South Atlantic. In the first week the sailing was inconclusive as the contrary winds and currents off Cape Agulhus slowed the fleet considerably. Then when the ships finally emerged and headed southeast, Phillip announced that he was changing the sailing arrangements. This came as a surprise to his officers, especially his most senior officers Major Ross and Captain Hunter. Some complained later of Phillip's secrecy. But in fact, Phillip had planned the alteration before the fleet's departure from Portsmouth and Sydney had authorised it in advance. Thus, approximately 100 leagues east of the Cape, Phillip moved to the *Supply*, taking with him the chronometer, Gidley King and Lieutenant Dawes. Also joining them were six artificers and a few convicts with carpentry and trade skills. He left Hunter behind in command of the *Sirius* with its great cabin stuffed with seedlings and plants and its menagerie of animals taken on board in Cape Town. He ordered the better sailers in the convoy – the *Alexander*, the *Scarborough* and the *Friendship* – to accompany him, if possible. But if they could not keep up, Lieutenant Shortland, the government agent for the transport ships, was instructed to make his own way with them as best he could. The *Sirius* would lead the remainder of the convoy. Phillip hoped to make haste, unencumbered by the wallowing store ships and slower transports. His objective was to arrive at Botany Bay a fortnight ahead of the rest of the convoy.

All were now aware that they were leaving the known world for a state unknown. And some of them engaged in melancholy reflection, poignantly contrasting what lay ahead with what they were leaving behind. Looking back later, Collins wrote that 'The land behind us was the abode of a civilised people; that before us was the residence of savages. When, if ever, we might again enjoy the commerce of the world was doubtful and uncertain.'

The potential for ignominious disaster could not have been lost on Phillip. At a future date, Jeremy Bentham, the British philosopher and social reformer, who had a vested interest in his own prison design known as the panopticon, would parody transportation to New South Wales, highlighting the uncertainties of convict exile. He illustrated his point with an imaginary sentence imposed by an imaginary judge: 'I sentence you, but to what I know not – perhaps to storm and shipwreck – perhaps to infectious disorders – perhaps to famine – perhaps to be massacred by savages – perhaps to be devoured by wild beasts. Away – take your chance – perish or prosper – suffer or enjoy: I rid myself of the sight of you!' In the next five years, Phillip would encounter almost everything that Bentham foretold – shipwreck, disease, famine and Aboriginal attack, though there were no wild beasts. But before reaching New South Wales, the fleet had to cross an unknown and unfamiliar ocean.

The Southern Ocean is the largest stretch of unbroken water on earth. It extends continuously around the globe separating America, Africa and Australia from Antarctica. Nowhere else does the sea roll uninterrupted around the world, nor the winds have such an unimpeded range. The zone that lies between approximately 40°S and 50°S is known as the Roaring Forties. In those latitudes the continuous flow of air in a westerly direction across the surface of the ocean is disturbed only by the southern extremity of South America. Without any wind from the opposite direction, the ocean current, powered by a consistent westerly wind, becomes continuous. And waves, which develop with the strength and consistency of the wind, almost never dissipate. The convergence of wind and current creates a perpetual swell that rolls inexorably towards the west coast of Tasmania then known as

Van Diemen's Land. In mid-ocean, the ever-present swell sometimes combines with local waves, borne out of gales and generated by storms, to create waves of extraordinary length and unmanageable height 'extending well over a mile in length and achieving a vertical frontal face just before it breaks'. Wave heights of 60 feet are not uncommon. On rare occasions freak waves of considerably greater height occur.

Into this treacherous ocean, Phillip ran down the 40th parallel of latitude on the diminutive *Supply*, endeavouring to keep within a few degrees either side. He knew from his study of Cook's expeditions that this must bring him to Van Diemen's Land, which lay between the latitudes of 40°S and 44°S. But the route due east along the 40th parallel was little known to Englishmen. This was the southern route to the East Indies, known since 1610 as the Brouwer Route after Hendrik Brouwer of the Dutch East India Company. The Brouwer route required ships to stay on an easterly course after rounding the Cape of Good Hope and sail with the westerlies 'for a thousand miles' before turning north for Bantam at the western end of Java. Whatever the precise meaning to the Dutch of 'a thousand miles' at that time, it became generally recognised that the islands of St Paul and Amsterdam were the marker points beyond which ships should change course and head north and northeast. These islands are almost precisely in mid-ocean, approximately halfway between the continents of Africa and Australia and nearly 2000 miles from either coast. Although the Brouwer route was of interest to the British, it remained a largely Dutch preserve, convenient for the Dutch trade to Java, but not particularly well known and hardly ever used by the British. India was Britain's principal possession in south Asia and the passage along the East African coast, passing Madagascar on the inside or the outside, was the orthodox and commonly used route. It was the one that Phillip had himself taken on the *Europe* in 1783. That is not to say that some British ships of the East India Company did not venture along the southern route. In 1622 the *Trial* did so and suffered the misfortune of sailing so far east that she was shipwrecked on a reef near the Montebello Islands of Western Australia. She was not the only one, but such adventures were isolated and infrequent.

This uncertainty of navigation was nervously reflected by Gidley King when in early December he noted in his journal that their situation in fog was perilous 'as no Ship ever ran in this parallel of Latitude before, so far to the Eastward'. He was more or less right – except perhaps for stray ships of the Dutch and English East India Companies and the seventeenth-century voyages of Tasman, Vlamingh and Dampier. He would not have known of the secret French expedition led by de Kerguelen that landed on the West Australian coast in March 1772. By any yardstick, this was a route less travelled, still exploratory at least beyond St Paul and Amsterdam, and quite unlike the relative security of an Atlantic voyage or the well tried passage to India – for which navigators had many precedents and much accumulated information. On his second and third voyages, Cook had sailed in different waters closer to the Antarctic landmass. On this voyage, Hunter chose to take the *Sirius* a little further south than Phillip, hoping for even stronger winds. But in the latitudes in which Phillip and Hunter both sailed, they were in unfamiliar waters without wholly reliable charts and could not know what lay in front of them. They would only know that they had reached Van Diemen's Land when it was sighted. On this leg of the voyage, the sailor's proverbial adage that 'it is better to trust a good lookout than a bad reckoning' must have had a particular significance for the hapless seamen who were compelled to follow Phillip and Hunter.

As the *Supply* sailed before the westerly winds, pushing further and deeper east into the unknown, Kendall's chronometer and Maskelyne's lunar table calculations were in frequent use. As often as possible, their results were anxiously compared one against the other and dutifully averaged. The differences between the 'time-keeper' and the 'lunars' were a constant subject of consideration. In these unfamiliar waters, latitude was not the issue. It could be gauged with reasonable approximation by the length of the day, the height of the midday sun or the position of known guide stars above the horizon. The real problem was longitude – knowing how far to the east the ship had sailed. That is why Phillip was entrusted with Kendall's chronometer. Sometimes tempestuous weather caused matters to go awry. In mid December 1787, after days of strong gales and heavy seas, Gidley King's journal recorded with alarm that 'the Time Keeper was not thought of till about 6 o'clock in the Evening'. The next day Dawes could not conceal his anxiety when he wrote that 'some very good altitudes were taken, from which the longitude of the ship was found – (supposing that the Time Keeper had not stopped)'. In fact, it had stopped and was down about an hour, something that added yet another layer of complication and necessitated ongoing adjustments to the readings derived from it. It was later alleged, contentiously, to be 'useless for the rest of the passage'.

On the *Sirius*, Hunter had to get by without a chronometer as he sailed across the Southern Ocean. This he did with great success. Sailors know the satisfaction gained when navigation by celestial observation leads with pinpoint accuracy to a ship's arrival at the anticipated destination at the very time that was predicted. Hunter was entitled to be satisfied, a fact reflected in Collins' subsequent words of admiration when describing the sighting of Van Diemen's Land. Looking back a decade later, he wrote, 'Nothing could more strongly prove the excellence and utility of lunar observations, than the accuracy with which we made the land on this long voyage from the Cape of Good Hope, there not being a league of difference between our expectation of seeing it, and the real appearance of it.'

But it was not plain sailing, not for the *Sirius* or the *Supply* or for any of the merchant vessels. For many days during the journey across the southern Indian Ocean and the Southern Ocean the ships experienced heavy gales and huge seas. For a great deal of the time the wind blew hard, generally ranging from the northwest to the southwest, sometimes veering around from the south bringing cold and misery. Severe gales were frequent and squalls were common. For day after day in late November, mid December, the week before Christmas and again until 3 January 1788, storms battered the ships. Gidley King recorded that from 18 to 24 December the very heavy sea that was running kept the *Supply* 'almost constantly under water and renders the situation of everyone on board of her, truly uncomfortable'. In the language of professional sailors accustomed by training and temperament to making weather observations muted by their objectivity, the seas at various times were heaving – running very high – frequently irregular. Sometimes they were the most confused and tumbling seas ever seen. Occasionally they were prodigious or mountains high. At least once they were a rage all over as white as snow.

In the big seas and constant swells that confronted Phillip's fleet, the most critical situation was in the troughs, in the valleys between the waves. If a ship wallows, losing some of her way at the bottom, she runs the risk that she will not have the speed to outrun the following sea. If the sea overtakes her, a mass of breaking water will crash over the stern. If that occurs, the ship will be 'pooped' as the sailors say.

More likely than not, she will slew around, presenting her broadside, and the next sea will overwhelm her, turning her on her beam-ends, carrying away her masts and rigging and consigning all on board to a watery grave. On the crests of the waves the danger is different. As the crest breaks and curls, streaming in a white cascade down the leeward side of the wave, the air is filled with flying spume, the wind shrieks and the ship simply slides, practically rudderless, barely in control.

The heavy seas meant that water frequently broke over all the vessels in the fleet. On the *Supply* and probably on others, it came over the head of the foresail. On another it crashed through the weather scuttle of the great cabin at the stern. On the *Lady Penryhn*, it threw weed and grass from the bottom of the ship halfway up the mainsail. On another, probably on most of them, the sea ran from the quarterdeck into the great cabin. All the vessels shipped seas both fore and aft. Great quantities were taken not only above board but also below and between decks, washing convicts and marines out of their beds and drenching everything. Blankets and bedding floated away, sloshing back and forth in the watery chaos. Everything movable was thrown down, in every part of every ship. Injuries and bruises were commonplace. Convicts were tossed around, tumbling every which way, as the tiny vessels were buffeted and bashed. The position of the marines was little different from that of the convicts. There was much howling, shrieking and cursing. Female convicts went down on their knees praying. Bowes Smyth, a surgeon, thought that his legs would be 'crushed to atoms' as heavy furniture tore apart from its fixtures and sliced across the deck floor. On some ships, probably most, it sometimes seemed as if the vessel would go under – for the immense water pressure generated by waves far exceeds the pressure that any wind can create.

The livestock, but especially the cattle on the *Sirius*, suffered dreadfully. Hunter, who had something of the country squire about him, sympathetically recorded their plight in his journal. The cattle were discomforted almost from the outset by the large head sea off Cape Agulhas. When westerly gales struck the convoy in the Southern Ocean, the cattle had difficulty withstanding the ship's rolling and labouring and became more distressed. Hunter noted that the 'poor creatures were frequently thrown with much violence off their legs and were exceedingly bruised'. After six weeks they were in a weakly state. The large quantities of sea water shipped during the storms aggravated their distress. When the cattle slipped, their legs buckled and they crashed to the floor. When they struggled to right themselves, their hooves slid on the wet timbers and they lost their balance again and again. The seamen were unable to assist them. The cattle were awkward, helpless, terrified. In the worst weather, it was proposed that slings be placed under their bellies. But this would leave their bovine limbs dangling and the idea was rejected for fear that the cattle might lose the use of their legs. Their physical discomfort was made worse because they were nearly starved. Three cows calved on the voyage but the fodder was scarcely sufficient to sustain them, let alone their progeny. The calves all died, as did a fourth cow that was big with calf. It is no wonder that the surviving cattle – an unhappy bull, four miserable cows and a bull calf of Afrikander breed – later escaped when they reached New South Wales. They found their way to a distant irenic place where they lived contentedly, and multiplied considerably. When the herd was found in 1795, it consisted of over 60 head, young and old.

There were interludes at sea between the gales, storms and violent squalls. At those times, Gidley King recorded his observations of the super-abundance of whales and albatrosses that the *Supply* encountered. By 8 December, in the vicinity of the island of St Paul, he noticed that the albatrosses were not merely abundant but were now enormous. There were the great albatrosses of the genus *Diomedea*, unique to the southern hemisphere. There were other natural wonders. A few days before sighting Van Diemen's Land, Bradley noted that the *Aurora Australis* was 'very bright with many beautiful red streamers that appeared to run from about 45° of altitude to the clouds that were in that part of the horizon'.

There is no indication of Phillip's interest in these diversions. He was approaching the end of a voyage that by virtue of its length, its route and the nature of the human cargo he carried, was unprecedented in complexity and responsibility. After taking readings at the South West Cape of Van Diemen's Land in early January 1788 and comparing them favourably with the longitude that Cook had recorded, the *Supply* rounded the island and charted a course northwards, soon followed by the *Sirius* and the other ships of the fleet. The sight of patches of snow on the peaks in mid summer was perplexing and caused some concern, but the storms which they then encountered along the south coast of New South Wales ensured that there were no premature celebrations. The ships received another battering before eventually limping into Botany Bay and mooring in its shallow and exposed waters between 18 and 20 January 1788. Then on 24 January, to the surprise and consternation of the English, two large ships under French colours appeared off the entrance to the bay. The ships, poignantly named after navigational aids – the *Astrolabe* and the *Boussole* (compass) – were those of the Comte de Lapérouse.

Lapérouse had not come to establish a settlement and was not equipped to do so, but his arrival was not a coincidence. Although he had sailed from Brest before the British decision to settle New South Wales had been announced, he was informed of Phillip's expedition in September 1787 while his ships were moored at Kamchatka in the Russian Far East. There he received an official communiqué from Fleurieu, the Minister of Marine, that had made its way by despatch riders via St Petersburg to Petropavlovsk across four thousand miles of steppe and tundra. Fleurieu's letter was dated 15 December 1786 and reached Lapérouse only two days before he was due to depart. It directed him to alter his route and proceed to Botany Bay to investigate whether the British had indeed established a presence there.

The sighting of the French ships was an unwelcome development for Phillip but his priority was to land the convicts and for the time being he ignored them. On 25 January he took the *Supply* three leagues north to Port Jackson. On the next day the remaining ships followed. A week later, amid the hubbub and bustle of unloading at Port Jackson, he sent Gidley King back to Botany Bay to pay his respects and to ascertain Lapérouse's intentions, instructing him that on his return he should immediately take the *Supply* with a group of marines to occupy and secure Norfolk Island. This was, clearly enough, 'to prevent its being occupied by the subjects of any other European power'. Phillip himself kept his distance from Lapérouse and the two did not meet in New South Wales. As Lapérouse was ranked as a rear admiral and Phillip was a captain, Phillip's behaviour was impolite by the standards of the day, especially among naval officers. Deference to more senior officers of foreign navies was usual, whether at peace or at war. Even at the height of war – before Napoleon changed the rules – relations between English and French naval officers were respectful. This attitude was best exemplified by the convention that was followed when, upon capture of his ship, an officer could secure his release by giving his word of honour as a gentleman that he would not serve in his country's navy until a suitable exchange had been arranged.

However, the dimensions of Phillip's appointment were complex and subtle and he had been appointed partly because he was a 'discreet' officer. The respected historian Alan Frost has suggested that Phillip's failure to meet Lapérouse may have reflected some fear that 'he might be known as a spy' and that he did not wish the French to perceive the excellence of Port Jackson. Both seem reasonably likely. Phillip's lengthy period under cover in the naval ports of France between 1784 and 1786 may well have made him apprehensive that he would be recognisable to Lapérouse. And his high opinion of the strategic utility of Port Jackson, which had never been charted and was barely known, explains his reluctance to allow the French to appreciate its advantages. He, of course, understood Whitehall's strategic and commercial objectives. The reality is that the two commanders were circling each other in New South Wales, neither willing to reveal the true scope of his expedition or the aspirations of his government.

GOVERNOR

The practicalities of transforming Phillip's
ideas into practice; his egalitarianism and
his attitude to the convicts, marines and
Aborigines, including his spearing and illness

Travelling north was Phillip's genius. Something about Cook's chart, or the overly rapturous descriptions of Sir Joseph Banks, caused Phillip to doubt the suitability of Botany Bay as the seat of settlement. Even before the fleet set sail from Portsmouth in May 1787 he had identified Port Jackson as a possible alternative, informing the administration that he should be free to make the settlement in such other port as he might find most convenient. It was with this possibility in mind that he planned, and hoped, to arrive two weeks ahead of the rest. When he reached Botany Bay, its open, exposed and waterless situation quickly confirmed his reservations. Thus on 21 January 1788, after the arrival of the *Sirius* and the last remaining ships in the convoy, Phillip departed with three longboats for a reconnaissance of Port Jackson.

Until that day, no white man had passed through the soaring sandstone cliffs that mark Port Jackson's entrance – the awesome portal that is known today as the Sydney Heads. Phillip could not know what to expect. But when he gradually saw what lay before him, he reacted favourably to its maritime potential, famously recording that he 'had the satisfaction of finding the finest harbour in the world, in which a thousand sail of the line may ride in the most perfect security'. This was not mere exuberance. For Phillip was familiar with the greatest harbours in the world, among them of course the vast bay at Rio de Janeiro, the deep water at Havana with its secure narrow inlet and the substantial anchorage at Toulon. Nor was he alone in his judgment. John White was emphatic: 'Port Jackson I believe to be, without exception, the finest and most extensive harbour in the universe, and at the same time the most secure, being safe from all the winds that blow.' And among others Ralph Clark, a 25-year-old officer of marines, wrote that Port Jackson was 'one of the finest harbours in the world – I never saw any like it – the river Thames is not to be mentioned to it and that I thought was the finest in the world'.

But there was more to Port Jackson than its maritime potential. As Phillip's men slipped quietly up the harbour and moved their attention from its sparkling ultramarine waters to its shoreline, they were taken by the tall trees, the rocky outcrops, the exotic flora and the sense of untouched Edenic beauty. The intense light and the brilliant colours filled them with eager curiosity and wonder. Singing from the tree tops were strange and unusual birds – raucous shrieking cockatoos, absurd laughing kookaburras and brightly coloured lorikeets. Worgan thought its beauty beggared all description. Bowes Smyth said that the flight of the parrots and the singing of the birds 'made all around appear like an enchantment'. And on the cliff-tops and at the water's edge were the local 'natives', members of the Eora people, the coastal Aborigines of this region. They were agitated, shouting and waving spears, and their numbers appeared more numerous than Cook and Banks had ever suggested.

Phillip's senior officers were mostly young men, educated and shaped by the late Enlightenment, romantic, well meaning and impressionable. They considered themselves to be serving the Empire and the cause of humanity, taking possession of a pure state of nature for noble objectives. Collins earnestly hoped that the convicts might be reformed and that 'we might not sully that purity [of nature] by the introduction of vice, profaneness and immorality'. Paraphrasing the poet John Milton, he evoked a sense of the founding of a new civilisation, writing later of the cove where they made their first settlement and 'the run of fresh water which stole silently along through a thick wood, the stillness of which had then for the first time since creation, been interrupted by the rude sound of the ... axe'.

The tranquillity of this sublime wilderness was soon rudely interrupted. The little cove that Phillip would later name 'Sydney' in honour of the Home Secretary became a scene of earnest bustling industry. The thud of the axe, the rasp of the saw and the crash of fallen timber soon became the predominant daily sounds. Gradually a semblance of physical order emerged as regimental rows of tents appeared, cabbage tree huts were constructed and stores were unloaded from the ships. A hospital for the sick was one of the first structures established. By March and April a barracks for the marines had been commenced and some store-houses constructed. This transformation was a source of satisfaction to Phillip, for his was an eighteenth-century view of improvement. The imposition of purpose and order, the cultivation of land and the taming of nature were regarded without demur as laudable achievements. Fixing a settlement of civilised people on a savage coast was chivalric. The words which Stockdale attributed to Phillip reflected this attitude:

> There are few things more pleasing than the contemplation of order and useful arrangement, arising gradually out of tumult and confusion; and perhaps this satisfaction cannot any where be more fully enjoyed than where a settlement of civilised people is fixing itself upon a newly discovered or savage coast.

Physical order was one thing, but the establishment of civil order was more problematic. Phillip was no longer in command of a well-run naval vessel, where he could count on the services of an experienced crew and the loyalty of professional officers. He now exercised a civilian authority and had to contend with complex relations among diverse persons most of whom did not share his vision, or care a fig about it. His experience as a captain of a ship of the line, as patron and protector of upwards of 600 men united in the furtherance of a common object, was valuable but it could not equip him for all of the difficulties he would now face. New South Wales may have been 'a newly discovered or savage coast' but in the main it was not 'a settlement of civilised people'. Many of the convicts were indolent. And once on land the marine officers, led by the churlish and dissembling Major Ross, would not accept responsibility for their supervision, contending that the policing of the settlement was not part of their duty.

Ross, who suffered from a 'warmth of temper', was 'perverse, sullen, litigious and unhelpful'. His appointment as Lieutenant Governor was a signal failure. His soldiers, drawn from the same social order as the convicts, were mostly recalcitrant and lawless. And many of his officers, riven by dissensions and jealousies, were little better than the men they commanded. Phillip remarked in a report to Sydney how 'so little harmony prevails between the commandant [Ross] and his officers' that there was friction everywhere. He explained:

The strength of the [marine] detachment consists of only eighteen officers, one of whom is on duty at Norfolk Island, and a second has never done any duty since he was appointed by Major Ross; of the sixteen remaining for the duty of this settlement, five have been put under arrest by the commandant, and are only doing duty till a general court-martial can be assembled, in consequence of a sentence passed by them at a battalion court-martial; a sixth officer is suspended in consequence of a representation made by the corps of his unofficerlike behaviour in taking a soldier who had been abused by a convict to make his complaint to the magistrates.

From the beginning, the marines almost as much as the convicts threatened the fragile civil order by stealing food from the public stores. And within a fortnight of landing Phillip moved rapidly to establish the criminal court, which promptly handed out heavy sentences of 150 or 200 lashes. At the end of the month, three convicts were sentenced to death and a fourth to 300 lashes, all for theft from the public stores. As theft escalated, the punishments increased in severity and frequency. For one seventeen-year-old man named Barrett, who was said to be the head of the gang, Phillip even arranged a public execution in front of the entire convict population. Increasingly, however, Phillip reprieved the convicts who were sentenced to death. But when six marines who had systematically plundered the stores they were assigned to guard were sentenced to death by court martial, Phillip showed no mercy. The scaffold was erected before their sentences were passed and their hangings proceeded with grim solemnity. Phillip had no time for persons in positions of authority who abused their trust.

Phillip's relationship with the marines was often poisonous but it later became farcical when he instituted a night watch of twelve worthy convicts to prevent robberies from the public stores and vegetable gardens. The night watch was highly successful but when it occasionally stopped marines who were acting suspiciously, or worse, Major Ross histrionically remonstrated with Phillip, complaining that it was 'an insult to the corps' and that Phillip had 'put the soldiers under the command of the convicts'. In his bitter report to Sydney, Phillip explained how he had been compelled reluctantly to abandon this useful initiative.

This antagonism towards Ross and his marines may have contributed to the perception that Phillip was partial to the convicts at the expense of the seamen and marines. But there were other factors. The settlement at Sydney Cove was no ordinary convict colony. There was no stockade. And Phillip did not confine the convicts behind prison walls. Nor did he require them to wear leg irons, unless they re-offended. He even allowed them to wear their own clothes and build their own huts of cabbage tree or wattle and daub. Within a month of arrival, Bowes Smyth noted that 'the marines and sailors are punished with the utmost severity for the most trivial offences, whilst the convicts are pardoned (or at least punished in a very slight manner) for crimes of the blackest die'. One marine captain righteously queried whether the administration had really intended that 'the only difference between the allowance of provisions served to the officer and served to the convict, be only half a pint [per day] of vile Rio spirits'. And the execrable Major Ross expostulated, 'Could I possibly have imagined that I was to be served with, for instance, no more butter than any of the convicts ... I most certainly would not have left England.' Their indignation could only have been heightened as famine threatened in the early years. Phillip progressively reduced everyone's rations, including for himself, without distinction between convict and free man. He would give himself and his officers no more than the meanest of those he governed. Some Englishmen found his egalitarianism baffling and unsettling.

There were other manifestations of Phillip's egalitarian benevolence. In England, before his departure, he had written that 'the Laws of this Country will, of course, be introduced in New South Wales'. There was a remarkable, if unorthodox, instance of this in July 1788 when he convened the first sitting of the civil court. He did so to enable two convicts, Henry and Susannah Kable, to sue a ship's captain for the theft of their personal property during the voyage. But even under English law, convicts had no right to sue. As the jurist William Blackstone graphically described it, they were 'civilly dead, unable to sue, unable to be a witness and unable to hold property and make contracts'.

Phillip assuredly knew this, but the formal records of sentence relating to each convict had not been delivered to him before the fleet sailed from Portsmouth. In the absence of documentary proof of their obvious convict status, Phillip chose to ignore the reality. He clearly believed that Henry and Susannah Kable should have the opportunity of redressing the wrong that had been done to them. He appointed the chaplain (Johnson) and the surgeon (White) to sit with the judge-advocate (Collins) as members of the court and allowed the action to proceed. In due course the property of Henry and Susannah Kable was restored to them and their rights against the dishonest ship's captain historically vindicated.

Curiously, Phillip's generous reaction to Susannah Kable had a direct connection with that of Sydney. For Sydney had shown compassion towards the very same convict woman before the fleet's departure. She had been brought from Norwich Gaol to Plymouth with her baby son to board one of the transports. At Plymouth the ship's captain refused to allow the baby on board. The Norwich gaoler, Mr Simpson, who had accompanied Susannah and her baby from Norwich, was so affected that he left the tearful mother behind and travelled post haste all the way from the west of England to London with the child in his lap. In London he proceeded to Whitehall where he waited for Sydney and engaged him on the steps of the Home Office. Sydney was understandably disconcerted, but so moved that he promptly announced that the child should be restored to its mother. At the same time he commended Simpson for his spirit and humanity. Naturally, the London newspapers delighted in the story, as did their readers. In fact, so many of the public were moved that £20 was raised in donations for the maintenance and welfare of mother and child in the colony. The goods purchased with these donations, and subsequently stolen by the ship's captain, then became the subject of the colony's first civil action.

Phillip's fair mindedness and sense of equality were singular but he did not abandon entirely all pretensions to Georgian gentility and personal aggrandisement. On 15 May 1788 he commenced the construction of a suitable Governor's residence to replace the pre-fabricated canvas tent which served as his first home and was neither wind- nor waterproof. The building's copper foundation plaque, duly inscribed and laid in the southeastern corner, referred to Phillip landing with the first 'settlers' not with convicts. When completed in the following year, the new residence displayed a number of emblematic Georgian architectural features that reflected the era but which were incongruous in their raw physical setting. The building was a square two-storey pilastered structure with a pared-down Palladian style, central pedimented breakfront, glass windows and the only set of stairs in the colony. There were even quoins and a roundel. A disgruntled few thought it a *folie de grandeur* constructed with an eye to posterity. Like the symbolism of Albion, however, it was a conscious transplantation of English cultural tradition and a symbol of authority. But its use would not be exclusive to Phillip and in due course he would share its kitchen with kangaroos and its dining room with Aboriginal guests.

Another early transplantation of English cultural tradition was the first town plan, created in July 1788. The central feature of Phillip's 'Albion' was a triumphal avenue 200 feet wide, running northeast toward the harbour's entrance. The planned avenue led to an expansive public square that was proposed for the waterfront, around which there were to be no commercial buildings. From there, one would look back and along the grand avenue. The whole concept radiated a formality and grandeur not unlike Greenwich itself, with its stately square beside the Thames. In truth, however, it was a dream, a flight of fancy, and was soon put to one side. Phillip was too pragmatic, and the exigencies of the settlement too pressing, to allow this original town plan to represent anything more than a passing vision. Although it remains Phillip's earliest telltale aspiration for the nascent settlement, the plan never left paper and the name of Albion went with it.

The greater priority was the cultivation of the land. Not only did the subsistence of the settlement depend on it but successful agricultural development was the core of the social experiment. Phillip could not have achieved this without Henry Dodd. This little-known man was the only one in the colony with substantial rural experience and a serious claim to agricultural proficiency. Phillip had known him during his days at Lyndhurst in Hampshire where Dodd was one of the farm servants. It is not clear how he and Phillip remained in contact following Phillip's separation from Charlott or when they were reunited. But Dodd sailed with Phillip on the *Sirius* as his personal servant and was a member of the official party. Watkin Tench said that he was a member of Phillip's household.

In November 1788 Phillip sent Dodd to Rose Hill, at the headwaters of the harbour, with a hundred convicts and a detachment of marines. At Sydney Cove, with its weathered sandstone and nutrient-poor soils, agriculture never really extended beyond kitchen gardens. The colony's survival depended on grain farming and the broad-scale planting of wheat, oats, corn, maize and barley. This only became achievable when the rich dark loams at Rose Hill were discovered and cultivated under Dodd's dedicated supervision. This was the colony's turning point. Phillip visited Dodd at Rose Hill, even sleeping humbly on the floor of his hut. Henry Dodd excelled himself, commanded the respect of everyone and laid the foundations for the colony's agricultural subsistence. Collins wrote that he 'acquired an ascendancy over the convicts, which he preserved without being hated by them'. By February 1790, Phillip was able to report with satisfaction that the corn produced by the convicts under the direction of 'this very industrious man ... was exceedingly good'.

The agricultural subsistence to which Dodd so substantially contributed eventually enabled Phillip to issue convict land grants. These land grants represented the first steps away from public farming and towards the intended new society – an idealistic rural society where ex-convicts became settlers working their 30-acre grants, cultivating their lots and improving their lives. The hoped-for transformation of 'villains into villagers' was the dream of Phillip's powerful and visionary supporters watching in England. It is no wonder that they saw the experiment in New South Wales as a subject 'affording the political philosopher new material for calculation, on a subject so interesting, so important to the civilised world'. A mere convict dumping ground was never envisioned. It was neither Sydney's ambition nor Phillip's intention. It was not the way in which Phillip saw himself as serving the cause of humanity.

Developing cordial relations with the Aborigines was another way in which Phillip saw himself as serving the cause of humanity. His instructions required him to 'conciliate the affections' of the Aborigines, to encourage everyone to 'live in amity and kindness with them' and to punish all who should 'wantonly destroy them, or give them any unnecessary interruption in the exercise of their several occupations'. All of this Phillip embraced, while at the same time demonstrating that well-intended but innocently superior loftiness of the age. He nurtured the hope that he might 'cultivate an acquaintance with them, without their having an idea of our great superiority over them, that their confidence and friendship might be more firmly fixed'. Unlike Cook, Phillip did not let fly with shot, at least at the beginning. And his approach was more gentle than that of Lapérouse, who regarded the Aborigines as malevolent savages to be avoided.

But Phillip and his officers were contradictory. They genuinely wished to be friends but could not see that they were invaders. They were enlightened, tolerant and chivalrous, in accordance with the spirit of the age, but they viewed the Aborigines through the lens of prevailing European preconceptions. Their instructions were to achieve amity and kindness not to pillage or harm. But they appropriated Aboriginal lands and ruined Aboriginal hunting and fishing grounds. There was no generalised racist terror. That would only come later, after Phillip's time, when commerce, greed and land ownership took root and a prevailing sentiment of hostility towards the Aborigines emerged.

To Phillip's dismay the early promise of peaceful co-existence with the Aborigines did not bear fruit. In the first few days at Botany Bay, seamen and marines had danced and jigged on the beach with the curious and good-natured 'natives', as they referred to them. Some called them 'indians'. Phillip walked forward with open arms and forbade any shooting. He handed out gifts – beads and mirrors and bright cloths. But the Eora stayed away from the settlement at Sydney Cove. They had good reason to be wary, watching from a distance as their fish and oysters were depleted, their trees cut down and their land transformed. After almost a year of disappointment, Phillip adopted a new strategy. He desperately wanted the Eora to appreciate the kindness and peaceful intentions that the British brought with them and the advantages of civilised life that they offered. And he hoped to learn about Aboriginal culture and language. In December 1788, he chose to take an Aboriginal man forcibly from Manly Cove. This man was Arabanoo. A few months later, when some convicts formed vigilante groups seeking reprisals for occasional Aboriginal attacks, Phillip took great exception to their conduct, knowing how such brutality would undo his good intentions. Wishing to demonstrate his bona fides to the Aborigines, he had the perpetrators publicly whipped and put in chains. Some convicts who had received spear wounds were allowed to recover. Then they were also whipped. But rather than being impressed, Watkin Tench said that Arabanoo displayed 'symptoms of disgust and terror'.

A greater terror was the arrival of the smallpox. It was Phillip's first real calamity in New South Wales. It descended like a cloud on the Aboriginal population in April, May and June 1789 and carried off at least half of its members living around the harbour, although not a single European was affected. The disease was well known in western Europe and was regarded as the most dreadful scourge of the human species. It decimated Native Americans when it was carried across the Atlantic by settlers and slaves. And it probably attacked more people in Georgian England than any other disease. But there had been no sign of it on the voyage or during the fifteen months of settlement. The first disturbing reports of the presence of the disease came to Phillip in April when men went down the harbour and found in the coves and inlets dead and dying Aborigines huddled among the rocks and lying on the beaches.

When Phillip learned of an Aboriginal family lying sick in a nearby cove, he took a boat and personally attended on the family with Arabanoo and a surgeon. They witnessed a scene of despair. The man was stretched out on the ground before a few burning sticks. The boy was trying to cool himself, pouring water on his head from a shell; nearby was the dead body of a female child and a little further away the corpse of a woman. Arabanoo was overcome and would not leave until he had buried the child. He did not see the mother's corpse and Phillip did not show it to him. Phillip brought the elderly man and boy to the hospital where they were placed in a separate hut. He had 'hopes that being cured and sent away with the many little necessaries we could give them would be the means of reconciling them to live near us'. The man died within hours but the boy recovered. White the surgeon adopted him, allowing him to live in his home. A few days later two more sick and diseased Aborigines were collected in Phillip's boat and brought to the hospital. Only one survived, a fourteen-year-old girl. When she recovered, she was also taken in, this time by the chaplain's wife, Mrs Johnson. Later, when Arabanoo himself became sick and died on 18 May, Phillip was deeply affected, attending his funeral and having him buried in his own garden.

The presence of the disease was perplexing and unfathomable and Phillip could not account for it. Some Francophobes blamed Lapérouse's men but their suspicion was baseless as the French ships had left in March of the previous year. Watkin Tench wondered about the smallpox virus that surgeons usually kept in vials secured in their medicine chests. But he dismissed the idea that it might have been the cause and there is no support for the speculation that any vials were unaccounted for. The calamity was a humanitarian disaster and a setback in Phillip's quest for peaceful co-existence with the Aborigines. He was deeply concerned but confident that the British were not to blame. And he may well have been justified. The English and the French were not the only voyagers to the Australian continent in the late eighteenth century. Recent opinion suggests that the virus may have originated with Macassan fishermen and been transported overland. They came seeking trepang and traded with the Aborigines.

By the time spring arrived, the smallpox had receded and perceptible signs of Aboriginal life reappeared around the harbour. Phillip continued his quest for engagement with the Aborigines. In November 1789 he chose once again to kidnap two more men at Manly Cove. One of the captured men was Bennelong, who was clever, gregarious and open to being civilised. Phillip took a deep personal interest in Bennelong's welfare, believing that he represented the longed-for breakthrough. Soon Bennelong and Phillip could be seen walking together and making little trips to South Head by boat. Bennelong used an Aboriginal term of endearment for Phillip which meant 'father' and he referred to himself as 'son'. But then after six months, Bennelong disappeared. And still the Eora stayed away. Phillip wistfully, and perhaps insightfully, wrote to Sir Joseph Banks saying that 'nothing will make these people amends for the loss of their liberty'. It was not until September that a resolution occurred, and then only after a pre-meditated act of retribution.

On 7 September 1790, without warning or provocation, an Aboriginal man standing in a throng at Manly Cove launched his weapon at Phillip. The shaft of the spear was not less than twelve feet long. Its head was a single wooden barb without any jagged bone or broken oyster shell fixed to it. Bennelong was in the throng and may have been responsible for what occurred. For it was he who had laid the spear in front of the assailant, pointing to him and calling his name. The assailant was between twenty and 30 yards from where Philip stood. With considerable dexterity, he flicked the spear upwards with his foot, fixed it to his throwing stick and thew it violently towards Phillip. The spear entered just above Phillip's right clavicle and exited near the third thoracic vertebra, high up on his back. It protruded 'about three inches just behind the shoulder blade and close to the back bone'.

Collins and the midshipman Henry Waterhouse were with Phillip. Collins turned and ran towards the beach, calling the crew to bring up the muskets. Waterhouse concluded that 'the Governor was killed'. But Phillip struggled for the boats, holding the shaft of the spear in both hands, unsuccessfully trying to keep the end of the shaft up. The shaft was too long, however, and its end kept striking the ground, stopping him short. Phillip called out to Waterhouse, begging him to haul the spear out. Waterhouse complied but made a hash of it and must have caused Phillip considerable further pain. At first he started to pull but realised that he was only drawing the single barbed head back into the flesh. Then he tried to break the shaft, bending it down. Having no success, he then bent it upwards. But still he could not break the hardwood shaft. Adrenalin must have then taken over. Another spear whistled towards him, grazing his right hand. In his own words 'it frightened me a good deal and I believe added to my exertions, for the next sudden jerk I gave it [the shaft] broke short off'. Spears were then flying thick.

With the help of a seaman, Waterhouse lifted Phillip into one of the boats. He was very faint. Shock must surely have begun to set in. The crew rowed for two hours while Phillip's wound bled a good deal. Waterhouse held Phillip in his arms. He said that Phillip was 'perfectly collected but conscious that a few hours must fix the period of his existence'. Phillip was taken to his house where he expected to die. He insisted that Balmain, one of the assistant surgeons, tell him candidly how many hours he had to settle his affairs. He warned Balmain not to deceive him as he was not afraid to meet his fate. 'Let it be whatever it would,' he said. Phillip was justified in feeling pessimistic but the place of entry of the spear may explain his good fortune. It must have gone through the fleshy part above the mid-clavicle. The trapezius muscle would have been savagely ripped and torn at the point of entry. But if the trajectory of the spear were slightly downwards, it is conceivable that the head of the spear could have passed through Phillip and emerged from his back without causing injury to any major anatomical structures.

It was still necessary of course for a surgeon to remove the shaft, to treat any shock, to reduce the pain and, most important of all, to prevent infection. Fortunately, spear and arrow wounds have a long history. Homer's anatomically accurate descriptions of removing spears and cutting out arrows in the *Iliad* had provided the basis for the practices used by military surgeons for thousands of years. Balmain had received a classical medical education at Edinburgh University and whether or not he read Homer, he would have followed the time-honoured practice of bathing and dressing Phillip's wound with tepid water and red wine. Spirit of turpentine and aloes may also have been used. When the wound was cleaned, a soft lint bandage would have been applied to the entry point on Phillip's shoulder, perhaps over a compress soaked in warm wine. For pain relief, if it were necessary, Phillip would have been given laudanum, an alcohol extract from opium, and perhaps a draught of red wine. For shock, if there were any signs, little could be done other than to keep the patient warm, comfortable and calm. In Phillip's case, his wound healed well. Waterhouse said that 'in six weeks he was able to get about again'.

It was then that Phillip's hoped-for reconciliation occurred. In October Bennelong returned with a retinue of friends – like a king returning in triumph. Phillip opened the settlement to the Aborigines, allowing them to come and go freely as they chose. Soon the Eora were constantly among the British and became very familiar. Many of them slept in the houses of officers that clustered on the eastern side of the cove, around the newly built Governor's residence. Phillip was delighted by the improvement in relations and was personally generous. He allowed Bennelong and his friend Barrangaroo to dine at Government House and had a small brick house built for them on the point that became known as Bennelong's Point. Here in November, the Eora staged their first corroboree to which the British were invited.

The improvement in relations, however, was not uniform and some sporadic attacks continued. And a serious setback occurred when Phillip's gamekeeper McIntyre was savagely speared in December 1790 and died a lingering death. McIntyre had apparently committed some atrocious offence against the Eora for which he was speared with a *cannadiul*, an Aboriginal death spear studded with lethal jagged stones. When Phillip had been speared three months earlier, he pointedly directed that there be no retaliation. He now took a different approach, ordering Watkin Tench and Dawes to take a party of marines to Botany Bay with instructions to bring back the heads of ten men of the Botany Bay tribe and to capture two men alive for execution. Dawes initially refused, then relented, but regretted doing so and fell out with Phillip. Watkin Tench at least successfully bargained with Phillip to reduce the number of heads to six. Eventually on 14 December a troop of over 50 men departed for Botany Bay armed with muskets, hatchets for beheading, and bags for carrying heads.

This seemed unlike Phillip. He knew the man who speared McIntyre. His name was Pemulwuy. On its face the object of the hunting party was to take the lives of the innocent instead of the guilty. In reality, it was an extravagant charade. It could not have been otherwise. The marines did everything possible to draw attention to themselves. A string of redcoats lumbered out to Botany Bay, with packs, kettles and cooking utensils bouncing around on their backs, muskets on their shoulders, eyes front, watching every step, feet thudding into the ground, twigs, branches and debris trodden underfoot, everything nosily snapping and cracking. The Aborigines watched from behind trees and among the rocks. They moved silently, stealthily. Few were seen and none was captured. The expedition served only as a melodramatic show of force – to reassure the convicts and to impress the Aborigines. Unless he was unwell, and his judgment impaired, Phillip could not have had a different objective.

In fact, there were ominous signs of the deterioration of Phillip's health. He now referred in his letters and despatches to a telltale pain in his side with repetitive regularity. In February 1790, he informed Nepean that his complaint had emerged in the first year of the settlement. In July he told Sir Joseph Banks that 'I find my health declines fast' and that he had at times 'a severe pain in my side', adding that he was 'getting little sleep'. In March 1791 he told Sydney in a private letter, 'For more than two years, I have never been a week free from pain in the side, which undermines and wears me out.' The following month he told Banks that the pain in the side 'has almost worn me out. I think it proceeds from an inflammation in the kidney'. In November he told Sydney, once again privately, that he had lately suffered more frequently than ever 'from a violent pain in the left kidney'. In April 1792 he wrote to Banks complaining of the pain in his side that seldom left him for more than a few days. In May the young William Chapman, with whose family Phillip was on close terms, arrived in Port Jackson and called on Phillip. In his letter to his parents Chapman provides the only firsthand account. He said that he was 'sorry to inform them that [Phillip] was not very well; his health now is very bad, he fatigues himself so much, he fairly knocks himself up, and won't rest, till he is not able to walk'. Phillip could now barely continue. His slight, angular body was brittle and his constitution sickly.

Phillip's symptoms were indicative of the presence of kidney stones – small solid concretions formed in the kidneys from dietary minerals in the urine. Most stones pass in the urine stream but some cause obstruction of the ureter, which in turn leads to intermittent pain that comes in waves and is felt in the flank between the ribs and hip. It can be one of the strongest known pain sensations. Phillip is unlikely to have lightly described his pain as 'severe' and 'violent'. Dietary factors are the primary cause of stone formation and some have suggested that the affliction was one of the occupational hazards of seafaring life. In Phillip's case, isolated in a far-flung colony, without adequate food, there was little that the surgeons could do. As the waves of pain coursed through his side, he would have doubled up, colour draining and facial muscles tensing. His sleepless nights would have made him disorientated, perhaps mildly delirious, certainly exhausted and debilitated. Laudanum, if administered, would have added to his disorientation.

While so afflicted, unable to walk, confined to his chair or forced to seek comfort in his bed, Phillip could no longer function effectively as His Majesty's representative. In November 1791 he had made his first official request to resign his commission. There had been an earlier private request in April 1790 for leave of absence to attend to his 'private affairs' in England but this was refused. Phillip's health, not his private affairs, was now the overwhelming factor. He told the new Home Secretary, Grenville, that he was 'induced to request permission to resign the Government that I may return to England in hopes of finding that relief which this country does not afford'. In March 1792 he pressed his request, stating, 'As my bad state of health continues without any hopes of a change for the better, I have to request that you, Sir, will move his Majesty to be graciously pleased to grant my request, if it has not been complied with before receipt of this letter.' By October Phillip seems to have been almost desperate. At the beginning of the month, he sent an official despatch with a long list of requirements, adding a final plaintive note in which he observed that 'the wants of the colony had made it a duty the severest I have ever experienced'. A few days later on 4 October, he wrote again, repeating that his state of health 'obliges me to hope I shall be at liberty to leave the country'. He did not know that Dundas, who replaced Grenville, had already approved his request and that the official response was on board the

Royal Admiral, which was only a few days out of Port Jackson. Dundas' letter arrived on 7 October. To Phillip's relief, the new Home Secretary was understanding, graciously lamenting that 'the ill state of your health deprives his Majesty of your further services in the Government of New South Wales'.

One might have thought that was all Phillip required. But he was now ambivalent and uncertain. Perhaps he was overwrought. Perhaps it was difficult for him to sever the emotional ties that bound him to the colony he had guided and nurtured from its conception, whose destiny he had shaped, whose people he had struggled to keep alive. Phillip had a profound sense of duty and he would not have wanted any odour of precipitous departure or abandonment – nothing to suggest that by leaving at this point he had failed in his duty. Within days he replied, inexplicably expressing his doubt whether Dundas' letter was really intended to convey the King's permission to return. He added that he feared that 'there is a possibility of its being expected that I should remain until permission to quit the Government is more fully and clearly expressed'. Despite these diffident remarks, there were no further communications. Phillip decided to leave on the first available ship. He was miserable but stoic. His pinched face now creased only rarely into the most formal of smiles. He was suffering, as one historian surmised, from 'exhaustion of spirit and decay of body'. When White and Collins heard of Phillip's plans to depart, they also requested permission to return. Collins said that he had lived so long with Phillip that 'I am blended in every concern of his'. But it would be some years before he or White would see England again.

Phillip could leave with a clear conscience. He had put the colony on a sound footing. In his final year in New South Wales the settlement's relative hardships diminished and perceptible signs of a sustainable community emerged. The colony stabilised. The drought that had nearly caused famine in 1790 and 1791 had ended. And the autumn harvest in 1792 was copious. In February, Major Grose arrived with the final company of the New South Wales Corps to replace the vexatious marines. The New South Wales Corps introduced its own problems and brought irreversible changes. Many of its officers were robust entrepreneurs who had purchased their commissions with an eye to profit. The buccaneering free enterprise of these 'trading officers' contributed to the settlement's economic progression in ways that Phillip did not approve and Sydney had not envisaged. But the metamorphosis from the heady idealism with which Phillip founded the colony to the free trade and rumbustious commerce for which the soldiers, settlers and newly emancipated convicts clamoured, was inevitable. As Phillip prepared for the resumption of his English life, a new chapter was opening in the colony that he had founded.

CHAPTER 12

SOCIETY GENTLEMAN

Phillip's return voyage to England, the recovery of his health, his second marriage and life in Georgian Bath

O n 10 December 1792 Phillip embarked on the *Atlantic*, saluted by a guard of honour from the New South Wales Corps. On the following morning, in the pre-dawn light, the ship weighed anchor and slipped out of Sydney Cove. All of the principal officers of the colony accompanied the *Atlantic* to the Heads, the entrance to the harbour through which Phillip had first nudged in a longboat on 21 January 1788. The officers then gave three cheers before parting and returning. Also on board the *Atlantic* was a remarkable coterie. Phillip brought with him four fine kangaroos that were accustomed to sleeping beside the fire in his kitchen at Government House. He also brought dingoes, birds, other animals, plants and timber samples. In addition, he was accompanied by two Aboriginal men, Bennelong and his younger friend Yemmerrawannie. They boarded the ship willingly, despite the distress of their wives and the dismal lamentations of their friends. Another passenger was returning marine private John Easty, who privately recorded in his journal that 'the state of the colony at this present time seems far better than at any time since the settlement was made'.

Even for the fit and able-bodied, the homeward passage via Cape Horn was arduous and not without considerable danger. For Phillip, ill and in pain, it must have been a sufferance. Ships such as the *Atlantic* sailed south from Port Jackson towards Stewart Island at the tip of New Zealand. There at latitude 47°S, they turned east and ran more or less within the ice zone, staying as far south as possible and seeking the strongest winds until they reached Cape Horn, where they kept the rocky, barren and southernmost headland of Tierra del Fuego on the port bow. In the Drake Passage, between Cape Horn and the South Shetland Islands of Antarctica, the unimpeded westerly winds of the Southern Ocean and the waters of the Antarctic circumpolar current funnel together, surging in the same direction. The result is a matchless intensity of atmospheric phenomena that causes the sailing conditions to be frequently hazardous and often violent. The winds moan and keen and the waves and icebergs sometimes dwarf passing ships. But for all its dangers, when travelling east, the Drake Passage was preferred to the treacherously narrow in-shore routes known as the Strait of Magellan and the Beagle Channel that thread between the archipelago of islands to the north.

The *Atlantic* made rapid progress, reaching the latitude of 47°S by 19 December before changing course and steering east by south into the ice zone. Keeping more or less to the 55th parallel, the latitude of

Cape Horn, she bowled along with the westerly winds, encountering much rain, snow, hail and storms, as well as icebergs. In fact, in early January 1793 the passengers and crew had the surreal experience of encountering at least 60 or 70 icebergs. It was like the ice scene in the Southern Ocean graphically depicted five years later in Samuel Taylor Coleridge's *The Rime of the Ancient Mariner* (1798).

By 8 January 1793 the *Atlantic* had sailed 4500 miles and was still 1300 miles from Cape Horn. A week later she cleared the snow-covered headland and beat up through the South Atlantic against the wind, into the teeth of rain and squalls, reaching Rio de Janeiro on 7 February. We know not what Phillip did at Rio de Janeiro or where he stayed, although it has been suggested that he was 'honoured with extraordinary attention'. This seems likely given his reception there in 1787. Easty was given shore leave and recorded in singular and amazed detail the 'grand and magnificent Romish churches, the statuary, the altars, the candlesticks and the constant blessings and genuflections by the citizens'. This had a familiar ring. The observations of Collins, White and Watkin Tench when the First Fleet visited Rio de Janeiro in 1787 were similar but Easty's observations have the hilarious intolerance and refreshing frankness of a simple man. He thought their practices were 'a thing so absurb that is Enough to make a prodstant Shuder' [sic]. He worried that 'so Great is thier idolatry thay kneel down when Ever any Images Pass them in the street' [sic]. And he felt sorry for them, saying that 'the Ignorance of the Lower Class of people makes me to pity them'.

It was in Rio de Janeiro that the first indication emerged of another war with France. On 23 February Captain Colnett, who was six weeks out of England, gave an account of 'great disturbances' in England and 'every preparation of war with the French'. During Phillip's absence in

New South Wales, France had been torn apart. In July 1789, while he was puzzling over the smallpox that struck the Aboriginal population, a Parisian mob had stormed the Bastille in Faubourg Saint-Antoine. And only a few weeks before the *Atlantic* arrived at Rio de Janeiro, Louis XVI had been executed at the guillotine. Then on 1 February 1793, the French revolutionary government declared war on Great Britain and the Dutch republic. Neither Phillip nor anyone on the *Atlantic* knew of these dramatic events and would not learn of them until they encountered a Portuguese ship in April. Wisely nonetheless, the *Atlantic*'s captain proceeded with caution, exercising the ship's great guns with increasing frequency as she moved into the waters of the North Atlantic. When the ship crossed the Equator, the crew amused themselves with the usual equinoctial ceremonies. And if Easty can be believed, Bennelong and Yemmerrawannie were convinced that Neptune was a king who lived in the sea. But the reality soon hit home when the *Atlantic* was fired upon by a French privateer in the approach to the English Channel. It is not difficult to imagine Phillip's depth of feeling a few days later when the English coast was sighted. Easty recorded in his journal 'our unspeakable Joy [at landing] in old England'. On 19 May 1793, almost exactly six years after he had sailed from Portsmouth with his complement of 800 convicts, Phillip returned to England with two Aboriginal men of the Eora people. They went ashore at Falmouth, Cornwall and took the coach to London.

Phillip's first priority on his return was the restoration of his health. He had been travelling at sea for almost six months and the long coach trip from the Cornish port of Falmouth to London was gruelling. For

Falmouth is only a little less distant from London than Penzance, England's most westerly town. The journey along the coaching road from Falmouth to London, frequently used by returning naval officers, involved over twenty stops to change horses at coaching inns. On arrival in London, Phillip needed to rest, to make arrangements for Bennelong and Yemmerrawannie and to attend to his financial affairs. He was anxious about his wife's will and the obligations that he had entered into upon marriage and separation. In particular, he had been concerned for several years about the two annuities he had secured. These were the 'private affairs' to which he referred in his unofficial letters to Sydney and Nepean in April 1790, when he sought leave of absence to return to England for twelve months. To make matters worse, the onset of war had caused great uneasiness in London's financial district, resulting in many failures, especially among firms trading with North America. John Lane's banking firm, Lane Son & Fraser, was one such casualty.

In London, Phillip consulted his physician and his lifelong friend and banker, John Lane. And he learned that his wife Charlott had died during the previous year. Phillip must have read her will anxiously. It contains many references to him but the terms of the will could only have given him solace. After recounting Phillip's financial commitments under the marriage agreement dated 18 July 1763 and the separation deed dated 22 April 1769, Phillip's eyes would have lit upon the comforting words 'I well and sufficiently release and discharge the said Arthur Phillip'. They were repeated, with excessive lawyerly thoroughness, several times. Charlott released Phillip from the obligations that he had entered into when they married and separated; freed him of the requirement to secure the annuities and to repay his debts to the estate; and left him a legacy of £100 – all on condition that he did not challenge any other provisions of the will, which he did not do.

When well enough, Phillip attended to official business. In late June 1793 he reported to the Home Secretary, Dundas. And afterwards he discussed the colony's agriculture and natural products with Banks and Hawkesbury, the President of the Board of Trade, explaining that he would have presented his returns earlier 'but that I have been much indisposed for several days'. In late July he discussed the formal resignation of his commission as Governor of New South Wales and sought from Dundas the grant of a lifetime pension in recognition of his service. Dundas promised to speak to Pitt on the matter. In due course the administration approved Phillip's pension effective from the date of his departure from New South Wales, namely 11 December 1792. The pension was half Phillip's salary as Governor: £500 a year in addition to his naval pay, which would continue to rise as he advanced in seniority. Nor would the pension cease on Phillip 'attaining any one of those places to which officers look up as rewards for past services' or to which a commanding officer might in due course expect to be appointed. Phillip had himself suggested the possibility of appointment to a seat on 'either of the Naval Boards, Colonel of Marines or Greenwich Hospital'. The honour of election as one of the governors of the Greenwich Hospital would have had a touching symmetry given his early education there, but Phillip may have overreached and the Lords Commissioners of the Admiralty demurred to his request.

Upon arrival in London, Bennelong and Yemmerrawannie were outfitted in accordance with the fashion of the time, for which Phillip paid the £30 bill. Each was supplied with two coats – one green and one of pepper and salt mixed cloth – a blue and buff striped waistcoat, slate-coloured ribbed worsted knee breeches, silk stockings, two pairs of fine cotton under-waistcoats faced with spotted muslin dimity, a double-breasted spotted quilted waistcoat and a pair of drab-coloured striped breeches. To complete their transformation, hats, shoes, buckles, shirts and cravats were also added to their wardrobe.

William Waterhouse, the father of Henry Waterhouse, the young man who had cradled the bleeding governor in the boat after his spearing, assisted Phillip in the care of the Aboriginal men. Waterhouse must have been an enlightened and liberal man of his time. He lived in Mount Street, in the heart of Mayfair, one of London's finest residential precincts. For much of their time in England, Bennelong and Yemmerrawannie lodged there. Sydney, who had retired in 1789, also had a town house nearby. Waterhouse allowed his home to be used as the venue for what now seems to have been a bizarre process of acculturation. Language tutors were assigned to the Aboriginal men to improve their reading, writing and spoken English. And Edward Jones, a classically trained musician who lived two doors away and was a favourite of the Prince of Wales, patiently recorded their music and their words while they sang to him in Waterhouse's drawing room. Waterhouse hired carriages for them, took them to the theatre at Covent Garden and Sadler's Wells, provided each of them with a new pair of gloves and a walking stick, and endeavoured to expose them to many facets of English life. They were taken to visit the sights of London – St Paul's Cathedral, the Houses of Parliament, the Tower arsenal and the Woolwich Docks. They were even taken to the biggest news story of the day – the trial of Warren Hastings, the former Governor-General of India.

This curious social experiment obviously had approval from the highest levels of government and Phillip and Waterhouse were duly reimbursed for all of the expenses of food, clothing, entertainment and lodging they incurred. The Aboriginal men were not taken to meet the King but they did meet Sydney, if not in Mayfair, certainly when they stayed at rural Eltham, near Sydney's country house at Chiselhurst southeast of London. When Yemmerrawannie sickened, Phillip arranged for the leading naval physician Sir Gilbert Blane to 'bleed and blister' him. And when he died on 18 May 1794, Phillip ensured that he received a respectable funeral and entry in the burial registry at Eltham Parish Church. Naturally it was a Christian funeral conducted in accordance with the Anglican rite. And Phillip ensured that there was a modest tombstone, which, like Blane's fees, was paid for by the Crown.

In retrospect, the whole sorry exercise was marred by pathos and incongruity. Unlike the fanfare that greeted Omai, the South Sea islander brought to London by Sir Joseph Banks in 1774, Bennelong and Yemmerrawannie never excited the interest of Londoners and appear to have attracted remarkably little attention. Perhaps Londoners had become more worldly in the preceding twenty years. More likely they were distracted by the war with France and the social upheaval, financial instability and political agitation that accompanied it. They were not so distracted, however, that they ignored the kangaroos that Phillip brought with him. One was placed on display at the Lyceum Museum in the Strand and was on show every day from morning until 8 o'clock in the evening. Many hundreds swarmed to view this curious marsupial – for the not inconsiderable entry price of one shilling.

In July 1793 Phillip asked Dundas whether he was 'at liberty to leave town' for Bath. He said that he had given up hope that the Bath waters might remove the pain in his side but he thought that they might 'in other respects be beneficial'. Each day in Bath a seemingly unending supply of hot water ascends from below the earth's crust. This iron-rich water originates as rain in the nearby hills, percolates to a great depth through limestone aquifers, and then, under pressure from geothermal energy, rises to the surface along fissures and faults in the limestone. The Celts built a shrine to the hot springs at Bath but the Romans went further and constructed a temple and bathing complex, including a *caldarium* (hot bath), *tepidarium* (warm bath) and *frigidariuim* (cold bath).

In Georgian England, taking the waters became a fashionable pastime for the wealthy and the well-to-do. The water cure involved the repeated imbibing of the unpleasant-tasting mineral waters and a certain amount of discreet bathing, selective immersion and douches of various strengths and concoctions. But drinking was the key. In 1781, John Elliott published an influential account of the medicinal properties of the mineral waters of Great Britain and Ireland. He advised that, 'The usual method of drinking the water is a glass or two before breakfast and about five in the afternoon. The next day, three glasses before breakfast and as many in the afternoon.' Of the waters at Bath, Elliott said that they had a slight saline, bitterish and iron taste and sometimes a somewhat sulphurous smell. Although these do not seem to be attractive features, he told his readers that the waters were beneficial in treating many maladies including 'the stone and gravel', complaints of the stomach and bowels, disorders of the head and the nerves, and gouty and rheumatic complaints. Kidney stones were a frequent target of the water cure. And it is not inconceivable that the drinking of copious amounts of Bath's mineral-rich water flushed out the renal stones with which Phillip was probably afflicted. Certainly there is no further reference to the pain in his side suffered in New South Wales.

Not everyone went to Bath for the cure. This Georgian spa town was fashionable throughout most of the century because of its beautiful buildings, its amiable society and the galvanising effect of royal patronage. It had none of London's squalors and all seemed to be as the architects intended. The Circus, inspired by the Coliseum, actually made you feel as if you were in ancient Rome. And when war with France started in 1793 and European spas became inaccessible, Bath's popularity increased further. The social life that whirled around the city extended beyond the curative effects of its water. It was all to do with the opportunities for social interaction that it provided, especially in the winter season from October to Easter. These were glamorous events attended by like-minded and often eligible people – fashionable and beautiful as they thought of themselves. Central to the social whirl was the building known as the Upper Assembly Rooms. In his retirement, Phillip would become the owner of an elegant terrace house just along from this emblematic centre of social activity.

The Upper Assembly Rooms were the venue for orchestrated dancing, cards, tea-drinking and a great deal of polite flirtation. Each night the master of ceremonies presided over dancing. Every week there were dress balls and fancy balls. Charles Dickens knew of the allure of these balls. And Jane Austen attended them. Writing decades later, Dickens said that the balls in the Upper Assembly Rooms at Bath 'are moments snatched from Paradise; rendered bewitching by music, beauty, elegance, fashion, etiquette'. In the ballroom, he explained, and in the long card room, the octagonal card room, the tea room, the staircase and in the passages, in fact everywhere throughout the Upper Assembly Rooms, 'dresses rustled, feathers waved, lights shone and jewels sparkled … brilliant eyes, lighted up with pleasurable expectation, gleamed from every side; and look where you would, some exquisite form glided gracefully through the throng'.

The physician Dr Hutton Cooper carried on practice in Bath and Phillip placed himself under his care. By August Phillip had taken up residence at No. 3 South Parade, a grand terrace situated on one of Bath's better streets. Hutton Cooper was not the only reason for Phillip's visit. Also in town were members of the Chapman family, at least the mother and several sisters of the young William Chapman, the boy who had written home from New South Wales in May 1792 on the sad state of Phillip's health. He was regarded, at least by his family, as Phillip's protégé. Phillip had certainly tried to assist the young William by offering him a place in the First Fleet in 1787 but his mother thought him too young and made him wait another four years. What is clear, however, is that Phillip was much admired by the Chapman family and was on affectionate terms with them. They pursued genteel leisure activities together, including cards and reading.

Reading was both a fashionable pastime and an indirect means of social introduction. The latest novels were available from circulating libraries. Like the Upper Assembly Rooms, the circulating library in Bath was an important feature of the cultural and social life of its residents and visitors. Subscription libraries focussed on scholarly materials but circulating libraries developed to serve general reading interests – in line with popular literature. In fact, the rise of the novel coincided with the rise of the circulating library. For a small fee, readers who belonged to a circulating library could have access to a wide selection of fiction writing, magazines and newspapers. These new libraries proliferated in most major centres, especially in resort and spa towns like Bath, Ramsgate and Cheltenham, where visitors came in the pursuit of leisure. For in truth, the circulating library was a fashionable daytime lounge for ladies and gentlemen that was as indispensable by day as the local assembly rooms were by night. The contemporary *Guide to All the Watering & Sea-Bathing Places* said that circulating libraries 'are frequented by all fashionable people'. Indeed, it continued, 'the taste and character of individuals may be better learned in a library than in a ball-room; and they who frequent the former in preference to the latter, frequently enjoy the most rational and the most permanent pleasure'.

Whether it was to enjoy the most rational and most permanent pleasure of other persons or simply to read books, Phillip joined one of Bath's circulating libraries on 12 August 1793, probably Marshall's in Milsom Street. On the following day, Isabella Whitehead joined the same library. It was the custom to subscribe to the library upon arrival in such a place as a means of announcing one's presence. Phillip and Isabella may not have known each other, and their joining on consecutive days may have been a coincidence, but sooner or later they would inevitably have encountered each other in Bath. Phillip was an eligible and distinguished naval officer whose reputation as the Governor of New South Wales no doubt preceded him. Isabella Whitehead was 43 years of age, unmarried and the daughter of a gentleman of affluent means who was in Bath for the recovery of his heath. In the small community of visitors to Bath, it would have been difficult for Phillip and Isabella not to meet. Each of them represented a slight variation on Jane Austen's universal truth. He may not have been the archetypal 'single man in possession of a good fortune' who 'must be in want of a wife' but at her age, Isabella was in need of a husband and she may have been the one with a fortune.

Her parents were both from prominent families involved in the cotton and linen weaving trade in the industrial northwest around Blackburn, Preston and Manchester. The region was littered with hundreds of collieries and produced most of the world's manufactured cotton. The prestige of Isabella's father Richard Whitehead was such that in 1759 George II appointed him as the high sheriff of Lancashire, making him the monarch's sole representative in the county. Fate thus ordained that Phillip and Isabella Whitehead would meet and marry. Like Phillip's first wife Charlott Denison, Isabella was probably too old to have children but still young enough to enjoy the companionship and comforts, not to mention the respectability, that usually accompany marriage. Their wedding took place on 8 May 1794 at St Marylebone in London, a few weeks before Phillip buried Yemmerrawannie. Within months of the union, Richard Whitehead was also dead. Isabella may not have been her father's only child, but there is every reason to assume that she was comfortably provided for. And Phillip, it seems, inherited some of his personal effects.

Whatever the precise level of affluence they enjoyed, Phillip and Isabella appear to have spent the first two years of their married life enjoying a charmed social existence, oscillating between Bath and London, entertaining and being entertained, attending card parties, concerts and balls. For card games, they would have played whist, piquet and casino, possibly also commerce, speculation and loo depending on their inclination. They would have listened to music by Handel and Haydn, Corelli, Albinoni and Gluck, as well as that of John

Christian Bach – the English Bach. The music of his ultimately more famous father, Johann Sebastian Bach, was not then fashionable. And at the Upper Assembly Rooms, if they chose to participate, Phillip and Isabella would have danced in formation the quadrilles and cotillions of the day. Fashions had changed since the 1760s. The heights of fantasy and outrageous ornamentation to which the French aristocracy adhered before the Revolution, and which the English copied, slipped out of favour. There was a movement towards simplicity, at least relatively speaking. To a greater or lesser extent, powdered wigs, rigidly boned bodices, extravagantly low-necked gowns and ostentatious hoops receded from fashion. The elaborately embroidered silks and velvets of which gentlemen were previously fond gave way to woollen cut-away tail coats in plainer colours, short satin waistcoats, breeches and stockings.

As to transport, this was still the pre-industrial era in which everyone depended on a horse-drawn carriage of one sort or another, or they walked or rode a horse. The 100 mile trip from London to Bath was usually undertaken either by the public stagecoach over several days with multiple changes of horses or in a private coach. Better still was a chaise, a smaller carriage where the horses were controlled by boys riding postilion on the nearside horses. Chaises could be hired, but an Englishman's dream was to own his own. For shorter distances, and around town, there were lighter vehicles such as the two-wheeled curricle, the pretty landaulet and the barouche. The last was a somewhat superior vehicle suitable for a dowager or a duchess. The phaeton was the young man's sports car of the horse age. Sedan chairs still existed of course and served a useful purpose within the limits of the strength of two men. They had right of way over pedestrians but they would soon pass out of fashion.

Phillip's early married life with Isabella was not all frippery. As persons who have held high office are sometimes inclined to do, Phillip remained interested, even active, in the subject of his former responsibilities. For a time at least, he was frequently in London 'on matters relative to the colony'. A new office had been established for Dundas, who became known as the Secretary of State for War and took with him the responsibilities of the former Home Office. Phillip volunteered advice to the administration, emphasising the need, among other things, to have a suitable naval vessel stationed permanently in New South Wales. And he communicated with Sir Joseph Banks, expressing his concerns about soldiers selling liquor and settlers profiteering. He was, as always, troubled by 'individuals making fortunes at the expense of the Crown' and distressed by the morals and commercial avidity of the 'trading officers' from the New South Wales Corps.

Phillip also took the opportunity to assist officers who had served under him, writing and making representations on their behalf. Foremost among them was Gidley King, for whom he sought valiantly and ultimately successfully to obtain an increase in his remuneration. Gidley King was also an intimate friend of the Chapman family and he and Phillip went back a long way together. It was Gidley King who wrote excitedly to the Chapman family when he was appointed to the *Ariadne* in 1781, informing them that the ship was commanded by Captain Phillip, which he said promised a great deal of happiness. This seems to be the communication that is the origin of the description of Phillip as someone in whom is blended the gentleman, the scholar and the seaman. Others whose interests Phillip sought to advance were

Henry Waterhouse, in whose father's home in Mayfair Bennelong and Yemmerrawannie had been lodged; a midshipman named Donovan who had behaved valorously at the wreck of the *Sirius* on Norfolk Island; George Johnson, whom Phillip regarded as the most deserving of all the marine officers to come out with the First Fleet; his loyal deputy Hunter, who became Governor of New South Wales in 1795; and Collins, who was the closest of all to Phillip and served as his secretary as well as the colony's judge-advocate.

In the meantime, the wars waged by the French revolutionary government continued against a number of European states. Austria was the first opponent and from 1 February 1793, Great Britain and the Dutch republic were drawn in. After Napoleon seized power from the revolutionary government in 1799 there was a brief period of peace in 1802–03. But this 'Peace of Amiens', as it was known, was only a short interlude between a revolutionary storm that had blown itself out and a Napoleonic storm that was gathering. In May 1803 Great Britain resumed hostilities against France and continued them inexorably until Napoleon's defeat at Waterloo in June 1815 and his eventual surrender and exile. This second phase was known as the Napoleonic Wars.

The French Revolutionary and Napoleonic Wars represented a gilded period for Britain's navy. The number of naval personnel and the extent of shipbuilding expanded rapidly. And enhanced opportunities for professional advancement proliferated. The figures provide a clear picture. When Phillip sailed for New South Wales in 1787, the number of officers and men borne in navy ships was only 14,514. By 1799 the number had increased almost tenfold to 128,930. The number of ships also increased dramatically – from 411 at the start of the war to 722 by 1799. This was the age of Nelson: a time when chivalric medievalism reached new levels of ambition, when popular culture idealised naval officers, and when Jane Austen's heroine in *Persuasion* could say of Captain Wentworth that she loved him because he belongs to 'a profession which is, if possible, more distinguished in its domestic virtues than in its national importance'.

As he readjusted to married life, Phillip must have followed the newspaper accounts of the progress of the war with a keen eye. On the continent, the French mobilised huge armies, supported by mass conscription, and rapidly achieved military success, taking San Sebastian from Spain in 1794, occupying all of Belgium and the Rhineland, and in the following year seizing the Netherlands. By late 1795 Prussia and Spain had ceded substantial territories to France in return for peace. At sea, however, Great Britain prevailed. On 1 June 1794, a few weeks after Phillip's wedding, the first and largest naval action of the war took place. It became known as 'The Glorious First of June'. The playwright Richard Brinsley Sheridan even wrote a play by the same name. Although the battle was only a partial success, it stimulated British patriotism and must have made Phillip's blood quicken. In the following months, his desire to return to active service could only have increased as newspapers reported that squadrons of the Royal Navy had progressively captured Martinique, Guadeloupe and St Lucia in the West Indies. Then in 1795 other British squadrons captured the strategic ports of Cape Town, Trincomalee and Malacca along the route to the East Indies. Phillip, in the meantime, like every other half-pay officer, waited to be called.

CHAPTER 13

INSPECTOR

Phillip's war service at sea and on shore during the French Revolutionary and Napoleonic wars

The opportunity for which Phillip had been waiting finally arrived in early 1796. There was no sign now of the ill-health that had plagued him in New South Wales. In February the Admiralty recalled him to active service to take command of the *Atlas,* a 98-gun ship of the line moored at Portsmouth. Phillip had not had command of a fighting ship for twelve years – not since he took the *Europe* to the India Squadron and back in 1783–84. He was now 57 years old and in the twilight of his active service career. The path that his professional life had taken – Portuguese service, espionage and colonial governor – had kept him out of sight and removed him from those opportunities for distinction at sea that were usually essential for a senior naval appointment in an active post. The command of the *Atlas* was a last chance, but it was a false start. In one of those mix-ups and miscommunications that are a by-product of war, he arrived in Portsmouth to be informed by Admiral Parker that another captain was already in command of the *Atlas*. Phillip had no choice but to return disconsolately to Bath in Somerset, duly claiming and receiving the expenses of his futile journey – all £12.18s.

It was not long before Phillip received another command. In March he was directed to Plymouth to take command of the *Alexander*. This was a twist of fate. For in 1778, just as the *Alexander* was launched at Deptford, Phillip had returned from his Portuguese service in South America. The circumstances at that time combined to ensure that he was appointed as the ship's first lieutenant and for eleven months in 1778–79 he sailed with her as part of the Channel Fleet. He was now about to do so again, this time as her captain. The *Alexander* was a 74-gun ship of the line with a complement of approximately 650 men. Her two gun decks each had 28 gun ports. The heaviest guns were always on the lower gun deck. The upper gun deck carried eighteen-pound cannon. Some lighter guns and carronades were situated on the quarterdeck and the forecastle. Nothing much had changed in the intervening years since Phillip had been her first lieutenant – except the ship's ownership. For a short time at the beginning of the war, after being captured near the Scilly Isles, the *Alexander* became French property, serving under the name *Alexandré*. On board at the time of her capture was Watkin Tench, the same marine captain who served with Phillip in New South Wales. His adventurous life took a turn for the worse when he became a French prisoner of war. As for the *Alexander* herself, her role as a French warship was only brief and within seven months she was recaptured and soon once again flew the red ensign of the Royal Navy.

Phillip's command of the *Alexander* was uneventful, and it concluded with disappointment. For three months she undertook coastal patrol duties along the southern coast between Plymouth and Portsmouth. Then in July she escorted nineteen vessels bound for the East Indies as far as Madeira, followed by more patrolling in the Channel. In October Phillip's tenure came to a sudden and unexpected end. He was superseded, required to relinquish the *Alexander*'s command and briefly returned to half pay. His successor was Captain Alexander John Ball, a youthful and charismatic officer who was destined for a baronetcy. Ball's time as the *Alexander*'s captain marked the beginning of an illustrious period of service for the ship and indeed for Ball – something that Phillip must have watched with chagrin. The ship served with distinction at the Battle of the Nile and throughout the Mediterranean. Nelson called Ball 'My dear, invaluable friend'.

Phillip was not long on half pay. Within days he was given command of the *Swiftsure*, to which he brought Isabella's brother as his third lieutenant. She was another 74-gun ship of the line and his third ship in the space of eight months. He was proud of the *Swiftsure* and later said that she was 'one of the best ships in His Majesty's Service'. She was also destined to achieve distinction at the Battle of the Nile – but not with Phillip as her captain. Phillip took over the *Swiftsure*'s command in October 1796 while she was fitting out in Portsmouth Harbour in readiness for sea service. While in port, captains frequently entertained aboard their ship, bringing on wives, friends and relations. In Phillip's case, we have just a glimpse of one such occasion when he made an unsuccessful attempt to entertain aboard the *Swiftsure* at Cawsand Bay. Phillip invited on board Isabella, his old friend Isaac Landmann and Landmann's son George. The ship could only be reached by going out into the sound in a small lugger. However, a southwest wind and waves that were 'exceedingly high and everywhere washing over us' thwarted the planned adventure. After a short and miserable sail, they reached the stern of the *Swiftsure* but it was evident that they would have difficulty getting on board in the conditions. Phillip took the decision to return to shore, gave some orders to the first lieutenant who was standing at the gangway, and turned the boat about with sails close-reefed. Everyone was extremely discomfited but to George Landmann's surprise, Phillip's suffering was the worst. He recorded the following unflattering but very human picture of Phillip:

> Well I remember his little figure smothered up in his brown
> camlet cloak lined with green baize, his face shrivelled, and
> thin aquiline nose under a large cocked hat, gathered up in
> a heap, his chin between his knees, sitting under the lee of
> the main mast; his sharp and powerful voice exclaiming: 'I
> cannot bear this, I am as sick as a dog!'

Phillip's discomfiture was only temporary and he would not have been the first captain of a ship of the line who had trouble finding his sea legs in a small boat in choppy waters close to shore. Back on the *Swiftsure*, he patrolled with the Western Squadron at the entrance to the Channel throughout the winter of 1796–97. In the early spring, after a Spanish fleet was defeated at the great battle off Cape St Vincent, the *Swiftsure* and several other warships were ordered to escort a convoy being sent to resupply the strategic British port of Gibraltar at the entrance to the Mediterranean. By 9 April the *Swiftsure* was off Cape Finisterre and a week later off Cape St Vincent, the southwestern point of Portugal. In these waters, an encounter with a French or Spanish warship was more likely, but to Phillip's disappointment no action eventuated. He then took his ship out into the Atlantic as far as Madeira before returning in June to join Nelson's blockading squadron at Cadiz, the Spanish Atlantic port 60 miles west of Gibraltar.

For the next four months Phillip remained on the *Swiftsure*, maintaining her station at the entrance to Cadiz harbour, blockading the Spanish ships inside, some of which had survived the battle off Cape St Vincent. In June Nelson himself came on board and inspected Phillip's ship. He reported to the Commander of the Mediterranean Fleet, who was now known as Earl St Vincent after the battle of the same name, that the *Swiftsure* was 'in most excellent order and fit for any service'. That was more than could be said for many other ships of the Royal Navy at the time. Insubordination was always a daily part of life at sea but never more so than in 1797 when perceived class interests united lower deck and quarterdeck against each other. In April of that year the crews of the Channel Fleet mutinied over pay and conditions. Murmurings and discontent soon spread throughout all the fleets of the Royal Navy. In the Mediterranean fleet, severe measures were necessary on St Vincent's flagship but Phillip kept any disaffection on the *Swiftsure* firmly under control without excessive belligerence. His captain's log and journal records no shortage of punishments, even for relatively minor offences, but they were usually limited to one or two dozen lashes. The mutiny did not spread to his ship.

September 1797 brought another change of command. St Vincent thought well of Phillip and knew of his prior Portuguese service and the glowing reports he had received. He had plans for a joint Anglo–Portuguese naval force, which included Phillip. In May and June 1797 St Vincent was in negotiations for the Portuguese to provide four 'well-manned, commanded and appointed' Portuguese warships to form 'an Auxiliary Naval Force of Co-Operation'. His idea was to augment this force with three English ships. The combined squadron would, he anticipated, patrol the Atlantic between the entrance to the Tagus River at Lisbon and Cape St Vincent. Naturally, he thought that the squadron would be commanded by 'a Native of Great Britain'. And St Vincent seems to have had Phillip in mind. However, the Portuguese resisted any notion of foreign authority and announced that the Marquis of Niza would command their ships. At the time St Vincent wrote regularly to Evan Nepean about his plans and proposals. Nepean then held the wartime post of Secretary to the Admiralty. When the appointment of the Marquis of Niza was announced, St Vincent informed Nepean that 'the moment he appears, I will unite the *Swiftsure*, *Bellerophon* and *Audacious* to it, under the command of Captain Phillip who is an officer of merit, and temper, and I am informed gave great satisfaction to the Government of Portugal while he was employed in the Portuguese Service'. One may safely assume that Nepean supported Phillip's credentials.

St Vincent's aspirations for Phillip were not to be. The reason for the alteration was a bitter difference that did not involve Phillip but of which he was an unfortunate casualty. The two most senior admirals serving under St Vincent were Horatio Nelson and Charles Thompson. Rather astutely as it turned out, St Vincent tended to favour Nelson, something that Thompson bitterly resented. Matters came to a head when St Vincent had two mutinous sailors executed on a Sunday. Thompson launched a public attack on his commanding officer, accusing St Vincent of profaning the Sabbath. This of course would not do, however devout Thompson may have been. The Admiralty recalled him, rendering vacant the command of the *Blenheim*. St Vincent told Phillip to take it, intending it to be a compliment, for the *Blenheim* was a 90-gun three-decker and until recently the flagship of an admiral. But she turned out to be a poisoned chalice and would be Phillip's last ship.

In September 1797 the *Blenheim* needed to go to Lisbon for repairs and St Vincent sent Phillip with her. The strategic landscape had begun to change and St Vincent and the administration wanted Phillip on the ground in Portugal so that he might be in a position to co-operate with General Stuart, who had been sent to command a military force in anticipation of an expected invasion by the French and Spanish armies. Whitehall feared that Portugal would not resist, or was incapable of resisting, any such invasion. Britain was therefore prepared to offer massive military and naval assistance to Portugal, hoping that doing so would justify it taking practical control of Portugal's naval and military forces. If that occurred, Stuart would inevitably become commander of the troops and Phillip commander of the naval forces. For three months in Lisbon Phillip worked in readiness for the expected invasion, renewing acquaintances, fostering links with the Portuguese administration and carrying out orders transmitted to him by St Vincent.

It was all to no avail. By February 1798, the expected invasion by French and Spanish forces had not eventuated. Worse still, Phillip's command of the *Blenheim* was abruptly taken from him when the newly arrived Rear-Admiral Frederick, accompanied by his own captain, insisted on hoisting his own flag on the recently repaired *Blenheim*. This was a perquisite of rank that St Vincent was unable to resist. Nor did he consider it appropriate to return Phillip to the *Swiftsure*, which was now ably commanded by the soon to be famous Benjamin Hallowell, another intimate of Nelson. Under Hallowell's command, the *Swiftsure* achieved the glory that Phillip so keenly desired – no more so than at the Battle of the Nile in August later that same year, when she bombarded the French flagship *L'Orient* and played the major role in her destruction.

Phillip was left high and dry. In his letter to Nepean he said that he was 'obliged to come on shore under the most mortifying circumstances'. Neither malice nor professional rivalry had been his undoing, just an unhappy combination of circumstances. And age was now also a factor. Nelson's leading captains, his revered 'band of brothers' who fought alongside him at the Battle of the Nile, were much younger men. His flag-captain, Edward Berry, was 30 years younger than Phillip. Ball on the *Alexander* was almost twenty years younger. Hallowell on the *Swiftsure* was 22 years younger. And Nelson himself was twenty years younger. None of the others was remotely close to Phillip in age. He was old enough to be the father of each of them. It was a testament to St Vincent's high estimation of Phillip that he had gone so close and progressed so far. But the command of a ship of the line in time of war was, for the most part, a young man's game and Phillip was at a temporal disadvantage.

Once again Phillip took the packet service from Lisbon, coming ashore at Falmouth on 2 March 1798. He had written to Nepean from Portugal and again on his arrival in England. He knew there were always more officers than ships and he must have wondered what, if anything, the Admiralty could provide for him. As his post chaise clipped and jolted along the coaching road to London, it is reasonable to assume that he ruminated on the future. His situation was like that of Patrick O'Brian's aging fictional captain Jack Aubrey, to whom the First Sea Lord said: 'I can hold out no hope of a ship. However, there may be some slight possibility in the Sea-Fencibles or the Impress Service. We are extending both, and they call for active, enterprising men.' Captain Aubrey, who was not enamoured of the First Lord's proposal, thought to himself that the Sea Fencibles and the Impress Service 'were landborne posts: [for] comfort-loving men, devoid of ambition or tired of the sea, willing to look after a kind of fishermen's militia or to attend to the odious work of the press-gang'.

Phillip was not yet entirely devoid of ambition nor tired of the sea but the best that Nepean could do was to find him an appointment as commander of the Hampshire Sea Fencibles. The Sea Fencible service was not quite a fishermen's militia. It was a form of naval home guard that fulfilled an important function at a time when there were realistic apprehensions of a French invasion of the south coast of England. The strategic thinking behind the service was that while the navy would seek to stop and destroy any invasion force off the French coastal ports, the Sea Fencibles would if necessary attack any French landing barges and hoys that reached the English beaches. The timing of Phillip's return was fortuitous because the establishment of an organisation to be known as the Sea Fencibles was a current topic of discussion within the Admiralty at the very time that Phillip had written to Nepean.

Phillip was not alone in his appointment as a commander of Sea Fencibles. There were many post captains in a similar position – without a ship and willing to take a shore job. On 6 April 1798 the Lords Commissioners of the Admiralty issued to the Navy Board

'A list of Post Captains appointed to superintend the Enrolment of Sea Fencibles'. Phillip was one of a number on the list. By 1805 there were 70 captains commanding groups of Sea Fencibles along sections of the coastlines of England, Scotland, Wales and Ireland. The service was attractive to unemployed officers because they became entitled to full pay rather than the half pay they would otherwise have received. And civilian recruits – for whom the major incentive was an entitlement to immunity from militia service or the press gang – were easily found.

For most of the next six years Phillip was engaged, with his usual painstaking conscientiousness, on the business of the Sea Fencibles and the Impress Service. And in January 1799, when he had reached the top of the captains' list, he was promoted to rear admiral of the blue. It was the final stage of his naval career – a career which he had officially commenced in 1755 as one of Captain Everitt's servants on the *Buckingham*. His work in the administration of the Sea Fencibles was unglamorous but Phillip was well suited to it. He supervised the recruitment and training of the local volunteers who made up the fencibles, he inspected the men and their posts, and he attended to the inevitable administrative responsibilities that go with the position of commanding officer. The men were trained in the use of cannon and pike and expected to man the signal stations on the coast as well as the Martello towers then being built. One of the recurring burdens for the commander was the necessity from time to time to secure the release of Sea Fencibles men who had been wrongly pressed, notwithstanding the exemption to which they were entitled. And of course there were always reports to the Admiralty, in Phillip's case invariably lengthy and careful.

From April 1798 Phillip made his home and his headquarters at Lymington, an old narrow-laned port west of Portsmouth. Isabella lived with him there. It was not far from Lyndhurst where he had farmed with Charlott 30 years before. Timber from the New Forest came to the port at Lymington before being shipped along the coast to the dockyards at Portsmouth. Lymington was not quite Bath, but like Lyme Regis and many other south-coast seaside towns of the period, it had its own assembly rooms, sea-baths, theatre and circulating library. And the mail coach to London left the Angel Hotel in the High Street every afternoon. Phillip was often away, and despite all that Lymington had to offer, this does not appear to have been an entirely happy period for Isabella – at least from 1801. In March of that year Pitt went out of office and the new government commenced the negotiations that culminated in the Peace of Amiens in March 1802. An interregnum in the hostilities with France followed until 1803 when the second stage of the long conflict erupted. As the peace discussions rolled on, the new administration disbanded the Sea Fencible service and closed down the signal stations. And the Admiralty, of which St Vincent was now the First Sea Lord, found other work for Phillip that required more and more time away from Lymington.

In April 1801 Phillip was sent to inspect and report on the facilities for French and Spanish prisoners of war throughout Hampshire. Among other places, the prisoners were confined in ships and hospitals at Portsmouth, Porchester and Forton. Phillip reviewed the health and conditions of the prisoners, paying particular attention to the cleanliness of their living quarters, listening to their complaints and being alert for abuses by supervising officers, surgeons and contractors. In July, having duly reported on the prisoners of war, the Admiralty requested him to undertake a thorough inspection and review of the operation and effectiveness of the Impress Service.

Phillip's review of the Impress Service was an extensive undertaking, requiring lengthy and arduous travel. Accompanied by a secretary, he travelled by post chaise on a lengthy tour of the principal ports of England and Scotland, beginning in Scotland in August and then travelling south through Yorkshire, Lincolnshire, Norfolk and Suffolk. In September and October, he continued along England's southern coast, visiting the port towns of Deal, Gosport, Southampton, Exmouth, Plymouth and Falmouth. In December 1801 he produced a comprehensive report. Isabella, it seems, did not find Phillip's hard work and lengthy absences agreeable. During his travels, she wrote a letter to her husband that appears to have indicated that she was an unhappy wife. All marriages are secrets of course and we will never know but Phillip's response dated 4 October 1801 reveals a distinct tension. He commenced by saying how truly sorry he was that Isabella persisted in groundless ideas 'that your husband and all your friends are plotting against your happiness'. He told her that her letters were painful to read and he asked her no longer to write to him 'unless you can write in a different language'. If she could do so, he said, he would be happy to hear from her in the following week when he expected to be at Appledore in Devon. But he repeated, 'My Bel, you had better not write, than write letters filled with charges which only exist in your imagination.' He concluded by informing her that, 'Your friends still love you, and respect you, but you drive them from you, by your unjust suspicions.'

By 1803 matters had only become worse – requiring more travel and resulting in more unhappiness. When the renewal of war became obvious at the beginning of 1803, and a Napoleon-inspired invasion of England once again became a threat, the Admiralty revived the Sea Fencibles and appointed Phillip to carry out inspections of the force along the south coast. From January he was back on the coaching roads of southern England inspecting the volunteer defenders along the coastline and reporting on their state of readiness to repel a French invasion. His unhappiness with Isabella continued. In April he wrote to her, again in the same vein, telling her 'for God's sake let me hear no more of doubts for which there is no reason' and finishing his letter with a plea that would be almost comic if it were not so sad – 'I see no reason for [the use of] the word afflicted at the conclusion of your letter, and if that is repeated, I shall think I have too good reason to conclude myself an afflicted husband. Think more justly my Dear Bel ...'

Whether truly afflicted or not, Phillip threw himself into his work and travelled ever more extensively. At the end of 1803, the Admiralty appointed him as Inspector of the whole of the Sea Fencible service, in addition to his role as Inspector of the Impress Service. This required constant travel. In days of bouncing coaches, rudimentary springs, wooden wheels and dirt roads, not to mention the constant changes of horses and the overnight stays at coaching inns, Phillip's exertions were remarkable. Between December 1803 and February 1805, accompanied only by a secretary, he traversed the whole of the coast of England and as far north as Forfarshire on the east coast of Scotland. One historian expressed his incredulity at Phillip's punishing schedule in these terms: 'Fourteen months spent on a trip that covered almost the whole coast of England and part of Scotland; fourteen months, day after day in post chaises, accompanied only by a secretary; fourteen months contact with the seafaring men of England ... such experience could have fallen to the lot of very few of his contemporaries.' There was some overstatement in that description, as Phillip's journeying was not continuous and he did have time out with Isabella in the village of

Bathampton in the summer and some time with friends and colleagues in London. But it must certainly have been arduous.

In fact, Phillip's ceaseless travel seems to have been exactly the sort of thing that Charles Dickens had in mind when he wrote the vivid opening lines of his essay 'Early Coaches' in *Sketches by Boz*: 'We have often wondered how many months' incessant travelling in a post chaise it would take to kill a man; how many months of constant travelling in a succession of early coaches, an unfortunate mortal could endure.' Despite the hardships, however, there was no realistic alternative to travel by post chaise, and a senior naval officer on official business, such as Phillip, would not have travelled any other way. When compared to the stagecoach, the post chaise was more gentlemanly. The stagecoach, a heavy, jolting vehicle, carried six inside passengers of every social status who got on and off at different places along the road. Like a modern bus, it arrived at inns at inconvenient hours and allowed insufficient time out for eating and sleeping. In a chaise you travelled all the way with only one other person, picked your own inns, and were sure of spending the nights in bed. Jane Austen's Mr Bingley, a young man with a large fortune, travelled to Netherfield to inspect the property in a chaise and four. Journeying by chaise was faster and more fashionable, and discretion was assured. And the only practical difference between a chaise and a post chaise was that a post chaise was hired, using rented horses that were changed at posts or stations, and was generally painted yellow.

Phillip's work with the Sea Fencibles and the Impress Service was significant and his reports were thorough and comprehensive. A national coastal defence force of volunteers was an innovation at the time but its establishment and manning were affected by political considerations. Within the navy, the work was not generally highly regarded and Phillip could not have failed to be aware of the subtle disdain in which it was held. By 1803 St Vincent had apparently decided that the Sea Fencibles were of little use other than 'to calm the fears of old ladies'. Nonetheless Phillip was instrumental in ensuring that the service operated efficiently. He made clear his concerns that too many suitable candidates for impressment avoided naval service by volunteering for the Sea Fencibles. At some ports, where there were no gun batteries or armed boats, he queried the utility of the Sea Fencibles at all. And he saw the need for a single command so as to avoid the inherent conflict between the Impress Service and the Sea Fencibles, who were competing for the same pool of men. This was a matter on which the Admiralty subsequently acted by adopting Phillip's recommendations and amalgamating the two services. This no doubt gave him a degree of satisfaction but it was no consolation for the loss of opportunity to distinguish himself in a sea command. And it is not clear how much attention the Admiralty gave to the separate recommendations in Phillip's December 1801 report for reform of the Impress Service. His proposals were principally concerned with changes in bookkeeping and reconciliation of accounts, the standardisation of expenses allowed to regulating captains and the maintenance of registers of exemptions. Despite Phillip's proposals, the system continued, essentially unchanged, until the end of the Napoleonic Wars.

It is clear that Phillip had now begun to consider his future, despite several last flickers of ambition. In 1803 he wrote to Lord Hobart, then Colonial Secretary, requesting that an arrangement be made to secure his pension rights for the benefit of Isabella after his death. He said that Dundas had promised this but 'for various causes' had quitted office without carrying out his promise. Phillip's request appears to have fallen on deaf ears and the administration does not seem to have subsequently provided for Isabella. It would have been exceptional to do so, and after Phillip's death his annual pension payment of £500 ceased to appear in the budget estimates for New South Wales.

For a brief time, he appears to have entertained a slender hope of a further sea command but in truth Phillip was probably ambivalent. In July 1802 he asked to be appointed as Admiral in the Leeward Islands but nothing eventuated. Early the next year, St Vincent offered him command of the naval force based in Ireland but Phillip did not accept. As far as active service was concerned, he seems to have chosen his end point. By the middle of 1803, Phillip was preparing for life after Lymington and was inspecting homes in Bath and Clifton. The addresses in Bath which he proposed for Isabella's consideration were among the most salubrious – Camden Place, the upper Crescent and Green Park Place. In Jane Austen's *Persuasion*, Sir Walter Elliot chose Camden Place because it was 'a lofty and dignified situation, such as becomes a man of consequence'. Pending a move to Bath, the village of Bathampton seems to have served as their new place of residence from 1804. Isabella moved there to be near members of the Chapman family. And in the summer months of that year Phillip spent some weeks with her before continuing his inspections.

There were now no more offers of active service from the Admiralty and no further requests by Phillip. He continued his work with the Sea Fencibles and the Impress Service and even revived his once secret South American charts and lent them to the Hydrographic Office for copying. In the end, the final chapter closed suddenly at the end of 1804. In December, the Admiralty replaced him as Inspector of the eastern half of the country and in the following February Phillip was told to close his books and consider his appointment at an end.

As was customary, Phillip's rank and remuneration continued their stately progress by seniority. There was then no retired list for admirals except unofficially for those (yellow) admirals who were in disfavour or were old or incapable and unsuitable for active flag rank. All of the remaining admirals, from the most junior rear admiral of the blue onwards, moved steadily up through the ranks and squadrons – rear admiral of the blue, then of the white, then of the red; then vice admiral and full admiral of the same coloured squadrons. Progressively, over the following years, Phillip continued through all the gradations of rear and vice admiral until he reached full admiral of the blue in 1814 – more senior even than Nelson, who had died a vice admiral of the white. The nine ranks of admiral, known as 'the last nine stages of increasing splendour', were a reward for length of service. Progress was automatic, devoid of uncertainty or surprise, depending only on death and seniority. And with each step upwards, there was an incremental increase in the half pay to which the admiral became entitled.

CHAPTER 14

FINAL YEARS

Phillip's retirement and death, the suicide theory, his last will and testament and the memorials in Australia and England

Retirement commenced at the beginning of 1805. The village of Bathampton, where Isabella resided during 1804, was two miles from Bath. The Chapman ladies – Jemima Powell and her niece and constant companion, Miss Fanny Chapman – lived in nearby Batheaston. They were among Isabella's closest friends. And they were great admirers of Phillip. Indeed they seemed to rejoice in their happy association with such a distinguished admiral, and they delighted in the attention he gave to the young William Chapman, Fanny's adored brother and Jemima's nephew. A social circle existed around Jemima in which Phillip's physician, Hutton Cooper, who was also part of the extended family, was a frequent participant. Phillip had consulted

Hutton Cooper on his return from New South Wales and continued to receive treatment from him. Miss Fanny's diary for the years 1807–12 includes frequent references to Hutton Cooper's fashionable ways and spendthrift habits, and there are several amusing references to him being tipsy 'but not unpleasantly so'.

Jemima Powell and Hutton Cooper were both in the full swing of fashion. And for the time being each of them was relieved of the burdens and responsibilities of marriage. In Jemima Powell's case, her husband, who later achieved infamy by killing Lord Falkland in a duel, had deserted her shortly after their marriage. Courtesy of her father, she was a woman of independent means who still managed to live in a liberal style – although not quite so well off as to be able to avoid always having to take the public stagecoach to London. Hutton Cooper on the other hand was briefly Jemima's brother-in-law through his second marriage and was now a widower. He also lived well but the source of his means is less certain. One of his descendants called him 'a rake and a fortune hunter' but that may simply reflect some unreliable family prejudice. The same descendant said, 'For some years he was equerry with I think the title of House Physician to William, Duke of Clarence.' In fact, he was a medical practitioner who held office as Groom of the Bed Chamber from 1812 and was also a Fellow of the Royal Society. Prince William, who would eventually succeed his brother as future King, favoured Bath and held an informal court there when in town. It seems that Jemima Powell, Hutton Cooper and their set, presumably including Phillip and Isabella, were on the periphery of the royal orbit. And Phillip was financially comfortable. As well as his pension of £500, his half pay as an admiral was now '£750 a year or more'. And he had a substantial investment in Old South Sea Annuities.

In December 1806 Phillip and Isabella moved closer to the centre of Bath's social life. Phillip, now aged 68, purchased the leasehold of a large and commodious house at No. 19 Bennett Street for £2200. This was a substantial acquisition. The property was just along from the Upper Assembly Rooms, a short walk to the Royal Crescent and even closer to the Circus. The building had all the features that a gentleman might require; even the design was by John Wood the Younger, who also designed the Royal Crescent. A contemporary description emphasised its central and fashionable situation near the Upper Assembly Rooms. Phillip and Isabella occupied three floors. The fine entrance hall and the breakfast and dining rooms were on the ground floor. A suite of three drawing rooms filled the first floor. And four bedrooms and dressing rooms were on the second floor. As was usual, the servants' rooms were in the attic. Below ground level in the basement were the kitchen, scullery, pantry and cellar.

Jemima Powell and Miss Fanny often visited Phillip and Isabella at Bennett Street. Fanny recorded in her letters and diaries their daily lives, their mutual comings and goings and the periods of illness that they shared or experienced. She and Jemima appear to have moved according to the seasons, fluctuating between their home at Batheaston and a town house in Milsom Street. The latter address was more convenient for visiting friends in Bath, especially in the winter months, and was only a few minutes' walk from Phillip and Isabella. On the other hand, village life was bucolic in the spring and summer. Milsom Street was Bath's most exclusive shopping precinct where Josiah Wedgwood had showrooms and the best haberdashers, milliners and dressmakers could be found. Miss Fanny, the diarist, reportedly watched the fashionable beau-monde stream by from 'her upstairs parlour window at No. 19 Milsom Street, over the shop of Mr Vezey, the coach-builder'.

Phillip, it appears, enjoyed wine and carriages – as a connoisseur of the former and devotee of the latter. In his new home he laid down some 30 dozen 'singularly choice' madeira, sherry and port which were 'fifteen to thirty five years in bottle'. And he acquired a particularly smart and colourful carriage for getting around town. With Isabella beside him, he is said to have derived pleasure from 'taking the Bath air in the barouche seat of his new, fashionable and well-built landaulet, with its bright yellow body lined with blue morocco squab, and with the uniformed Jehu in the dickey seat'. This is what you might have expected in Jane Austen's image-conscious Bath – an emphasis on fashion, perhaps even ostentation, where the streets were filled with parties of ladies 'in quest of pastry, millinery … or young men', and where ownership of a landaulet was a singular mark of affluence. Jane Austen would have warmly approved of Bennett Street, at the 'upper' end of town, as a suitable location for someone of Phillip's rank and status.

Not surprisingly, Phillip continued to enjoy the company of fellow naval officers. According to one account, his home was 'the constant resort of his naval friends'. Fanny Chapman records some of them – Admirals Christie, Dacres and Macdonald and Captain Munn, as well as John Hunter, Philip Gidley King and Henry Waterhouse from his New South Wales days. The predominant entertainment was tea and conversation, dinner and cards, perhaps coffee, certainly madeira and sherry. Isabella shopped with the ladies and visited her friends. She and Phillip sometimes strolled. In truth it would have been a promenade. Sometimes they took the pretty landaulet. Regularly, one suspects, they visited Marshall's circulating library at No. 23 Milsom Street where there was more on offer than books. The pace was restrained. Like most Georgian gentlemen, Phillip possessed fine china, crystal and glassware and a 'large and valuable quantity of silver'. He also had an extensive collection of books which he had inherited from Isabella's father, Richard Whitehead. It was, by all accounts, a pleasant retirement.

This agreeable but subdued lifestyle came abruptly to an end on a particularly cold night in February 1808. Phillip and Isabella had only been in Bennett Street for just over a year. During the night Phillip suffered a paralytic stroke, losing the entire use of his right side, both his arm and leg. He was approaching 70 years of age and had lived longer than many of the men who had shaped his life. His early patrons Michael Everitt and Augustus Hervey had died at the ages of 60 and 55 years respectively. And of his close friends and colleagues with whom he was associated in the great experiment of New South Wales, Gidley King would die in a few months' time at the age of 50; Collins would die two years later at the age of 54; and Nepean would die at the age of 69. Sydney was already dead. Only the robust Hunter would live to the grand age of 83.

Understandably, the stroke caused Isabella to become distraught. And in the blackness of night there must have been confusion, commotion and probably panic among the servants. Early in the morning, Isabella sent for Jemima Powell, begging her to request the trusted Hutton Cooper to come at once. When Jemima and Miss Fanny arrived shortly afterwards, they found Isabella 'as mad as a March hare'. Jemima went in to see the poor admiral and was distressed by what she observed. The ladies feared he would not recover. Phillip's paralysis was on the right side and was therefore a function of left brain damage. His speech is likely to have been affected, but contemporary accounts make no mention of it. He was, however, 'very much altered'.

From late March visitors from out of town commenced to arrive. The loyal Henry Waterhouse was the first to see Phillip. Then came Gidley King, himself feeble with gout. Afterwards he wrote to his son, Phillip Parker King, whom he had proudly named after Phillip, informing him that the admiral 'may linger on some years under his present infirmity, but from his age, a great reprieve cannot be expected'. In September Gidley King visited again, a week before his own death, this time informing his son that Phillip 'is quite a cripple ... but his intellects are very good, and his spirits are what they always were'. Hutton Cooper attended – to 'bleed' the patient, it seems. Bleeding was one of those treatments that was thought to be a cure for almost everything. And Phillip became sentimental, more than once crying violently and kissing Miss Fanny's hand two or three times.

Phillip may have had some good fortune, however. Depending on the location of the affected brain cells, damage caused by a stroke may turn out to be temporary. Sometimes the cells resume functioning or reorganise themselves. Occasionally stroke survivors experience an unanticipated recovery. Symptoms such as paralysis, blindness, memory loss, aphasia, loss of vision, numbness, confusion and even deafness can recede. This is what appears to have happened to Phillip. After eighteen months, there was a marked improvement in his health. Mobility and sociability returned and he was on his feet again, despite Gidley King's pessimistic prognosis and notwithstanding Hutton Cooper's almost certainly unhelpful 'bleeding'. But the risk of recurrence of stroke remained – a stroke survivor is always the most vulnerable.

In late October 1809, at the celebrations to mark the 50th year of the reign of George III, Phillip and Isabella stepped out one evening, calling on Jemima Powell and Miss Fanny, presumably at Milsom Street. Phillip even went upstairs. In November he and Isabella travelled to Oxford. And they now entertained more often, receiving visits and making up a foursome at cards after dinner. Casino seemed to be their game of choice. In May 1810, they even received Jemima Powell and Miss Fanny as house guests in their home for four days. Twelve months later Miss Fanny's diary records Phillip and Isabella 'strolling' in the Circus. And in June 1811, Phillip's health was sufficiently robust to allow him to undertake with Isabella a two-month summer holiday at Clifton near Bristol – from which they did not return until late August.

There are no more direct accounts of Phillip but in 1812 the *Naval Chronicle* published an extensive biographical memoir about him. Among other things, it recorded his service on the 90-gun *Union* under Captain Everitt between August 1757 and November 1758. This was not official information, for Phillip's name does not appear in the ship's muster book and Phillip's service in that period is otherwise a blank. As Everitt was long dead, the source of the information must have been Phillip himself who, one might reasonably infer, was consulted about his entry and was well enough in 1812 and sufficiently interested to assist in setting the record straight.

During the same period, Phillip appears to have developed and maintained a connection with Francis Greenway, the architect who was later responsible for some of the earliest and most important public buildings in colonial Sydney. History does not reveal the reason or the circumstances, but it appears that Phillip was friendly with the much younger Greenway, whom he may have met in Clifton where Phillip and Isabella holidayed during the previous summer. Greenway's sentence for forgery at the Bristol Assizes in March 1812 has the faint suggestion of favour and influence. Greenway pleaded guilty to the forgery charge 'under the advice of his friends' and duly received the death sentence, knowing, one suspects, that it would be commuted to transportation to New South Wales. Phillip then made it his business to recommend Greenway to Macquarie, the current Governor of the colony. Phillip's testimonial was so effective that within a few months of Greenway's arrival in New South Wales, Macquarie consulted him about several government commissions. And within a few short years, he was emancipated.

Greenway regarded Phillip as 'his friend and patron'. And at an official ball held at Government House on 26 January 1818 to commemorate 30 years since Phillip came ashore at Sydney Cove, Greenway recorded his gratitude publicly by presenting a 'likeness' of Phillip which he had executed. The *Sydney Gazette* responded to this gesture by warmly announcing that Greenway 'felt much pleasure in this opportunity of celebrating the memory of the Vice Admiral who had ever been his friend and patron'.

Death eventually came on 31 August 1814. There were no suspicious circumstances and there is no record of a coronial inquest. When a person died a natural death, he or she had a common law right to be buried in the parish churchyard or burial ground. The honour of interment within the walls of a sacred church building was reserved for 'persons of great sanctity or considerable wealth'. In the case of suicide, both church and state law not only proscribed a Christian burial but specified other grim and salutary consequences. As the 1811 edition of the venerable *Blackstone's Commentaries on the Laws of England* noted, the law enacted vengeance on the dead person's reputation and fortune – 'on the former by an ignominious burial in the highway, with a stake driven through his body; on the latter, by a forfeiture of all his goods and chattels to the King: hoping that his care for his own reputation, or the welfare of his family, would be some motive to restrain him from so desperate and wicked an act'.

Phillip died at home and was buried at the medieval church of St Nicholas, Bathampton on 7 September. Just a few friends made the journey from Bath. The funeral cortège consisted only of a coach and carriage. The vicar was the Reverend Richard Bedford. Phillip and Isabella had a connection with Bathampton, where they had resided in 1804, and their closest friends Jemima Powell and Miss Fanny had an even closer connection with adjoining Batheaston. The two neighbouring villages are linked by the River Avon. Both are two miles from Bath and each of them has a parish church dating from the Middle Ages. The grounds of St Nicholas' church include an ancient graveyard filled with crooked headstones and dotted with the ubiquitous yew trees whose resinous scent was once thought to repel the noxious vapours of the dead. The choice of the village church of St Nicholas, and not Bath Abbey, was in keeping with 'the uniquely English tradition of the country's elites being buried not in a grand metropolitan church but in the local parish church'.

The actual place of burial was inside the church, just beyond the entrance. Consistent with his status and indeed his wealth, Phillip was not buried in the graveyard. A slate slab that was for a long time concealed beneath a floor covering in the church bears the following inscription: 'Underneath lie the remains of Arthur Phillip, Esq., Admiral of the Blue, who died 31st of August 1814 in his 76th year. Also of Isabella relict of above Admiral Phillip, who died the 4th of March 1823, in the 71st year of her age'. High up on the north wall of the church tower, accessible only by a ladder, is another unobtrusive plaque on which the following words are written: 'Near this tablet are the remains of Arthur Phillip Esq., Admiral of the Blue, first Governor & Founder of New South Wales.' The death was routinely noted in all the usual places and no suggestion of scandal accompanied its announcement in the *Bath Chronicle* and the *Bath Journal*. Nor was there a hint of controversy in the *Naval Chronicle* or the *Sydney Gazette*. Isabella continued to live in their home at No. 19 Bennett Street and in her will she requested that she be buried alongside her husband in St Nicholas' Church.

Almost a hundred years after Phillip's death, an improbable theory of his suicide emerged. Its origin can be traced to a familiar and unreliable combination, all too capable of leading to a travesty of justice. It involved an elderly spinster called 'Miss Bowie', who believed that the former home of Isabella and Phillip was inhabited by the admiral's ghost. She was emphatic, she told a journalist in 1910, that not only had she seen the ghost but so had unnamed others. She asserted that on one occasion the ghost even brushed past her on the staircase and that its features were of 'quite an ugly little man'. The ghost behaved, she said, in a manner that was brusque, commanding and authoritative. She attributed the reason for the presence of the ghost to a family 'legend' that Phillip's death was suicide. Her story captured the imagination of John Francis Meehan, an enterprising Irishman – journalist, writer and minor publisher. His interest was the famous houses and celebrities of Bath, and he made it his business to be constantly on the lookout for unusual stories and fresh angles, real or imagined.

In the April 1911 edition of a local Bath paper called the *Beacon*, Meehan laid out the fanciful story of the recently deceased Miss Bowie in all its improbable detail and stitched it together with his own journalistic embroidery. Miss Bowie's family legend, which never descended to the detail of how the suicide supposedly occurred, took on a life of its own. Rumour subsequently piled on conjecture, which piled on speculation. The gullible and the irresponsible leapt to the assumption, for which there was never any contemporary foundation, that Phillip threw himself out of a sitting room window and that his body was found outside the basement cellar. A century after Phillip's death, a theory that started from nothing became Kafkaesque, entirely lacking facts, credibility and probability, failing the simplest tests of reliability. It should now be finally despatched, ignored and laid to rest. Neither Meehan nor Miss Bowie ever suggested that Phillip threw himself out of a window. Miss Bowie said nothing on the subject and Meehan merely speculated, with no basis other than idle conjecture, that Phillip might have died in one of two rooms, but possibly he thought in 'the back room on the drawing-room floor, for a long time occupied as a bed-room by the late Miss Bowie'.

More reliable are the inferences about Phillip's life that can be drawn from the terms of his will and the size of his estate. One of the most revealing features that emerges from Phillip's will is the magnitude of his estate and the degree of financial acumen that it reflects. And the terms of the will reveal some of Phillip's closest personal associations. Phillip's estate was valued for probate at £25,000 – a present value in excess of £40 million, once again depending on the methodology used and the assumptions adopted.

Naturally Isabella was the major beneficiary of Phillip's estate and the recipient of his first bequest. He left her £600 stock in four per cent annuities, explaining that this was in substitution for a legacy of £250 in 'Navy five per cents' left to her by a mutual friend 'but which was afterwards sold out by me and reinvested in my name in the four per cent annuities'. The financial instrument known as 'Navy five per cents' was a relatively high interest rate annuity backed by the Bank of England. It originated from debts incurred by the Royal Navy during the Napoleonic Wars and was a popular investment vehicle between 1810 and 1821. Phillip also held a parcel of Old South Sea Annuities in the precise sum of £8333 6s 8d. This was not a random number but the capital amount necessary on a 3 per cent return to produce an annuity of £250. It represented the security for the marriage bond that he had executed in favour of Isabella prior to their marriage – to provide for her future in the event that he died before she did.

The four per cent annuities and the Old South Sea Annuities were reliable and conservative investments that would have provided a generous income stream for Isabella. She also received the home at No. 19 Bennett Street for the remainder of her life. And Phillip gave her his household goods, although he only allowed her a life interest in the most valuable items – the Brazil diamond ring from Charles Slingsby

Duncombe and his extensive collection of silver. Isabella thus became the possessor for her lifetime of the ring and the silver and the outright owner of all of Phillip's linen, china, liquor, books, jewels, watches and trinkets as well as his 'horses, carriages and harness'. As Jane Austen frequently emphasised, ownership of a carriage was an undoubted status symbol at that time. It was always a matter of interest to the impertinent and the nosy whether a person kept a carriage and what kind. This is not difficult to understand given that a carriage was a significant luxury item, expensive to purchase and costly to maintain – both in the coachmen who were necessary to care for and operate it and in the horses that were required to be stabled or rented. The pretty yellow landaulet with its Moroccan leather seats became Isabella's. However, Phillip's drawings from New South Wales did not. No sentimentality seemed to attach to them. The will directed that they be sold.

Phillip's collection of Georgian silver was meticulously itemised in his will. Although he permitted Isabella to have the use of it during her life, he specified that the best items were to go to her nephew Newton Shaw after her death. Each item was individually described and its weight listed in ounces. All of the pieces would have been sterling silver. A quality piece of Georgian sterling silver often had its weight inscribed on the underside. Sheffield plate was not yet common and would not have formed part of Phillip's collection. The collection included a large oval 'waiter' or tray, a large cup, a tea urn, a coffee urn, a soup tureen cover and ladle, a bread basket, a pair of saltcellars, a teapot and a cream jug. The silver tray and the tea urn each weighed over a hundred ounces and the weight of most of the other items was also substantial.

Subject to Isabella's life interest, the valuable Brazil diamond ring went to Lady Nepean, wife of Phillip's loyal long-time supporter Evan Nepean, who did so much to advance his career in the 1780s. He stipulated that if she died before being able to enjoy it, the ring should go to her daughter, Harriet. It was obviously a prized possession of great sentimentality. Duncombe had been a friend to Phillip since at least the 1770s. And his family papers show a number of payments to Phillip in 1786-87 as well as transfers in the other direction. All were conducted through Duncombe's banker, Messrs Child & Co. Between 1788 and 1791 when Phillip was in New South Wales, Duncombe received on Phillip's behalf a number of substantial payments from 'Osborn Standert' and made investments in annuities for him. It is likely that these monies represented part of Phillip's remuneration as Governor of New South Wales, for Standert was a chief clerk of treasurer's accounts in the Navy Office. Indeed Phillip trusted Standert so much that he appointed him as one of his executors, along with John Lane.

John Lane features throughout the will. The relationship between Phillip and John Lane went right back to Everitt, Phillip's first patron and Lane's father-in-law. It is detectable at almost all stages of Phillip's life. When Phillip sailed on the *Europe*, John Lane was the one to whom Phillip entrusted his secret charts of the South American coast. And according to one source, John Lane also once fitted out a frigate in which Phillip sailed 'to the other side of the world'. Phillip therefore left John Lane a token of his appreciation. It was the largest single legacy in his will. After Isabella's death, he directed that Lane should have the interest on a principal sum of £2000. When he died, the interest and dividends were to go to Lane's wife Eleanor, the daughter of Michael Everitt. After her death, the whole of the principal sum of £2000 was to go to their daughter, another Harriet.

Many others were nominated to share in Phillip's estate. There was one legacy of £200 and nine legacies of £500 to cousins, nieces, nephews, friends and other relatives. One of those was Susannah Richardson, 'granddaughter of my late Uncle Pagester'. This brought the wheel of life almost full circle for she appears to have been the granddaughter of Susanna Breach, a relative of Phillip's mother Elizabeth Breach. In Phillip's early life, his mother moved to the docklands of Rotherhithe where, as it happens, in 1752 Susanna Breach married Charles Pagester, a shipwright at Rotherhithe. It was presumably from here in 1751 that Phillip went as an 'orphan of the sea' to the Charity School of the Royal Hospital for Seamen at Greenwich. And it was presumably from here in 1753 at the Greenland Dock that he commenced his apprenticeship on an Artic whaling ship.

Not everyone received what was due to them. One of the four main beneficiaries was Mary Ann Lancefield. Her grandson, who was christened 'Arthur Phillip Lancefield' in memory of the family's generous benefactor, grew up to become a clergyman. Years later, he wistfully recalled that his grandmother never received her entitlement. He wrote that 'all her share of the property was lost in the costs of a Chancery suit of the type of *Jarndyce v Jarndyce*'. He was referring to the fictional legal case in Charles Dickens' novel *Bleak House*, in which the litigation over an inheritance dragged on for so many generations that the legal costs eventually devoured the entire estate, leaving nothing for the claimants. Dickens used the case as a vehicle for satirising the complexity and torpidity that bedevilled proceedings in the Court of Chancery at that time.

Fact follows fiction and Phillip's estate suffered a similar, though not quite identical, fate. Thirty years after his death, legal proceedings over his will were still running. If you search carefully through the dusty law reports from the 1840s, only a few years before the publication of *Bleak House,* you will find an account of Phillip's will and the dispute over his estate that followed. It is hidden under the name *Attorney General v Potter.* Potter was Phillip's last living executor. The dispute, which commenced after Isabella's death in 1823, involved the competing rights of the principal beneficiaries of the estate and the purchaser of No. 19 Bennett Street. The unhappy case went through layer upon layer of the court system, finally ending up before the Lord Chancellor who was, historically and euphemistically, 'the keeper of the King's conscience' but is probably better known to non-lawyers as the fanciful and absurd 'Lord High Chancellor' of Gilbert & Sullivan's *Iolanthe.* In Phillip's case, the real Lord Chancellor deliberated for a year before finally giving an admirably concise decision allowing the sale to proceed. He did not subscribe to the theory that the validity of a judgment depends on the length of its reasons, and his explanation of its legal basis was only a paragraph long. By that stage all of Phillip's executors except Potter were dead, as no doubt were most of his beneficiaries.

There were many losers from the litigation, except of course the lawyers who fattened their wallets at every stage along the way. As usual their fees were paid out of the estate, constantly diluting its value and progressively thwarting Phillip's intentions. Until the Lord Chancellor's decision in 1844 the contract for the purchase of No. 19 Bennett Street by Dr Bowie, the father of the unreliable Miss Bowie, was still hanging in the balance, unable to be completed 21 years after it was entered into. And more than £1077 for unpaid duty was owed to Her Majesty's representatives, the Commissioners of Stamps and Taxes. As for the four principal beneficiaries to whom Phillip wished the bulk of his estate to go after Isabella's death, including Mary Ann Lancefield, the legal costs appear to have cut a swathe through his intended beneficence. We will never know how much they lost or how little they ultimately received. We have only the sad reflections of the Reverend Arthur Phillip Lancefield and the dry words of the Lord Chancellor's judgment.

Phillip's estate may have been depleted in death, and not everyone may have received what was due to them, but the most enduring legacy of his life remains the colony that he established; a colony that he thought would one day be 'the most valuable acquisition Great Britain ever made'. It has long since ceased to be an acquisition and for over a century has been a proud and independent nation state. Phillip's memory in Australia is perpetuated in the colossal monument by the Italian sculptor Achille Simonetti, commissioned by Sir Henry Parkes in 1889. The visionary Parkes, the father of federation, who brought the separate colonies together and laid the foundation for a single Australian Commonwealth of states and territories, understood Phillip's significance. The bronze statue, surmounted on a pedestal of Carrara marble and ringed by base statues of Agriculture, Commerce, Neptune and Cyclops, dominates the broad sweep from the Royal Botanic Gardens across Sydney Harbour and onwards to the Heads – that sandstone portal through which Phillip first came in a longboat in 1788; the same entrance that has since greeted so many ships and so many migrants from all corners of the world.

There are more memorials in England. One is a bust at St Mary le Bow, 'the Australian church in London'. It was rescued from the rubble of St Mildred's in Bread Street when that church was destroyed by German bombing during the Blitz in May 1941. Another monument is in nearby Watling Street, depicting scenes from the arrival of the First Fleet, surmounted by a bust of Phillip. In London's Guildhall there is a Phillip memorial tapestry commissioned by the Corporation of the City of London and woven in Melbourne. At St Nicholas, Bathampton, there is an Australian chapel. It is the only parish church in England with kangaroos in the stained glass windows. All of the woodwork in the chapel is of Australian black bean timber and the floor is of Wombeyan marble. In the south aisle is the Phillip memorial, which faces you as you enter the church and bears the words 'Founder of Australia'. In Bath Abbey the Australian government has erected a memorial tablet, above which hangs an Australian flag. The tablet describes Phillip as 'Founder and First Governor of Australia' to whose 'Indomitable Courage, Prophetic Vision, Forbearance, Faith, Inspiration and Wisdom was due the Success of the First Settlement in Australia at Sydney 26 January 1788.'

NOTES ON TRAVEL

The writing of this book was the result of a great deal of reading, even more thinking and quite a lot of travel. The City of London was my geographic starting point. I traipsed thoughtfully along its ancient lanes and narrow alleys; visited its churches and searched for the remains of its taverns and coffee houses, its prisons and poor houses. I plied the River Thames from city to estuary, imagining the bustle of London's eighteenth-century riverside docks and shipyards, and stared in wonder at the imperious buildings of Maritime Greenwich, where the naval pensioners and the 'orphans of the sea' once lived in architectural splendour.

In the south of England, I strolled with my wife through the village of Lyndhurst in Hampshire, picnicked in the New Forest and visited the sea at Lymington and Lyme Regis. At Portsmouth, I crawled all over the *Victory* from bow to stern and from top deck to hold, and spent hours in the Royal Naval Museum. In Bath, I sauntered around the Circus, imbibed the curative waters in the Pump Room, paid homage to Phillip's home in Bennett Street, sipped coffee in the Upper Assembly Rooms and marvelled at the eighteenth-century fashions on display.

On the continent, I visited Paris, Calais, Flanders and Lille, searching for clues of Phillip's 'lost years'. At Gibraltar, I climbed the Rock and looked across the strait to Jebel Musa in Morocco. In Lisbon, I absorbed the remnants of Portuguese historical grandeur and immersed myself in its Maritime Museum. On the Atlantic island of Madeira, I stared out across the ocean from Reid's Hotel and contemplated the enormity of the voyages of exploration and slavery that passed through the surrounding waters.

At Cape Town, I examined the harbour at Table Bay and travelled by small boat to Robben Island. And in the old Dutch town centre, I investigated with horror the Slave Lodge Museum, the Company Gardens where the slaves once toiled, and the Dutch fort known as the Castle of Good Hope. From the flat top of Table Mountain, I looked west across the South Atlantic, and from the rocky cliff tops of the Cape of Good Hope, I gazed at the turbulent seas that Vasco da Gama first conquered in the fifteenth century. In India, I travelled to Calcutta in Bengal and along the Coromandel Coast of Tamil Nadu, south from the coastal port once known as Madras.

On the far side of the Indian Ocean, I went to Fremantle in Western Australia, to the foremost maritime archaeology museum in the southern hemisphere, where the full extent of the early Dutch and French exploratory voyages to *Terra Australis* was revealed to me. In Sydney, on the Pacific coast of Australia, I studied firsthand the little coves and inlets, and the Heads at the entrance to the harbour, which remain virtually unchanged since Phillip's men first saw them in January 1788. And I crossed the Tasman Sea, to Stewart Island at the southern tip of New Zealand, where sailing ships returning to England turned east to run with the westerly winds and currents across the vast expanse of the Southern Ocean. As for Cuba, Brazil and Cape Horn, I relied on my own research and the accounts provided by friends and emissaries. Their assistance enabled me to form a clear and striking historical picture.

NOTES

Abbreviations used throughout the Notes:

HRNSW 1 Historical Records of New South Wales, vol. 1, part 2,
    Phillip, Government Printer, Sydney, 1892

HRNSW 2 Historical Records of New South Wales, vol. 2, *Grose &
    Paterson*, Government Printer, Sydney 1893

HRNSW 5 Historical Records of New South Wales, vol. 5, *King*,
    Government Printer, Sydney, 1897

NA National Archives, London:

– ADM Admiralty
– CO Colonial Office
– FO Foreign Office
– HO Home Office
– PRO Chatham Papers
– PROB Prerogative Court of Canterbury
– SP State Papers

PREFACE

Page ix **'a man with a good head ... plenty of common sense'**
    George Mackaness, *Admiral Arthur Phillip: Founder of New South
    Wales, 1738–1814*, Angus and Robertson, Sydney, 1937, pp. 464–65.

CHAPTER 1 Naval education

Page 1 **'starveling, barefoot, onion-nibbling peasants'** Roy Porter,
    England in the Eighteenth Century, Folio Society, London, 1998, p. 12.

Page 2 **'lazy, sotted and brutish'** Francois Lacombe, *Observations
    sur Londres ... par un Atheronome de Berne*, chez Lacombe, Paris,

1777, in Robert Hughes, *The Fatal Shore*, Collins Harvill, London, 1987 p. 24.

Page 2 'when trade is at stake' William Pitt, *The Speeches of the Right Honourable the Earl of Chatham in the Houses of Lords and Commons*, Aylott & Jones, London, 1848, p. 6; see also Porter, p. 411.

Page 2 'easy, glorious and profitable' NAM Rodger, *Command of the Ocean*, Penguin Books, London, 2005, p. 235.

Page 3 'obscure German wanderer' Alan Frost, *Arthur Phillip 1738–1814: His Voyaging*, Oxford University Press, Melbourne, 1987, p. 257.

Page 3 'a kapellmeister' Hughes, p .67.

Page 3 'un-English physiognomy' Alan Atkinson, *The Europeans in Australia: A History*, Oxford University Press, Melbourne, 1997, p. 94.

Page 3 'long hooked fleshy nose' Andrew Tink, *Lord Sydney*, Australian Scholarly Publishing, Melbourne, 2011, p. 220.

Page 4 'Mindful of the perils and dangers of the sea' PROB 6/108; PROB 11/653, NA.

Page 5 'a hell such as Dante might have conceived' *The Memoirs of Jacques Casanova de Seingalt 1725–1798, Vol. 5*, trans. Arthur Machen, GP Putnam's Sons, New York/Elek Books, London, 1894, p. 367.

Page 5 'an emblem of hell itself' Daniel Defoe, *Moll Flanders*, Pocket Books, New York, 1957, p. 296.

Page 6 'the Sons of disabled Seamen' *Establishment for Admitting, Maintaining, and Educating of Poor Boys in the Royal Hospital for Seamen at Greenwich* ..., n.p., London, 1732, article 2. See also John Cooke & John Maule, *An Historical Account of the Royal Hospital for Seamen at Greenwich*, G Nicol, T Cadell, J Walter,

GGJ & J Robinson, London, 1789, pp. 60–77; Pieter van de Merwe, *A Refuge for All: A Short History of Greenwich Hospital*, National Maritime Museum, London, 2010, p. 5; HD Turner, *The Cradle of the Navy*, William Sessions, London, 1990, pp. 1–5; *Articles and Instructions for the Better Government of His Majesty's Royal Hospital for Seamen at Greenwich ...*, 2nd edn, n.p., London, 1741, article 2.

Page 7 **'seamen, seafaring men and persons'** Christopher Lloyd, *The British Seaman 1200–1860: A Social Survey*, Paladin, p. 123.

Page 9 **'the darling object of her life'** van der Merwe, p. 4.

Page 9 **'one of the most sublime sights that English architecture affords'**, van de Merwe, p. 9.

Page 10 **'If any boy shall get in by false testimonials'** *Establishment for Admitting, Maintaining, and Educating of Poor Boys ...*, article 8.

Page 12 **'Arthur Phillip is noted for his diplomacy'** Nigel Rigby & Pieter van der Merwe, *Pioneers of the Pacific: Voyages of Exploration, 1787–1810*, UWA Press, Crawley, WA, 2005, p. 24.

Page 12 **'the best Way and Manner'** Turner, p. 157.

CHAPTER 2 Junior officer

Page 18 **'young gentlemen'** Michael Everitt to John Clevland, 30 June 1755, ADM 1/1758, NA.

Page 19 **'All ships sailing up the straits of Gibraltar'** R Baldwin, *The Importance of the Island of Minorca and Harbour of Port Mahon*, London, 1756, p. 40.

Page 21 **'no one can see two yards before him'** Roy Adkins & Lesley Adkins, *Jack Tar: Life in Nelson's Navy*, Abacus, London, 2009, p. 273.

Page 22 **'When Admiral Byng hoisted the Red Flagg'** Arthur
Phillip to [Rebecca] Phillip, 21 June, PRO 30/8/52, Chatham
Papers, NA.

Page 24 **'Indeed he shall be tried immediately'** Tom Pocock, *Battle
for Empire: The Very First World War 1756–63*, Caxton Editions,
London, 2002, p. 33.

Page 25 **'in England it is thought necessary to kill an admiral'**
Voltaire, *Candide*, J. Nourse, London, 1759, p. 95.

Page 26 **'are all turned over to the *Neptune*'** *The London Chronicle*,
6–9 August 1757, vol. 2, p. 134.

Page 27 **'Brightly dawned the auspicious morning'** Adkins &
Adkins, p. 23.

Page 29 **'our bells are worn threadbare'** Horace Walpole to George
Montagu, 21 October 1759, in Horace Walpole, *Letters from the
Hon. Horace Walpole, to George Montagu, Esq. from the Year 1736, to
the Year 1770*, Rodwell and Martin, Henry Colburn, London, 1818,
p. 180.

Page 29 **'Splice, Knot, Reef a sail'** Adam Nicolson, *Men of Honour:
Trafalgar and the Making of the English Hero*, Harper Perennial,
London, 2006, p. 25.

Page 33 **'altogether inexpressible'** David Syrett, *The Siege and
Capture of Havana 1762*, Navy Records Society, London, 1970,
p. xxix; Pocock, p. 212.

Page 34 **'sent ashore a Lieut and forty men to hawl Cannon'**
'Lieutenant's Logbook for HMS Stirling Castle 1759–1762',
ADM/L/S/447, National Maritime Museum, London.

Page 34 **'in assisting to raise new batteries'** Syrett, pp. xxix, 247.

Page 34 **'the seamen have performed extremely well'** George
Pocock to John Clevland, 17 July 1762, in Syrett, p. 247.

Page 35 **'represent his conduct'** Augustus Hervey to Augustus
  Keppel, 3 July 1762, in Syrett, p. 222.

Page 35 **'a conquest too dearly obtained'** Bennet Langton recalling
  a passage in a letter from Samuel Johnson to Topham Beauclerk
  on the death of Dr Bathurst in Havana in James Boswell, *The
  Life of Samuel Johnson, LL. D.: Including a Journal of a Tour to the
  Hebrides*, George Dearborn, New York, 1833, p. 104.

Page 36 **'the most difficult since the invention of artillery'** Duke
  of Cumberland to Earl of Albermarle, 2 October, 1762, in George
  Thomas, Earl of Albemarle, *Memoirs of the Marquis of Rockingham
  and His Contemporaries*, Vol. 1, Richard Bentley, London, 1852,
  p. 125.

Page 36 **'off Minorca; in the Channel and the Bay of Biscay'**,
  Frost, p. 44.

CHAPTER *3* Gentleman farmer
Page 40 **'master of the world'** See Frank McLynn, *1759: The Year
  Britain Became Master of the World*, Jonathan Cape, London, 2004,
  p. 1.

Page 40 **'no place on earth more tempting'** Stella Tillyard,
  'Foreword', in Frederick A Pottle (ed.), *Boswell's London Journal
  1762–63*, Folio Society, London, 1985 (1950), p. xi.

Page 40 **'without which a gentleman of the smallest fortune**
  Porter, p. 202.

Page 40 **'Boswell's whim'** Pottle, p. 233.

Page 45 **'principally in domestic disbursements'** *The Observer*, 15
  December 1793.

Page 45 **'acquiescently fertile'**, Eleanor Dark, *The Timeless Land*,
  Collins, London, 1941, p. 119.

Page 46 **'reason to believe that some days were more severe'**
Gilbert White, *The Natural History & Antiquities of Selborne*, Folio
Society, London, 1994 (1788), p. 38.

Page 48 **'some circumstances occurred'**, *The Observer*, 15 December
1793.

Page 52 **'constantly attend to what is passing'** Earl of Suffolk to
Horace St Paul, 23 July 1773, in Frost, p. 55.

Page 52 **' the recovery of his health'** ADM 106/2972, NA.

Page 52 **'superior to what it was'** 'Capt. Arthur Phillips. Intelligence.
Naval Force at Toulon', January 1785, 'Phillips. Intelligence from
Nice', 21 March 1785, FO 95/4/6, fols 499, 501 extract, NA.

Page 53 **'the unspeakable pleasure'** GT Landmann, *Adventures and
Recollections of Colonel Landmann*, Colburn & Co., London, 1852,
p. 121.

Page 54 **'the most difficult since the invention of artillery'**
Duke of Cumberland to Earl of Albermarle, 2 October, 1762, in
Thomas, p. 125.

Page 54 **'le Theorie avec beaucoup de Pratique'** Augustus Hervey
to Pinto de Souza, 25 August 1774, in Kenneth Gordon McIntyre,
The Rebello Transcripts: Governor Phillip's Portuguese Prelude,
Souvenir Press, London, 1984, p. 205.

Page 54 **'own little knowledge as a field engineer'** Arthur Phillip
memorandum, c. October 1786, in *HRNSW 1*, p. 52.

CHAPTER 4 Mercenary

Page 56 **'one hundred leagues west'** McIntyre, p. 26.

Page 57 **'apple of discord'** ibid, p. 44.

Page 57 **'there are 4,000,000 cruzadas in silver'** ... **'The
clandestine trade'** Allan Christelow, 'Great Britain and the Trades

from Cadiz and Lisbon to Spanish America and Brazil, 1759–1783', *Hispanic American Historical Review*, vol. 27, no. 1, 1947, pp. 5, 12.

Page 58 **'because on the contrary follows the ruin'**; Beaglehole (ed.), *The Journals of Captain Cook*, vol. 1, Cambridge University Press, Cambridge, 1955, p. 489.

Page 58 *'très bon officier de Marine'* Augustus Hervey to Pinto de Souza, 25 August 1774, in McIntyre, p. 205.

Page 58 **'the English Casanova'** David Erskine (ed.), *Augustus Hervey's Journal*, William Kimber, London, 1953, p. xi.

Page 58 **'princesses, marchesas, countessas'** NAM Rodger, *The Wooden World: An Anatomy of the Georgian Navy*, Collins, London, 1986, p. 255.

Page 59 **'in England, makes a great difference'** Pinto de Souza to Mello e Castro, 8 November 1774, in McIntyre, pp. 207–08.

Page 59 **'Apply yourself with diligence'** Christelow, p. 24.

Page 60 **'He gives way to reason'** Marquis do Lavradio to Mello e Castro, 10 May 1778, in McIntyre, pp. 233–34.

Page 61 **'a city of churches'** Rose Macaulay, *They Went to Portugal*, Cape, London, 1946, p. 91.

Page 63 **'conspicuous information concerning Phillip's intelligence'** Mello e Castro to Marquis of Lavradio, 24 January 1775, in Frost, pp. 69–70.

Page 64 **'a prison and the ruin of its inhabitants'** Governor Da Rocha to Marquis of Lavradio, 20 April 1775, in Frost, p. 75.

Page 64 **'had effectually put a stop to all the acts of daring'** Marquis of Lavradio to Mello e Castro, 18 August 1776, in McIntyre, pp. 216–18.

Page 66 **'made every effort to induce the Chief'** … **'imploring him for the sake of his own honour'** Marquis of Lavradio,

'List of Officers of the Fleet, Setting Forth the Merits of Each', 22 October 1777, in McIntyre, p. 232.

Page 67 **'no advantage to be gained by disobeying'** McIntyre, pp. 225–27.

Page 67 **'out of the great deference he renders'** Lavradio, 'List of Officers of the Fleet', in McInytre, p. 232.

Page 67 **'his countenance betrayed the anguish'** Marquis of Lavradio to Marquis of Pombal, 10 March 1777, in McIntyre, pp. 220–24.

Page 70 **'very clean-handed'** Marquis of Lavradio to Mello e Castro, 10 May 1778, in McIntyre, pp. 233–34.

Page 70 **'where ships that wanted to wood and water'** Arthur Phillip to Lord Sandwich, 17 January 1781, SAN/F/26, no. 23, National Maritime Museum, London; see also Frost, pp. 81–82.

Page 71 **'keys to empire' … 'way to wealth'** Rachel L. Carson, *The Sea Around Us*, Readers Union – Staples Press, London, 1953, p. 159.

Page 72 **'that I may reap the Credit'** Arthur Phillip to Lord Sandwich, 17 January 1781, SAN/F/26, no. 23, National Maritime Museum, London.

Page 73 **'the great advantage of the nation'** Phillip, Journal, William L Clements Library, University of Michigan, Sydney Papers 17.

Page 73 **'Views of the Diamond Works'** ibid.

Page 74 **'exposed for sale' … 'shaved, fattened, and if necessary, even painted'** Hugh Thomas, *The Slave Trade: The History of the Atlantic Slave Trade 1440–1870*, Picador, London, 1997, p. 432.

Page 75 **'as a token of my lasting friendship'** Will of Charles Slingsby Duncombe of Duncombe Park, Yorkshire, 12 October 1803, PROB 11/1399/276, NA.

CHAPTER 5 Captain of the *Ariadne*

Page 78 **'was at the masts and rigging'** NAM Rodger, *The Insatiable Earl: A Life of John Montague, 4th Earl of Sandwich*, WW Norton & Co., New York, 1994, p. 245; NAM Rodger, *Command of the Ocean*, pp. 336–37.

Page 78 **'great affright and terror'** Frost, p. 96.

Page 79 **'one of the officers of the most distinct merit'** Marquis of Lavradio to Mello e Castro, 10 May 1778, in McIntyre, pp. 233–34.

Page 79 **'many suitors and little to bestow'** Rodger, *The Insatiable Earl*, p. 180.

Page 80 **'that every man's comfort afloat'** Adkins & Adkins, p. 25.

Page 84 **'an opportunity of getting what is due'** Arthur Phillip to Lord Sandwich, 19 July 1780, ADM 1/2306, NA.

Page 85 **'from Lisbon to the Brasils'** For example, *St James Chronicle*, 2 February 1787, in Frost, p. 111; also *The World*, 16 April 1789.

Page 86 **'it is probable that I may be call'd forth'** Arthur Phillip to Lord Sandwich, 17 January 1781, SAN/F/26, no. 23, National Maritime Museum, London.

Page 86 **'being sent from Lisbon'** Luis da Cunha Menezes to D Luis de Vasconcelos, 7 May 1781, in Frost, p. 112.

Page 86 **'the scum of the earth'** PH Stanhope, *Notes of Conversations with the Duke of Wellington, 1831–1851*, Longmans, Green & Co., New York, 1888, p. 14; Philip J Haythornthwaite, *Wellington: The Iron Duke*, Potomac Books, Dulles, 2007, p. 52.

Page 87 **'You know how much I was interested'** Arthur Phillip to Evan Nepean, 2 September 1987, in *HRNSW 1*, p. 114.

Page 88 **'a mere fighting blockhead'** Rodger, *The Wooden World*, p. 297.

Page 90 **'take any further charge of her'** Arthur Phillip to Philip
Stephens, 20 December 1781, ADM 1/2306, NA; see also
Mackaness, pp. 24–5.

Page 91 **'Preparations and Plans for W. India'** Earl of Shelburne
to Thomas Townshend, 21 September 1782, Correspondence
and Papers of Thomas Townshend, 1st Viscount Sydney, F25,
Brotherton Special Collections, Leeds University Library,
Leeds.

Page 91 **'send him to his ship'** Augustus Keppel to Thomas
Townshend, 25 September 1782, William L Clements Library,
University of Michigan, Sydney Papers, box 9/10.

Page 91 **'to investigate the situation'** Pinto de Souza to Sá e Mello,
1 October 1782, in Frost, p. 114.

Page 92 **'Phillip plan'** Robert J King, 'An Australian Perspective
on the English Invasions of the Rio de la Plata in 1806
and 1807', *International Journal of Naval History*, vol. 8, no. 1,
2009.

Page 92 **'arms for the Chileans'** Sir Charles Middleton,
'Preparations Necessary for a Secret Expedition', 26 September
1782, William Petty, 1st Marquis of Lansdowne, 2nd Earl of
Shelburne Papers, Manuscripts M-66, vol. 151, item 28, William
L Clements Library, University of Michigan.

Page 92 **'give great alarm'** Sir Charles Middleton to Earl of
Shelburne, 3 October 1782, William Petty, 1st Marquis of
Lansdowne, 2nd Earl of Shelburne Papers, Manuscripts M-66,
vol. 151, William L Clements Library, University of Michigan.

Page 92 **'with all possible expedition'** Evan Nepean to Lords
Commissioners of the Admiralty, November 1782, SP 42/66,
no. 408, NA.

CHAPTER 6 Captain of the *Europe*

Page 96 **'our captain dreaded the idea'** Edward Spain, *The Journal of Edward Spain, Merchant Seaman and Sometimes Warrant Officer in the Royal Navy*, St Marks Press, Bankstown, 1989, p. 44.

Page 97 **'is blended, which is not common'** Frederick Chapman, *Governor Phillip in Retirement*, ed. George Mackaness, Halstead Press, Sydney, 1962, pp. 17–18.

Page 98 **'lest there be orders'** Spain, p. 44.

Page 101 **'I paid no attention'** Arthur Phillip to Philip Stephens, 25 April 1783, ADM 1/2307, NA.

Page 101 **'exaggerating the incident'** McIntyre, p. 175.

Page 101 **'such as I always thought them'** Arthur Phillip to Philip Stephens, 25 April 1783, ADM 1/2307, NA.

Page 102 **'this morning when I first came on deck'** Adkins & Adkins, p. 83.

Page 104 **'I cannot help reflecting'** ... **'the aromatic smell'** Spain, pp. 46–47.

Page 108 **'the difficulties which have attended the refitting'** Commodore King to Philip Stephens, 18 February 1784, ADM 1/54, NA.

CHAPTER 7 Secret Agent

Page 110 **'a national *magnum opus*'** Philippe Godard & Tudgual de Kerros, *1772: The French Annexation of New Holland. The Tale of Louis de Saint Aloüarn*, Western Australian Museum, Welshpool, 2009, p. 11; Rodger, *The Insatiable Earl*, p. 130.

Page 110 **'in order that we may ascertain the number of ships'** Lord Carmarthen to Duke of Dorset, 1 October 1784, FO 27/13, p. 1068, NA.

Page 110 **'India is the first quarter to be attacked'** Henry Dundas
to Lord Sydney, 2 November 1784, PRO 30/8/157, fo. 6, NA.

Page 110 **'Our wealth and power in India'** Sir James Harris to Lord
Carmarthen, 4 March 1785, FO 37/6, NA.

Page 111 **'the fullest and most accurate intelligence'** Lord
Carmarthen to Duke of Dorset, 19 October 1784, FO 27/13, fols.
1158–59, NA.

Page 111 **'on account of his private affairs'** Arthur Phillip to Philip
Stephens, 14 October 1784, ADM 1/2307, NA.

Page 111 **'to undertake a Journey'** Secret Service Ledger, 11
November 1784, Nepean Papers, William L Clements Library,
University of Michigan.

Page 115 **'before the War'** 'Capt. Arthur Phillips. Intelligence. Naval
Force at Toulon', January 1785, 'Phillips. Intelligence from Nice',
21 March 1785, FO 95/4/6, fols 499, 501 extract, NA.

Page 116 **'*débonnaire bourgeois commerçant*'** Myra Stanbury,
'The De Saint Aloüarn Voyage of 1772', in Jeremy Green (ed.),
*Report on the 2006 Western Australian Museum, Department
of Maritime Archaeology, Cape Inscription National Heritage
Listing Archaeological Survey*, Report 223, Special Publication
10, Australian National Centre of Excellence for Maritime
Archaeology, Western Australian Museum, Welshpool, 2007,
p. 14.

Page 116 **'prodigiously efficient'** Robert Lacour-Gayet, *A Concise
History of Australia*, trans. James Grieve, Penguin Books,
Melbourne, 1976, p. 81.

Page 118 **'likely places for French settlement'** ... **'which may be
interesting'** OHK Spate, *Paradise Found and Lost*, Australian
National University Press, Sydney, 1988, pp. 155–57.

Page 118 **'condition, strength and object'** Dunmore (ed.), *Journal of La Pérouse*, Vol 1, Hakluyt Society, London, 1994, p. cxxxvii.

Page 118 **'the French have a design'** Duke of Dorset to Lord Carmarthen, 5 May 1785, FO 27/16, fo. 553, NA.

Page 118 **'sixty criminals from the prison'** Duke of Dorset to Lord Carmarthen, 9 June 1785, FO 27/16, fols. 605–06, NA.

Page 119 **'turn his gaze entirely to his navies'** Lacour-Gayet, pp. 80–81.

Page 120 **'improving France's strategic position in the Indian Ocean'** Ted Gott & Katrine Huguenaud, *Napoleon: Revolution to Empire*, National Gallery of Victoria, Melbourne, 2012, p. 40.

Page 120 **'*secrète*'** Myra Stanbury, p.15.

Page 121 **'on his private affairs'** Arthur Phillip to the Lords Commissioners, 1 December, 1785, ADM 6/207, NA.

Page 122 **'other ports of France'**, Secret Service Ledger, 11 November 1784, Nepean Papers, William L Clements Library, University of Michigan.

Page 123 **'all the shipwrights and carpenters' and following quotations** 'Lieutenant Monke to Evan Nepean. Secret intelligence from Toulon', 24 October 1787, FO 95/4/6, fols 503–09, NA; also Alfred Cobban, 'British Secret Service in France, 1784–92' in *The English Historical Review*, Vol. 69, no. 271, p. 250.

CHAPTER 8 Pioneer

Page 128 **'the convicts were what they had always been'** KM Dallas, 'The First Settlement in Australia, Considered in Relation to Sea-Power in World Politics', *Papers and Proceedings (Tasmanian Historical Research Association)*, no. 3, 1952, pp. 4–12.

Page 129 **'the intentions of France'** Sir James Harris to Lord Carmarthen, 3 February 1786, British Library, Add. MS 28061, fo. 21.

Page 129 **'is drawing nearer and nearer every hour'** Sir James Harris to Lord Carmarthen, 8 August 1786, FO 37/11, p. 72, NA.

Page 129 **'France certainly under the name of *flûtes*'** George III to Lord Sydney, 16 August 1786 in Arthur Aspinall (ed), *The Later Correspondence of George III*, Vol. 1, Cambridge University Press, Cambridge, 1970, p. 244.

Page 130 **'But it is questionable'** Emer de Vattel, *The Law of Nations, or, Principles of the Law of Nature, Applied to the Conduct and Affairs of Nations and Sovereigns*, GG & J Robinson, London, 1797, (1758) book 1, chap. 18, section 208.

Page 130 **'a passing bird'** Godard & Kerros, p. 150.

Page 131 **'in case of being opposed'** Arthur Phillip, comments on a draft of his instructions, c. 11 April 1787, CO 201/2, fol. 131, NA.

Page 132 **'promote the interests of future commerce'** Lord Beauchamp, report, 28 July 1785, in *Journals of the House of Commons*, vol. 40 (18 May 1784 – 1 December 1785), n.p., London, 1803, p. 1164.

Page 133 **'above all, the cultivation of the flax plant'** Evan Nepean to Sackville Hamilton, draft, 24 October 1786, HO 100/18, fols 369–72, NA.

Page 133 **'a means of preventing the emigration'** Lord Sydney to chairmen, East India Company, 15 September 1786, in Tink, p. 222; Alan Frost, *The First Fleet: The Real Story*, Black Inc, Melbourne, 2011, pp. 20–21.

Page 133 **'to prevent its being occupied'** 'Phillip's Instructions', 25
     April 1787, in *HRNSW 1*, p. 89.

Page 133 **'superior excellence for a variety of maritime purposes'**
     ibid.

Page 133 **'the scheme of being able to assist the East Indies'**
     Watkin Tench, *Watkin Tench: 1788*, ed. and introduced by Tim
     Flannery, Text, Melbourne, 1996, p. 80.

Page 134 **'commanding influence in the policy of Europe'** …
     'we might very powerfully annoy' in King, esp. n. 32.

Page 135 **'the capital seat of plague'** … **'all life dies and all death
     lives'** Report of the debate, 16 March 1785, in William Cobbett,
     Cobbett's Parliamentary History of England, vol. 25, pp. 391–92.

Page 135 **'so dreary a coast'** Emma Christopher, *A Merciless Place*,
     Allen & Unwin, Sydney, 2010, p. 328; see also Alan Frost, *Botany
     Bay: The Real Story*, Black Inc, Melbourne, 2011, p. 194.

Page 136 **'essentially the government in all its departments'**
     Spencer Percival to William Huskisson, 21 August 1809, in A
     Aspinall & Anthony Smith (eds), *English Historical Documents:
     1783–1832*, vol.11, Eyre and Spottiswoode, London, 1959, p. 129.

Page 137 **'to Cruise as a Volunteer'** Arthur Phillip to Lord Sandwich,
     5 September 1779, in Frost, *Arthur Phillip 1738–1814*, p. 96.

Page 137 **'Adieu, my dear friend'** Arthur Phillip to Evan Nepean, 3
     September 1787, in *HRNSW 1*, pp. 116–17.

Page 138 **'austere, morose and inaccessible man'** Rodger, *The
     Insatiable Earl*, p. 309.

Page 138 **'for a service of this complicated nature'** Lord Howe to
     Lord Sydney, 3 September 1786, CO 201/2, fol. 31, NA.

Page 139 **'I do think God Almighty made Phillip'** Rev. W Butler
     of Cheyne Walk, Chelsea, letter, in Louis Becke & Walter Jeffery,

Admiral Phillip: The Founding of New South Wales, facsimile edn, T Fisher Unwin, London, 1899, p. 103.

Page 139 **'seen much of the service' ... 'made on purpose for such a Trial of Abilities'** Daniel Southwell to Rev. W Butler, 2 August 1787, Daniel Southwell—Papers, M 1538, State Library of New South Wales, Sydney.

Page 139 **'the Commodore ... had doubled every cape'** Landmann, p. 123.

Page 141 **'the Ancient Line of Separation' ... 'nearly corresponding'** McIntyre, *The Rebello Transcripts*, p. 160; Kenneth Gordon McIntyre, *The Secret Discovery of Australia: Portuguese Ventures 200 Years before Captain Cook*, Souvenir Press, Adelaide, 1977, p. 354.

Page 141 **'to omit any notice'** Sir Robert Peel to Sir Joseph Banks, 30 November 1811, in McIntyre, *The Secret Discovery of Australia*, p. 354.

Page 142 **'a more unlimited one'** Arthur Bowes Smyth, *The Journal of Arthur Bowes Smyth: Surgeon, Lady Penryhn*, ed. PG Fidlon & RJ Ryan, Australian Documents Library, Sydney, 1979, p. 68 (7 February 1788).

Page 144 **'the outstanding generosity of the Government'** Becke & Jeffery, p. 25.

Page 144 **'to submit to the consideration of Lord Chatham'** Arthur Phillip to Lord Sydney, 26 July 1790, DLMSQ 162, nos 1030–31, State Library of New South Wales, Sydney.

CHAPTER 9 Philosopher

Page 148 **'the garrison and the convicts' ... 'that it may be said hereafter'** Arthur Phillip to Lord Sydney, 12 March 1787, in *HRNSW 1*, pp. 56–57.

Page 149 **'obliged to put a stop to his wishes'** George Teer to
Navy Board, 4 December 1786, ADM 106/243, NA.

Page 151 **'rail'd around from deck to deck'** Philip Gidley
King, 'The Journal of Lieutenant King', in *HRNSW 2*, p. 514
(October–December 1786).

Page 152 **'They now have comfortable beds',** Letter in *The
Gentleman's Magazine*, 4 December 1786, vol. 56, pt. 2, p. 1019.

Page 152 **'he himself carrys out between thirty and forty'**
Ralph Clark to Lieutenant Bedlake, 10 May 1787, Ralph Clark –
Letterbook, 3 April 1787–30 September 1791, C 221, State Library
of New South Wales; see also Mackaness, p. 80.

Page 154 **'time is longitude and longitude time'** Dava Sobel,
Longitude, Fourth Estate, London, 1995, p. 168.

Page 154 **'our trusty friend' … 'never-failing guide'** JC
Beaglehole, 'Cook the Navigator', lecture delivered to the Royal
Society, London, 3 June 1969, in *Proceedings of the Royal Society
London. Series A, Mathematical and Physical Sciences*, vol. 314, no.
1516, 16 December 1969, p. 33.

Page 154 **'ordinary sea captain would take about four hours'** ibid.,
p. 31.

Page 154 **'ever-more entangled filigrees of arithmetic'** Simon
Winchester, *Outposts: Journeys to the Surviving Relics of the British
Empire*, Penguin Books, London, 2003 (1985), p. 17.

Page 155 **'Capt. Phillip, who with Capt. Hunter'** William Bradley,
'A Voyage to New South Wales', unpublished journal, December
1786 – May 1792 (compiled c. 1802), Safe 1/14, Mitchell Library,
State Library of New South Wales, Sydney, online at http://acms.
sl.nsw.gov.au/album/albumView.aspx?acmsID=412904&item
ID=823591.(11 May 1787), p. 11.

Page 155 **'the Empire of the East'** Frost, *Botany Bay – The Real Story*, p. 214.

Page 156 **'seat of Empire'** Arthur Phillip to Sir Charles Middleton, 6 July 1788 (privately owned).

Page 156 **'of the greatest consequence to Britain'** Arthur Phillip, comments on a draft of his instructions, c. 11 April 1787, CO 201/2, fol. 131, NA.

Page 156 **'no doubt but that this country'** Arthur Phillip to Lord Sydney, 9 July 1788, in *HRNSW 1*, p. 151.

Page 156 **'serving my country and serving the cause of humanity'** Arthur Phillip to Lord Sydney, 10 July 1788, in *HRNSW 1*, p. 179.

Page 157 **'with all convenient speed'** 'Phillip's Instructions', p. 90.

Page 157 **'Give them a few acres of ground'** ... **'it is very probable'** James Mario Matra, memoranda, attached to 'Proposal for Establishing a Settlement in New South Wales', 23 August 1783, in *HRNSW 1*, p. 7.

Page 157 **'It is sufficiently proved by ancient and modern history'** Atkinson, p. 68.

Page 158 **'together with an assortment of tools'** 'Phillip's Instructions', p. 91.

Page 158 **'without having any dispute with the Natives'** and **following quotations** Arthur Phillip, memorandum, c. October 1786, in *HRNSW 1*, p. 52.

Page 159 **'necessary to prevent the transport crews'** ... **'must have none'** ibid, p. 52.

Page 159 **'any man who takes the life of a Native'** Arthur Phillip, comments on a draft of his instructions, c. 11 April 1787, CO 201/2, fol. 131, NA.

Page 159 **'odious consequences' in** Frost, *The First Fleet: The Real Story*, p. 67.

Page 159 **'to pine away a few years in misery'** Arthur Phillip to Lord Sydney, 15 May 1788, in *HRNSW 1*, p. 127.

Page 159 **'the most abandoned of the female convicts'** ... **'At Mill Bank [jail in London] something of this kind'**, Arthur Phillip, memorandum, c. October 1786, in *HRNSW 1*, p. 52.

Page 159 **'and let them eat him'** ibid, p. 53.

Page 160 **'There can be no slavery in a free land'** ibid, p. 53.

Page 160 **'No nation in Europe'** 'The Speech of the Right Honourable William Pitt: On a motion for the abolition of the slave trade', 2 April 1792, *Cobbett's Parliamentary History of England*, Vol. 29, p. 1152.

Page 160 **'The Expedition to Botany Bay comprehends'** *St James Chronicle*, 16–18 January 1787 in John Gascoigne, *The Enlightenment & the Origins of European Australia*, Cambridge University Press, Cambridge, 2002, pp. 69–70.

Page 164 **'mirrored to perfection the taste'** Mary Webster, *Francis Wheatley*, Routledge & Kegan Paul Ltd, London, 1970, flyleaf.

CHAPTER 10 Commander

Page 168 **'At a future period when this country feels the advantages'** Arthur Phillip to Evan Nepean, 11 May 1787, in *HRNSW 1*, p. 103.

Page 168 **'the largest forced exile'**, Hughes, p. 2.

Page 170 **'seem as if expressly placed'** Arthur Phillip, *The Voyage of Arthur Phillip to Botany Bay*, John Stockdale, (1789), facsimile edn, Hutchinson, Sydney, 1982, p. 26.

Page 172 **'The calms so frequent'** ibid, p. 28.

Page 172 **'even to a Boatswain's Mate'** ... **'are all we have to depend on'** Joseph Nagle, *The Nagle Journal: A Diary of the Life of Jacob Nagle, Sailor, from the Year 1775 to 1841*, ed. John C Dann, Weidenfeld & Nicholson, New York, 1988, pp. 73–74.

Page 173 **'were no better than he was'** Nagle, pp. 73–74.

Page 174 **'a promiscuous intercourse'** ... **'uncontrollable'** John White, *Journal of a Voyage to New South Wales*, Angus & Robertson, Sydney, 1962 (1790), p. 63 (23 June 1787).

Page 176 **'faint silvery vapour'** Robert Louis Stevenson, *Travels with a Donkey in the Cevennes*, Folio Society, London, 1967 (1879), p. 83.

Page 176 **'Captain Phillip for the first time'** White, p. 69 (1 August 1787).

Page 177 **'daughters of the sun'** David Collins, *An Account of the English Colony in New South Wales ...*, vol. 1, T Cadell & W Davies, London, 1798, facsimile edn, Libraries Board of South Australia, Adelaide, 1971, pp. xviii–xxi.

Page 178 **'only out of absolute necessity'** Robert Ross to Philip Stephens, 10 July 1788, in *HRNSW 1*, p. 173.

Page 179 **'many of whom are nearly naked'** Arthur Phillip to Evan Nepean, 2 September 1787, in *HRNSW 1*, p. 112.

Page 179 **'We formed as tender an intercourse with them'** White, p. 87 (1 September 1787).

Page 181 **'found on enquiry that the last year's crops'** Arthur Phillip to Philip Stephens, 10 November 1787, in *HRNSW 1*, p. 118.

Page 181 **'abounding with the most luxurious flowers and aromatic shrubs'** White, p. 81 (1 September 1787).

Page 182 **'this is the last port'** Daniel Southwell to his mother, 11 November 1787, Daniel Southwell—Papers, M 1538, State Library of New South Wales, Sydney.

Page 183 **'Phillip's Cabbin was like a small Green House'** Francis
Masson to Joseph Banks, 13 November 1787, EN 1/36, Banks
Collection, Sutro Library, San Francisco.

Page 183 **'In a climate so favourable'** Phillip, (Stockdale), p. 129.

Page 184 **'The land behind us was the abode of civilised people'**
Collins, vol. 1, p. xxxiv.

Page 185 **'I sentence you, but to what I know not'** J Bowring
(ed.), *The Works of Jeremy Bentham*, vol. 1, *Principles of Penal
Law*, William Tait, Edinburgh, 1843, book 5, chap. 2, 'Of
Transportation'.

Page 186 **'extending well over a mile in length'** Robin Knox-
Johnston, *The Cape of Good Hope: A Maritime History*, Hodder &
Stoughton, London, 1989, p. 16.

Page 186 **'for a thousand miles'** JR Bruijn, FS Gaastra & I Schöffer,
Dutch-Asiatic Shipping in the 17th and 18th Centuries, vol. 1,
Martinus Nijhoff, The Hague, 1987, pp. 70–1.

Page 187 **'as no Ship ever ran in this parallel of Latitude'** Philip
Gidley King, p. 534 (7 December 1787).

Page 187 **'it is better to trust a good lookout'** Rodger, *The Wooden
World*, p. 48.

Page 188 **'the Time Keeper was not thought of till about 6
o'clock'** Philip Gidley King, p. 535 (17 December 1787).

Page 188 **'some very good altitudes were taken'** ibid, p. 535,
setting out an extract from Mr Dawes' journal.

Page 188 **'useless for the rest of the passage'** James Campbell to
Lord Ducie, 12 July 1788, nos 3–4, MLMSS 5366, Collection 16,
First Fleet Collection of Journals, Correspondence and Drawings,
Mitchell and Dixson libraries, State Library of New South Wales,
Sydney.

Page 189 **'Nothing could more strongly prove the excellence'**
Collins, vol. 1, p. xxxvii.

Page 189 **'almost constantly under water'** Philip Gidley King,
p. 536 (18 December 1787).

Page 190 **'crushed to atoms'** Bowes Smyth, p. 45 (29 November
1787).

Page 191 **'poor creatures were frequently thrown'** John Hunter,
journal, May 1787 – March 1791, DLMS 164, Dixson Library,
State Library of New South Wales, Sydney, online at http://acms.
sl.nsw.gov.au/album/albumView.aspx?acmsID=412913&item
ID=823673, pp. 50–1 (1 January 1788).

Page 192 **'very bright with many beautiful red'** Bradley, p. 51 (6
January 1788).

Page 193 **'to prevent its being occupied'** 'Phillip's Instructions',
p. 89.

Page 194 **'he might be known as a spy'** Frost, *Arthur Phillip
1738–1814*, p. 166.

CHAPTER 11 Governor

Page 196 **'had the satisfaction of finding the finest harbour'**
Arthur Phillip to Lord Sydney, 15 May 1788, in *HRNSW 1*,
p. 122.

Page 196 **'Port Jackson I believe to be'** White, p. 112 (26 January
1788).

Page 196 **'one of the finest harbours in the world'** Ralph Clark,
journal, 9 March 1787 – 17 June 1792, Safe 1/27a, Mitchell
Library, State Library of New South Wales, Sydney, online at
http://acms.sl.nsw.gov.au/album/albumView.aspx?acmsID=41290
5&itemID=823869, p. 93 (26 January 1788).

Page 197 **'made all around appear like an enchantment'** 'Extracts from the Journal of Arthur Bowes', HRNSW2, p.392 (26 January 1788).

Page 197 **'we might not sully that purity'** ... **'the run of fresh water'** Collins, p. 5.

Page 198 **'There are few things more pleasing'** Phillip, (Stockdale), p. 122.

Page 199 **'warmth of temper'**, Arthur Phillip to Evan Nepean, 12 February 1790 in *HRNSW 1*, pp. 301–04.

Page 199 **'perverse, sullen, litigious and unhelpful'** Patrick O'Brian, *Joseph Banks*, Harvill, London, 1994, p. 261.

Page 199 **'so little harmony prevails'** ... **'The strength of the [marine] detachment'** Arthur Phillip to Lord Sydney, 1 February 1790, in *HRNSW 1*, pp. 288–93.

Page 200 **'an insult to the corps'** ... **'put the soldiers under the command'**, ibid.

Page 201 **'the marines and sailors are punished'** Bowes Smyth, p. 74 (23 February 1788).

Page 201 **'the only difference between the allowance of provisions'** James Campbell to Lord Ducie, 12 July 1788, nos 3–4, MLMSS 5366, Collection 16, First Fleet Collection of Journals, Correspondence and Drawings, Mitchell and Dixson libraries, State Library of New South Wales, Sydney.

Page 201 **'Could I possibly have imagined'** Robert Ross to Philip Stephens, 10 July 1788, in *HRNSW 1*, p. 174.

Page 201 **'the Laws of this Country will of course be introduced'** Arthur Phillip, memorandum, c. October 1786, in *HRNSW 1*, p. 53.

Page 201 **'civilly dead, unable to sue'** William Blackstone, *Blackstone's Commentaries on the Laws of England*, Vol. 4, new edn, with notes by John Archbold, William Reed, London, 1811, pp. 373–82.

Page 205 **'acquired an ascendancy over the convicts'** Collins, Vol. 1, p. 148.

Page 205 **'this very industrious man'** Arthur Phillip to Lord Sydney, 12 February 1790, in *HRNSW 1*, pp. 296 and 299.

Page 205 **'villains into villagers'** ... **'affording the political philosopher'** Grace Karskens, *The Colony: A History of Early Sydney*, Allen & Unwin, Sydney, 2009, p. 110.

Page 206 **'conciliate the affections'** ... **'wantonly destroy them'** 'Phillip's Instructions', p. 89.

Page 206 **'cultivate an acquaintance with them'** WEH Stanner, 'The History of Indifference Thus Begins', *Aboriginal History*, Vol. 1, 1977, p.3.

Page 207 **'symptoms of disgust and terror'** Tench, p. 102.

Page 208 **'hopes that being cured and sent away'** Arthur Phillip to Lord Sydney, 13 February 1790, in *HRNSW 1*, p. 308.

Page 209 **'nothing will make these people amends'** Arthur Phillip to Joseph Banks, 26 July 1790, series 37.12, section 7, Papers of Sir Joseph Banks, State Library of New South Wales, Sydney, online at www2.sl.nsw.gov.au/banks/.

Page 210 **'about three inches just behind the shoulder blade'** ... **'Let it be whatever it would'** Henry Waterhouse, 'Account of Governor Phillip Being Wounded in September 1790 at New South Wales', item 2, Papers Relating to Waterhouse Family and Bass Family, Aw 109, Mitchell Library, State Library of New South Wales, Sydney.

Page 212 **'in six weeks he was able to get about again'** ibid.; Bradley, p. 230.

Page 214 **'I find my health declines fast'** … **'getting little sleep'** Arthur Phillip to Joseph Banks, 26 July 1790, series 37.12, section 7, Papers of Sir Joseph Banks, State Library of New South Wales, Sydney, online at www2.sl.nsw.gov.au/banks/.

Page 214 **'For more than two years'** Arthur Phillip to Lord Sydney, 24 March 1791, in GR Tipping (ed.), *The Official Account through Governor Phillip's Letters to Lord Sydney*, GR Tipping, Beecroft, 1988, p. 115.

Page 214 **'has almost worn me out'** Arthur Phillip to Joseph Banks, 23 April 1791, in Mackaness, pp. 333–34.

Page 214 **'from a violent pain in the left kidney'** Arthur Phillip to Lord Sydney, 11 November 1791, in Tipping, p. 117.

Page 214 **'sorry to inform them that [Phillip] was not very well'** Chapman, pp. 19–20.

Page 215 **'private affairs'**, Arthur Phillip to Lord Sydney, 15 April 1790 in *HRNSW 1*, p. 329; Arthur Phillip to Evan Nepean, 15 April 1790 in *HRNSW 1*, p. 330.

Page 215 **'induced to request permission'**, Arthur Phillip to William Grenville, 21 November 1791 in *HRNSW 1*, p. 559.

Page 215 **'as my bad state of health continues'** Arthur Phillip to Henry Dundas, 31 March 1792, in *HRNSW 1*, p. 613.

Page 215 **'the wants of the colony'** Arthur Phillip to Henry Dundas, 2 October 1792, in *HRNSW 1*, p. 646.

Page 215 **'obliges me to hope'** Arthur Phillip to Henry Dundas, 4 October 1792, in *HRNSW 1*, p. 651–2.

Page 216 **'the ill state of your health'** Henry Dundas to Arthur Phillip, 15 May 1792, in *HRNSW 1*, p. 625.

Page 216 **'there is a possibility'** Arthur Phillip to Henry Dundas, 11 October 1792, in *HRNSW 1*, p. 666.

Page 216 **'exhaustion of spirit and decay of body'** Frost, *Arthur Phillip 1738–1814*, p. 218.

Page 216 **'I am blended in every concern of his'** 'Collins, David (1756–1810)', in *Australian Dictionary of Biography*, vol. 1, Melbourne University Press, Melbourne, 1966, p. 237.

CHAPTER 12 Society gentleman

Page 220 **'the state of the colony'**, John Easty, journal November 1786 – May 1793, DLSPENCER 374, Dixson Library, State Library of New South Wales, Sydney, online at http://acms. sl.nsw.gov.au/album/albumView.aspx?acmsID=412912&itemID=823440, pp. 143–74.

Page 221 **'honoured with extraordinary attention'**, Robert J King 'Arthur Phillip, Defender of Colonia, Governor of New South Wales', presented to the V Simpósio de Historia Maritimo e Naval Iber – Americano, Ilha Fiscal, Rio de Janeiro, Brazil, 25–29 October, 1999.

Page 221 **'grand and magnificent Romish churches'** ... **'the Ignorance of the Lower Class'** Easty, journal, (14 February 1793).

Page 221 **'great disturbances'** ... **'every preparation for war'**, Easty, journal, (23 February 1793).

Page 222 **'our unspeakable joy'** Easty, journal, (23 May 1793).

Page 223 **'private affairs'** Arthur Phillip to Lord Sydney, 15 April 1790, in *HRNSW 1*, p. 329; Arthur Phillip to Evan Nepean, 15 April 1790, in *HRNSW 1*, p. 330.

Page 223 **'I well and sufficiently release'** 'Will of Margaret Charlotte Philip Otherwise Charlott Phillip, Wife of Gloucester, Gloucestershire', 6 October 1792, PROB 11/1224/98, NA.

Page 224 **'but that I have been much indisposed'** Arthur Phillip to
Lord Hawkesbury, 27 June 1793, fol. 44, Add MS 38229, vol. 40,
Liverpool Papers, Western Manuscripts, British Library, London.

Page 224 **'attaining any one of those places'** Arthur Phillip to
Henry Dundas, 21 October 1793, in *HRNSW 2*, pp. 74–75.

Page 224 **'either one of the Naval Boards'** ibid.

Page 226 **'bleed and blister'** Jack Brook, 'The Forlorn Hope:
Bennelong and Yemmerrawannie Go to England', *Australian
Aboriginal Studies*, vol. 1, no. 1, 2001, p. 40.

Page 227 **'at liberty to leave town'** ... **'in other respects be
beneficial'** Arthur Phillip to Henry Dundas, 23 July 1793, in
HRNSW 2, pp. 59–60.

Page 227 **'The usual method'** ... **'the stone and gravel'** John
Elliott, *An Account of the Nature and Medicinal Virtues of the
Principal Mineral Waters of Great Britain and Ireland*, J Johnson,
London, 1781, pp. 108, 115.

Page 228 **'are moments snatched from Paradise'** ... **'dresses
rustled, feathers waved'** Charles Dickens, *The Posthumous Papers
of the Pickwick Club*, vol. 2 in *Charles Dickens*, Complete Works
Centennial Edition, Heron Books, London, 1967, p. 109.

Page 230 **'are frequented by all fashionable people'** ... **'taste and
character of individuals'** Lee Erickson, 'The Economy of Novel
Reading: Jane Austen and the Circulating Library', *Studies in
English Literature, 1500–1900*, vol. 30, no. 4, 1990, pp. 574–75.

Page 231 **'single man in possession of a good fortune'** Jane
Austen, *Pride & Prejudice*, Penguin Classics, London, 2003 (1813),
opening sentence.

Page 233 **'on matters relative to the colony'** Arthur Phillip to
Henry Dundas, 21 October 1793, in *HRNSW 2*, p. 74.

Page 233 **'individuals making fortunes'** Arthur Phillip to Joseph
  Banks, 7 September 1796, series 37.29, section 7, Papers of Sir
  Joseph Banks, State Library of New South Wales, Sydney, online
  at www2.sl.nsw.gov.au/banks/.

Page 235 **'a profession which is, if possible, more distinguished'**
  Jane Austen, *Persuasion*, Penguin Classics, London, 2003 (1818),
  final sentence.

CHAPTER 13 Inspector

Page 239 **'My dear, invaluable friend'** Horatio Nelson to John Ball,
  4 June 1801, in Henry Frendo, *Ball, Sir Alexander John, Baronet
  (1756–1809), Naval Officer and Politician in Malta*, October 2007,
  Oxford Dictionary of National Biography, www.oxforddnb.com/
  view/printable/1210.

Page 239 **'one of the best ships'** Arthur Phillip to Evan Nepean, 17
  February 1798, ADM 1/2317, NA.

Page 240 **'exceedingly high and every one washing over us'** ...
  'Well I remember his little figure' Landmann, p. 123.

Page 241 **'in most excellent order and fit for any service'**
  Horatio Nelson to Earl St Vincent, 9 June 1797, ADM 1/396,
  NA.

Page 242 **'well-manned, commanded and appointed'** ... **'the
  moment he appears'** Earl St Vincent, letters, May and June
  1797, fols 158, 168 & 171, Add MS 31166, British Library,
  London; Earl St Vincent to Evan Nepean, 26 June 1797, Earl
  St Vincent to Souza Coutinho, 26 June 1797, both in ADM
  1/396, NA.

Page 244 **'obliged to come on shore'** Arthur Phillip to Evan
  Nepean, 17 February 1798, ADM 1/2317, NA.

Page 244 **'band of brothers'** See Brian Lavery, *Nelson & the Nile: The Naval War against Bonaparte, 1798*, Naval Institute Press, Annapolis, 1998, p. 154.

Page 245 **'I can hold out no hope of a ship'** Patrick O'Brian, *Post Captain*, HarperCollins, London, 2002 (1972), p. 141.

Page 246 **'A List of Post Captains'** 'Manuscript Book Listing Appointments to the 1798 Establishment, Instructions (Financial), Widows' Charity, Other Appointments, Leave of Absences, Expense of the Service & Promiscuous. Index', 1798–1810, ADM 28/147, pp. 16, 18, NA.

Page 248 **'that your husband and all your friends'** ... **'Your friends still love you'** Arthur Phillip to Isabella Phillip, 4 October 1801, Bath Archives, Bath & North East Somerset Record Office, Bath.

Page 249 **'for God's sake let me hear no more'** ... **'I see no reason'** Arthur Phillip to Isabella Phillip, 24 April 1803, Bath Archives, Bath & North East Somerset Record Office, Bath.

Page 249 **'Fourteen months spent on a trip'** Mackaness, p. 439.

Page 250 **'We have often wondered'** Charles Dickens, *Sketches by Boz*, vol. 1, in *Charles Dickens*, p. 154.

Page 251 **'to calm the fears of old ladies'** *The Letters and Papers of Admiral Viscount Keith* vol.3, Navy Records Society, 1955, pp. 133–4, 155 and 168 in Christopher Lloyd, *The British Seaman 1200–1860: A Social Survey*, Paladin, London, 1970, p. 188.

Page 252 **'for various causes'** Arthur Phillip to Lord Hobart, 5 April 1803, *HRNSW 5*, pp. 86–87.

Page 252 **'a lofty dignified situation such as becomes a man of consequence'** Austen, *Persuasion*, p. 128.

Page 253 'the last nine stages of increasing splendour' Patrick
O'Brian, *The Yellow Admiral*, Harper Collins, London, 1997,
p. 16.

CHAPTER 14 Final years

Page 256 'but not unpleasantly so' Chapman, p. 36.

Page 258 'her upstairs parlour window' Mackaness, p. 443-44.

Page 258 'taking the Bath air' ibid, p. 443.

Page 258 'in quest of pastry, millinery, or... young men' Jane
Austen, *Northanger Abbey*, Penguin Classics, London, 2003 [1818]
p. 13.

Page 258 'the constant resort of his naval friends' Mackaness,
p. 449; Frost, *Arthur Phillip 1738–1814*, p. 252.

Page 259 'large and valuable quantity of silver' Mackaness,
p. 458.

Page 259 'as mad as a March hare' Fanny Chapman, diary, 22
February 1808, in Frederick Chapman, p. 33.

Page 260 'very much altered' ... 'may linger on some years'
Philip Gidley King to Phillip Parker King, July 1808, in Frederick
Chapman, p. 35.

Page 260 'is quite a cripple' Philip Gidley King to Phillip Parker
King, September 1808, in Mackaness, p. 447.

Page 262 'under the advice of his friends' Percival Serle (ed)
'Greenway, Francis Howard (1777-1837)' in *Dictionary of
Australian Biography*, Angus & Robertson, Sydney, 1949, online at
Gutenberg.net.au/dictbiog/O-biog6.html#greenway1.

Page 263 'persons of great sanctity' James Brooke Little, *The Law
of Burial*, 3rd edn, Local Government Board and Home Office of
Great Britain, London, 1902, p. 18.

Page 263 **'on the former by an ignominious burial'** William
   Blackstone, *Blackstone's Commentaries on the Laws of England*,
   vol. 4, new edn, with notes by John Archbold, William Reed,
   London, 1811, p. 190.

Page 263 **'the uniquely English tradition'** Roy Strong, *Visions of
   England*, Bodley Head, London, 2011, p. 101.

Page 264 **'quite an ugly little man'** Mackaness, p. 456.

Page 265 **'in the backroom on the drawing-room floor'** ibid.,
   p. 457.

Page 268 **'to the other side of the world'** EM Green, 'Arthur
   Phillip: An Unwritten Chapter', in Harry Wilson & Edward
   Salmon (eds), *United Empire: The Royal Colonial Institute Journal*,
   vol. 12, new series, Sir Isaac Pitman and Sons, London, 1921,
   p. 734; see also Frost, *Arthur Phillip 1738–1814*, p. 112.

Page 269 **'all her share of the property was lost in the costs of a
   Chancery suit'**, Arthur Phillip Lancefield, letter, 8 March 1899,
   in Becke & Jeffery, pp. 256–58.

Page 271 **'the most valuable acquisition Great Britain ever made'**
   Arthur Phillip to Lord Sydney, 9 July 1788, in *HRNSW 1*, p. 151.

BIBLIOGRAPHY

Abbott, Graham, 'The Expected Cost of the Botany Bay Scheme', *Journal of the Royal Australian Historical Society*, vol. 81, no. 2, 1995, pp. 151–66.

Ackroyd, Peter, *London: The Biography*, Vintage, London, 2001.

——*Albion: The Origins of the English Imagination*, Anchor Books, New York, 2004.

Adkins, Roy & Lesley Adkins, *Jack Tar: Life in Nelson's Navy*, Abacus, London, 2009.

Alden, Dauril, *Royal Government in Colonial Brazil: With Special Reference to the Administration of the Marquis of Lavradio, Viceroy 1769–79*, Cambridge University Press, London, 1968.

An Account of Several Work-Houses for Employing and Maintaining the Poor ..., Joseph Downing (printer), London, 1732, cited in Peter Higginbotham, *City of London Parish Workhouses*, The Workhouse, www.workhouses.org.uk/CityOfLondon/parishes.shtml.

Arthur Phillip, Governor of NSW, Autograph Letters, 1786, 1788–92, DLMSQ 162, Mitchell Library, State Library of New South Wales, Sydney.

Articles and Instructions for the Better Government of His Majesty's Royal Hospital for Seamen at Greenwich ..., 2nd edn with additions, n.p., London, 1741.

Aspinall, A & Anthony Smith (eds), *English Historical Documents: 1783–1832*, vol. 11, Eyre and Spottiswoode, London, 1959.

Aspinall, Arthur (ed.), *The Later Correspondence of George III*, vol. 1, Cambridge University Press, Cambridge, 1970.

Atkinson, Alan, *The Europeans in Australia: A History*, Oxford
    University Press, Melbourne, 1997.

Austen, Jane, *Sense and Sensibility*, Penguin Classics, London, 2003
    [1811].

——*Pride and Prejudice*, Penguin Classics, London, 2003 [1813].

——*Northanger Abbey*, Penguin Classics, London, 2003 [1818].

——*Persuasion*, Penguin Classics, London, 2003 [1818].

Banks Collection, Sutro Library, San Francisco.

Banks, Joseph, *Notes Describing the Recovery of Diamonds in Brazil with
    Annotated List of the Accompanying 3 Water Colours and 5 Drawings*,
    unpublished manuscript, Manuscript Item 5c, n.d., Royal
    Geographical Society of Australasia (South Australian Branch),
    York Gate Library, Adelaide.

Bannerman, W Bruce (ed.), *The Registers of All Hallows, Bread Street,
    and of St John the Evangelist, Friday Street, London*, Harleian
    Society, London, 1913.

Barnard, Madeleine, *Cape Town Stories*, Struik Publishers, Cape Town,
    2007.

Barrington, George, *A Voyage to Botany Bay*, C Lowndes, London,
    1795.

Bateson, Charles, *The Convict Ships 1787–1868*, Brown, Son &
    Ferguson, Glasgow, 1959.

Baugh, Daniel A, *Naval Administration 1715–50*, Navy Records
    Society, London, 1977.

——'The Eighteenth-Century Navy as a National Institution, 1690–
    1815', in JR Hill (ed.), *The Oxford Illustrated History of the Royal
    Navy*, Oxford University Press, Oxford, 1995.

——*The Global Seven Years War 1754–63: Britain and France in a
    Great Power Contest*, Pearson Education Ltd, Harlow, 2011.

———(ed.), *British Naval Administration in the Age of Walpole*, Princeton University Press, Princeton, 1965.

Bauss, R, 'The Critical Importance of Rio de Janeiro to British Interests with Particular Attention to Australia 1787–1805', *Journal of the Royal Australian Historical Society*, vol. 65, no. 3, 1979, pp. 145–72.

Beaglehole, JC, 'Cook the Navigator', lecture delivered to the Royal Society, London, 3 June 1969, in *Proceedings of the Royal Society London. Series A, Mathematical and Physical Sciences*, vol. 314, no. 1516, 16 December 1969, pp. 27–38.

———(ed.), *The Journals of Captain James Cook on his Voyages of Discovery*, vol. 1, Cambridge University Press for the Hakluyt Society, Cambridge, 1955.

Becke, Louis & Walter Jeffery, *Admiral Phillip: The Founding of New South Wales*, facsimile edn, T Fisher Unwin, London, 1899.

Bentham, Jeremy, *The Correspondence of Jeremy Bentham*, vol. 3, *January 1781 to October 1788*, ed. Ian R Christie, Athlone Press, London, 1971.

Bergad, Laird, *Slavery and the Demographic and Economic History of Minais Gerais Brazil 1720–1888*, Cambridge University Press, New York, 1999.

Bishop, WJ, *A History of Surgical Dressings*, Robinson & Sons Ltd, Chesterfield, 1959.

Blackmore, HL, *The Armouries of the Tower of London*, vol. 1, *Ordnance*, Department of the Environment, Her Majesty's Stationery Office, London, 1976.

Blackstone, William, *Blackstone's Commentaries on the Laws of England*, vol. 4, new edn, with notes by John Archbold, William Reed, London, 1811.

Blainey, Geoffery, *The Tyranny of Distance: How Distance Shaped Australia's History*, Sun Books, Melbourne, 1966.

Bloomfield, Noelene, *Almost a French Australia: French–British Rivalry in the Southern Oceans*, Halstead Press, Ultimo, 2012.

Bold, John, *Greenwich: An Architectural History of the Royal Hospital for Seamen and the Queen's House*, Yale University Press, New Haven & London, 2000.

Bonwick, Colin, *English Radicals and the American Revolution*, University of North Carolina Press, Chapel Hill, 1977.

Borrow, George, *Celebrated Trials, and Remarkable Cases of Jurisprudence, from the Earliest Records to the Year 1825*, vol. 4, Knight & Lacey, London, 1825.

Boswell, James, *Life of Johnson*, Oxford University Press, Oxford, 1998.

Boulaire, Alain, *Kerguelen: Le Phénix des Mers Australes*, France-Empire, Paris, 1997.

Bowes Smyth, Arthur, *The Journal of Arthur Bowes Smyth: Surgeon, Lady Penryhn*, ed. PG Fidlon & RJ Ryan, Australian Documents Library, Sydney, 1979.

Bowring J (ed.), *The Works of Jeremy Bentham*, vol. 1, *Principles of Penal Law*, William Tait, Edinburgh, 1843.

Bradley, Margaret, *Daniel Lescallier, 1743-1822, Man of the Sea—and Military Spy? Maritime Developments and French Military Espionage*, Edwin Mellen Press, New York, 2005.

Bradley, William, 'A Voyage to New South Wales', unpublished journal, December 1786 – May 1792, Safe 1/14, Mitchell Library, State Library of New South Wales, Sydney, online at http://acms. sl.nsw.gov.au/album/albumView.aspx?acmsID=412904&item ID=823591.

Brewer, John, *The Pleasures of the Imagination: English Culture in the Eighteenth Century*, HarperCollins, London, 1997.

Briggs, Asa, *England in the Age of Improvement: 1783–1867*, Folio Society, London, 1999.

Broadbent, James, *The Australian Colonial House*, Hordern House, Sydney, 1997.

Brook, Jack, 'The Forlorn Hope: Bennelong and Yemmerrawannie go to England', *Australian Aboriginal Studies*, vol. 1, no. 1, 2001, pp. 36–46.

Brown, Colin, *Whitehall: The Street that Shaped a Nation*, Pocket Books, London, 2010.

Bruijn, JR, FS Gaastra & I Schöffer, *Dutch-Asiatic Shipping in the 17th and 18th Centuries*, vol. 1, Martinus Nijhoff, The Hague, 1987.

Burke, Peter, *Celebrated Naval and Military Trials*, WH Allen & Co., London, 1876.

Campbell, Judith, *Invisible Invaders: Smallpox and Other Diseases in Aboriginal Australia 1780–1880*, Melbourne University Press, Melbourne, 2002.

Carley, Mary Manning, *Jamaica: The Old and the New*, George Allen & Unwin, London, 1962.

Carson, Rachel L., *The Sea Around Us*, Readers Union – Staples Press, London, 1953

Carter, Harold, *Sir Joseph Banks, 1743–1820*, British Museum (Natural History), London, 1988.

Cavell, Samantha, *Midshipmen and Quarterdeck Boys in the British Navy, 1771–1831*, Boydell Press, Woodbridge, 2012.

Chambers, Neil (ed.), *The Letters of Sir Joseph Banks: A Selection, 1768–1820*, Imperial College Press, London & River Edge, 2000.

Champion, Shelagh & George Champion, *The Spearing of Governor*

Phillip at Collins Cove (now Manly Cove), 7 September 1790,
S Champion & G Champion, Killarney Heights, c. 1989.

Chapman, Frederick, *Governor Phillip in Retirement*, ed. George
Mackaness, Halstead Press, Sydney, 1962.

Christelow, Allan, 'Great Britain and the Trades from Cadiz and
Lisbon to Spanish America and Brazil, 1759–1783', *Hispanic
American Historical Review*, vol. 27, no. 1, 1947, pp. 2–29.

Christopher, Emma, *A Merciless Place*, Allen & Unwin, Sydney, 2010.

——, Cassandra Pybus & Marcus Rediker (eds), *Many Middle
Passages: Forced Migration and the Making of the Modern World*,
University of California Press, Berkeley, 2007.

Churchill, Winston, *A History of the English-Speaking Peoples*, vol. 3,
The Age of Revolution, Cassell, London, 1957.

Clark, Manning, *A History of Australia*, vol. 1, *From the Earliest Times
to the Age of Macquarie*, Melbourne University Press, Melbourne,
1962.

Clark, Ralph, journal, 9 March 1787 – 17 June 1792, Safe 1/27a,
Mitchell Library, State Library of New South Wales, Sydney,
online at http://acms.sl.nsw.gov.au/album/albumView.aspx?acmsI
D=412905&itemID=823869.

——letterbook, 3 April 1787 – 30 September 1791, C 221, Mitchell
Library, State Library of New South Wales, Sydney, online
athttp://acms.sl.nsw.gov.au/album/albumView.aspx?acmsID=412
907&itemID=823592.

Clark, Richard, *Capital Punishment in Britain*, Ian Allan, Hersham, 2009.

Clark, Robert, *Circulating Libraries*, 11 April 2005, The
Literary Encyclopaedia, www.litencyc.com/php/stopics.
php?rec=true&UID=189.

Clendinnen, Inga, *Dancing with Strangers*, Text, Melbourne, 2005.

Cobban, A, 'British Secret Service in France, 1784–1792', *English Historical Review*, vol. 69, no. 271, 1954, pp. 226–61.

Cobbett, William, *Cobbett's Parliamentary History of England Volumes 25 and 29: From the Norman Conquest, in 1066 to the Year 1803 ...*, rarebooksclub.com, 2012.

Cobley, John, *Sydney Cove*, vol. 1, *1788*, Hodder & Stoughton, London, 1962; vol. 2, *1789–1790*, Angus & Robertson, Sydney, 1963; vol. 3, *1791–1792*, Angus & Robertson, Sydney, 1965.

Coke, Edward, *The Third Part of the Institutes of the Law of England: Concerning High Treason, and Other Pleas of the Crown and Criminal Causes*, E & R Brooke, London, 1797.

Colledge, JJ & Ben Warlow, *Ships of the Royal Navy: The Complete Record of All Fighting Ships of the Royal Navy from the 15th Century to the Present*, Chatham, London, 2006.

Colley, Linda, *The Ordeal of Elizabeth Marsh*, HarperCollins, London, 2007.

Collins, David, *An Account of the English Colony in New South Wales ...*, 2 vols, T Cadell & W Davies, London, 1798, facsimile edn, Libraries Board of South Australia, Adelaide, 1971.

'Collins, David (1756–1810)', in *Australian Dictionary of Biography*, vol. 1, Melbourne University Press, Melbourne, 1966, pp. 236–40.

Cooke, John & John Maule, *An Historical Account of the Royal Hospital for Seamen at Greenwich*, G Nicol, T Cadell, J Walter, GGJ & J Robinson, London, 1789.

Correspondence and Papers of Thomas Townshend, 1st Viscount Sydney, Brotherton Special Collections, Leeds University Library, Leeds.

Cullinan, P, *Robert Jacob Gordon 1743–95: The Man and His Travels at the Cape*, Struik Winchester, Cape Town, 1992.

Cust, Lionel, *History of the Society of Dilettanti*, Macmillan, London, 1914.

Dallas, KM, 'The First Settlement in Australia, Considered in Relation to Sea-Power in World Politics', *Papers and Proceedings (Tasmanian Historical Research Association)*, no. 3, 1952, pp.4–12.

Daniel Southwell—Papers, 1783–93, M 1538, State Library of New South Wales, Sydney.

Dark, Eleanor, *The Timeless Land*, Collins, London, 1941.

de Vattel, Emer, *The Law of Nations, or, Principles of the Law of Nature, Applied to the Conduct and Affairs of Nations and Sovereigns*, GG & J Robinson, London, 1797.

Deacon, Richard, *A History of the British Secret Service*, Miller, London, 1969.

Defoe, Daniel, *A Tour through the Whole Island of Great Britain*, Folio Society, London, 2006 (1724–26).

Deptford, 1784–89, ADM 106/243, National Archives, London.

Dickens, Charles, *The Life and Adventures of Nicholas Nickleby*, vol.1, in *Charles Dickens*, Complete Works Centennial Edition, Heron Books, London, 1967.

——*Oliver Twist*, vol. 1, in *Charles Dickens*, Complete Works Centennial Edition, Heron Books, London, 1967.

——*Sketches by Boz*, vol. 1, in *Charles Dickens*, Complete Works Centennial Edition, Heron Books, London, 1967.

——*The Posthumous Papers of the Pickwick Club*, vol. 2, in *Charles Dickens*, Complete Works Centennial Edition, Heron Books, London, 1967.

Duke of Dorset, Daniel Hailes, and George Craufurd, September–December 1784, FO 27/13; January–June 1785, FO 27/16, National Archives, London.

Dull, Jonathan, *The French Navy and American Independence: A Study of Arms and Diplomacy, 1774–1787*, Princeton University Press, Princeton, 1975.

——*The French Navy and The Seven Years' War*, University of Nebraska Press, Lincoln, 2008.

Dunmore, John, *French Explorers in the Pacific*, vol. 1, *The Eighteenth Century*, Clarendon Press, Oxford, 1965.

——*Visions & Realities: France in the Pacific 1695–1995*, Heritage Press, Palmerston North, 1997.

——(ed.), *Journal of La Pérouse*, Hakluyt Society, London, 1994.

Easty, John, journal, November 1786 – May 1793, DLSPENCER 374, Dixson Library, State Library of New South Wales, Sydney, online athttp://acms.sl.nsw.gov.au/album/albumView.aspx?acmsID=412912&itemID=823440.

Eldershaw, M Barnard, *Phillip of Australia: An Account of the Settlement at Sydney Cove 1788–92*, George C Harrap & Co. Ltd, London & Sydney, 1938.

Elliott, John, *An Account of the Nature and Medicinal Virtues of the Principal Mineral Waters of Great Britain and Ireland*, J Johnson, London, 1781.

Erickson, Lee, 'The Economy of Novel Reading: Jane Austen and the Circulating Library', *Studies in English Literature, 1500–1900*, vol. 30, no. 4, 1990, pp. 573–90.

Erskine, David (ed.), *Augustus Hervey's Journal*, William Kimber, London, 1953.

Establishment for Admitting, Maintaining, and Educating of Poor Boys in the Royal Hospital for Seamen at Greenwich ..., n.p., London, 1732.

Fenner, F, DA Henderson, L Arita, Z Težek & ID Ladnyi, *Smallpox and Its Eradication*, World Health Organization, Geneva, 1988.

Fergusson, Lyn M, *Admiral Arthur Phillip: The Man*, Pilar Publishing, Killara, 2009.

First Fleet Collection of Journals, Correspondence and Drawings, ca 1786–1802, Mitchell & Dixson libraries, State Library of New South Wales, Sydney.

Fisher, David R & Terry Jenkins, 'Cooper, John Hutton (1765–1828), of Royal Crescent, Bath, Som.', in David R Fisher (ed.), *History of Parliament: The House of Commons 1820–1832*, vol. IV, Cambridge University Press, Cambridge, 2009, p. 733.

Fitzhardinge, LF, 'Watkin Tench (1758–1833)', *Australian Dictionary of Biography*, vol. 2, Melbourne University Press, Melbourne, 1967, pp. 506–07.

Fitzpatrick, William, *Secret Service under Pitt*, 2nd edn, Longmans, Green, & Co., London & New York, 1892.

Fletcher, BH, 'Balmain, William (1762–1703)', *Australian Dictionary of Biography*, vol. 1, Melbourne University Press, Melbourne, 1966, pp. 51–2.

Flynn, Michael, 'Appointed on Merit', *Inside History*, no. 4, May–June 2011, pp. 48–51.

Forester, CS, *Mr Midshipman Hornblower*, Little, Brown & Co., New York, 1984.

Fowell, Newton, letter to John Fowell, 12 July 1788, Fowell Family Collection, MLMSS 4895/1/18, Safe 1/188, Mitchell Library, State Library of New South Wales, Sydney, online at http://acms.sl.nsw.gov.au/album/albumView.aspx?acmsID=411983&itemID=824081.

Frendo, Henry, *Ball, Sir Alexander John, Baronet (1756–1809), Naval Officer and Politician in Malta*, October 2007, Oxford Dictionary of National Biography, www.oxforddnb.com/view/printable/1210.

Frost, Alan, *Convicts and Empire: A Naval Question 1776–1811*, Oxford University Press, Melbourne, 1980.

——'New South Wales as *Terra Nullius:* The British Denial of Aboriginal Land Rights', *Historical Studies*, vol. 19, no. 177, 1981, pp. 513–23.

——*Arthur Phillip 1738–1814: His Voyaging*, Oxford University Press, Melbourne, 1987.

——*Botany Bay Mirages*, Melbourne University Press, Melbourne, 1994.

——*The Global Reach of Empire*, Melbourne University Publishing, Melbourne, 2003.

——*Botany Bay: The Real Story*, Black Inc, Melbourne, 2011.

——*The First Fleet: The Real Story*, Black Inc, Melbourne, 2011.

Fullager, Kate, 'Bennelong in Britain', *Aboriginal History*, vol. 33, 2009, pp. 31–50.

Fuller, Edmund, *Bullfinch's Mythology*, Dell Publishing, New York, 1959.

Fullerton, Susannah, *A Dance with Jane Austen*, Frances Lincoln, London, 2012.

Garrow, David, *The History of Lymington, and Its Immediate Vicinity …*, C Baynes, London, 1825.

Gascoigne, John, *Joseph Banks and the English Enlightenment: Useful Knowledge and Polite Culture*, Cambridge University Press, Cambridge, 1994.

——*The Enlightenment and the Origins of European Australia*, Cambridge University Press, Cambridge, 2002.

George, Mary Dorothy, *London Life in the Eighteenth Century*, Harper & Row, New York, 1965.

George Raper—Papers, 1787–1824, M 1183, State Library of New South Wales, Sydney.

Gergis, Joelle, Phillip Brohan & Rob Allan, 'The Weather of the First Fleet Voyage to Botany Bay, 1787–1788', *Weather*, vol. 65, no. 12, 2010, pp. 315–19.

Gilkerson, William, *Boarders Away II, With Fire: The Small Firearms and Combustibles of the Classical Age of Fighting Sail, 1626–1826 ...*, Andrew Mowbray, Lincoln, RI, 1993.

Gillen, Mollie, 'The Botany Bay Decision, 1786: Convicts, Not Empire', *English Historical Review*, vol. 97, no. 385, October 1982, pp. 740–66.

Godard, Philippe & Tudgual de Kerros, *1772: The French Annexation of New Holland. The Tale of Louis de Saint Aloüarn*, Western Australian Museum, Welshpool, 2009.

Goldston-Morris, Maurine, *The Life of Admiral Arthur Phillip, RN, 1738–1814*, Naval Historical Society of Australian Monograph No. 58, Garden Island, NSW, 1997

Gossett, William, *The Lost Ships of the Royal Navy, 1793–1900*, Mansell Publishing, London, 1986.

Gott, Ted & Katrine Huguenaud, *Napoleon: Revolution to Empire*, National Gallery of Victoria, Melbourne, 2012.

Green, EM, 'Arthur Phillip: An Unwritten Chapter', in Harry Wilson & Edward Salmon (eds), *United Empire: The Royal Colonial Institute Journal*, vol. 12, new series, Sir Isaac Pitman & Sons, London, 1921, pp. 732–35.

Green, Harvey, *Wood: Craft, Culture, History*, Penguin Books, New York, 2007.

Green, Jeremy, *Australia's Oldest Wreck: The Historical Background and Archaeological Analysis of the Wreck of the English East India Company's Ship* Trial, *Lost off the Coast of Western Australia in 1622*, Supplementary Series 27, British Archaeological Reports, Oxford, 1977.

Greenfield, Amy, *A Perfect Red: Empire, Espionage and the Quest for the Colour of Desire*, Doubleday, London, 2005.

Greentree, David, *A Far-Flung Gamble: Havana 1762*, Osprey Publishing, Oxford, 2010.

'Greenway, Francis Howard (c. 1777–1837)', in Perceval Serle (ed.), *Dictionary of Australian Biography*, Angus & Robertson, Sydney, 1949.

Gregory, Desmond, *Minorca, the Illusory Prize: A History of the British Occupations of Minorca between 1708 and 1802*, Associated University Presses, London, 1990.

Grigsby, Joan, 'Dancing, Balls and Assemblies', in *The Jane Austen Companion*, ed. J David Grey, Macmillan, New York, 1986.

Hanaway, Lorraine, 'Travel and Transportation', in *The Jane Austen Companion*, ed. J David Grey, Macmillan, New York, 1986.

Hancock, David, *Citizens of the World: London Merchants and the Integration of the British Atlantic Community, 1735–1785*, Cambridge University Press, Cambridge, 1997.

Harlow, Vincent T, *The Founding of the Second British Empire 1763–1793*, vol. 1, *Discovery and Revolution*, Longmans, Green & Co., London, 1952.

Harris, JR, *Industrial Espionage and Technology Transfer, Britain and France in the Eighteenth Century*, Ashgate, Aldershot, 1998.

Hart, Francis Russell, *The Siege of Havana, 1762*, Houghton Mifflin Co., Boston & New York, 1932.

Hattendorf, John B (ed.), *Maritime History*, vol. 2, *The Eighteenth Century and the Classic Age of Sail*, Krieger Publishing Company, Malabar, Fla., 1997.

Hawes, Charles Boardman, *Whaling*, Doubleday, Page & Co., New York, 1924.

Haythornthwaite, Philip J, *Wellington: The Iron Duke*, Potomac Books, Dulles, 2007.

Heath, Byron, *Discovering the Great South Land*, Rosenberg Publishing, Sydney, 2005.

Hibbert, Christopher, Ben Weinrib, John Keary & Julia Keary, *The London Encyclopaedia*, 3rd edn, Pan Macmillan, London, 2011.

Hill, Constance, *Jane Austen: Her Homes & Her Friends*, Dodo Press, Gloucester, 2008.

Hill, David, *1788: The Brutal Truth of the First Fleet*, William Heinemann, Sydney, 2008.

——*The Great Race*, William Heinemann, Sydney, 2012.

An Historical Narrative of the Discovery of New Holland and New South Wales ..., John Stockdale, London, 1786.

Historical Records of New South Wales, vol. 1, part 2, *Phillip*, Government Printer, Sydney, 1892; vol. 2, *Grose and Paterson, 1793–1795*, Government Printer, Sydney, 1893; vol. 5, King, Government Printer, Sydney, 1897.

Hodgson, Godfrey, *Lloyds of London: A Reputation at Risk*, Allen Lane, London, 1984.

Holmes, MRJ, *Augustus Hervey: A Naval Casanova*, Pentland Press, Edinburgh, 1996.

Hoskins, Ian, *Sydney Harbour, A History*, UNSW Press, Sydney, 2009.

Hudson, Geoffrey L (ed.), *British Military and Naval Medicine, 1600–1830*, Rodopi, New York, 2007.

Hughes, Robert, *The Fatal Shore*, Collins Harvill, London, 1987.

Hunter, John, journal, May 1787 – March 1791, DLMS 164, Dixson Library, State Library of New South Wales, Sydney, online at http://acms.sl.nsw.gov.au/album/albumView.aspx?acmsID=41291 3&itemID=823673.

Ireland: Home Office Correspondence on Civil Affairs, 1786, HO 100/18, National Archives, London.

Jackson, C Ian (ed.), *The Arctic Whaling Journals of William Scoresby the Younger*, vol. 1, *The Voyages of 1811, 1812 and 1813*, Hakluyt Society, London, 2003.

Jackson, Melvin & Carel de Beer, *Eighteenth Century Gunfounding*, David & Charles, Newton Abbott, 1973.

Jenkins, James Travis, *A History of the Whale Fisheries*, Witherby, London, 1921.

Jiggens, John, *Sir Joseph Banks and the Question of Hemp: Hemp, Seapower and Empire, 1776–1815*, Jayjay, Indooroopilly, 2012.

John Montagu, 4th Earl of Sandwich (First Lord of the Admiralty), naval papers, 1781, SAN/F/26, National Maritime Museum, London.

Johnson, W, 'The Woolwich Professors of Mathematics, 1741–1900', *Journal of Mechanical Working Technology*, vol. 18, no. 2, 1989, pp. 145–94.

Journals of the House of Commons, vol. 40 (18 May 1784 – 1 December 1785), n.p., 1803.

Karskens, Grace, *The Colony: A History of Early Sydney*, Allen & Unwin, Sydney, 2009.

Keegan, John, *Battle at Sea*, Pimlico, London, 1993.

Keneally, Thomas, *The Commonwealth of Thieves*, Random House, Sydney, 2005.

——*Australians: Origins to Eureka*, Allen & Unwin, Sydney, 2009.

King, Dean H with John B Hattendorf, *Harbors and High Seas: An Atlas and Geographical Guide to the Complete Aubrey-Maturin Novels of Patrick O'Brian*, 3rd edn, Henry Holt & Co., New York, 2000.

—— with John B Hattendorf & J Worth Estes, *A Sea of Words: A Lexicon and Companion to the Complete Seafaring Tales of Patrick O'Brian*, 3rd edn, Henry Holt & Co., New York, 2000.

King, Jonathan, *The First Fleet: The Convict Voyage that Founded Australia*, Macmillan, Melbourne, 1982.

King, Philip Gidley, 'The Journal of Lieutenant King', in *Historical Records of New South Wales*, vol. 2, *Phillip and Grose, 1789–1794*, Government Printer, Sydney, 1893, pp. 513–660.

King, Robert J, 'What Brought Lapérouse to Botany Bay?', *Journal of the Royal Australian Historical Society*, vol. 85, no. 2, 1999, pp. 140–47.

—— 'Arthur Phillip Defender of Colônia, Governor of New South Wales', presented to the V Simpósio de História Marítimo e Naval Iber-americano, Ilha Fiscal, Rio de Janeiro, Brazil, 25 to 29 October 1999, available online at http://web.viu.ca/black/amrc/Research/Papers/PHILLIP2.HTM.

——'An Australian Perspective on the English Invasions of the Rio de la Plata in 1806 and 1807', *International Journal of Naval History*, vol. 8, no. 1, 2009, available from http://www.ijnhonline.org/wp-content/uploads/2012/01/Article-King.pdf

Knittle, Walter Allen, *Early Eighteenth Century Palatine Emigration*, Dorrance & Co., Philadelphia, 1937.

Knox-Johnston, Robin, *The Cape of Good Hope: A Maritime History*, Hodder & Stoughton, London, 1989.

Koebel, WH, *The Romance of the River Plate*, 2 vols, Hugh Ponsonby, London, 1914.

——*British Exploits in South America*, Century, New York, 1917.

Kohn GC (ed.), *Encyclopaedia of Plague and Pestilence: From Ancient Times to the Present*, 3rd edn, Facts on File, New York, 2008.

La Pérouse, Jean-François Galaup comte de, *The Journal of Jean-François Galaup de La Pérouse 1785–1788*, vol. 1, ed. & trans. John Dunmore, Hakluyt Society, London, 1994.

Lacour-Gayet, Robert, *A Concise History of Australia*, trans. James Grieve, Penguin Books, Melbourne, 1976.

Laing, John, *A Voyage to Spitzbergen* …, 4th edn, n.p., Edinburgh, 1822.

Lambert, Andrew, *War at Sea in the Age of Sail: 1650–1850*, Cassell, London, 2000.

Landmann, GT, *Adventures and Recollections of Colonel Landmann*, Colburn & Co., London, 1852.

Laughton, John Knox, rev Richard Harding, 'Temple West', in *Oxford Dictionary of National Biography, 1885–1900*, vol. 58, Oxford University Press, New York, 2004, pp. 241–42.

Lavery, Brian, *Nelson and the Nile: The Naval War against Bonaparte 1798*, Naval Institute Press, Annapolis, 1998a.

——(ed.), *Shipboard Life and Organisation, 1731–1815*, Navy Records Society, London, 1998b.

Lavrenov, IV, 'The Wave Energy Concentration at the Agulhas Current off South Africa', *Natural Hazards*, vol. 17, no. 2, 1998, pp. 117–27.

Leicester, Paul (ed.), *The Works of Thomas Jefferson in Twelve Volumes*, Federal Edition, Putnam, 1904.

Letter-Books of Secret Official Letters of Lord St Vincent, vol. 1, Add MS 31166, British Library, London

Letters from Keppel's Expedition to Senegal (1758), and Johnstone's and King's Expeditions to the Cape (1781, 1783), 1758–86, ADM 1/54, National Archives, London.

Letters from Captains, Surnames E, 1751–56, ADM 1/1758, National Archives, London.

Letters from Captains, Surnames P, 1780–81, ADM 1/2306; 1 January 1782 – 31 December 1784, ADM 1/2307; 1798, nos 151–322, ADM 1/2317, National Archives, London.

Letters from Commanders-in-Chief, Mediterranean, 1797, ADM 1/396, National Archives, London.

Letters of Henry Dundas, Visc. Melville, to William jun., 1784–1804, PRO 30/8/157, National Archives, London.

List of Officers on Leave, 1762–74, ADM 106/2972, National Archives, London.

Little, James Brooke, *The Law of Burial*, 3rd edn, Local Government Board & Home Office of Great Britain, London, 1902.

Liverpool Papers, Western Manuscripts, British Library, London.

Lloyd, Christopher, *The British Seaman 1200–1860: A Social Survey*, Paladin, London, 1970.

——& Jack Coulter, *Medicine and the Navy 1200–1900*, vol. 3, *1714–1815*, E & S Livingstone, Edinburgh & London, 1961.

Locke, John, *Two Treatises of Government*, ed. Peter Laslett, New American Library, New York, 1965 (1690).

Lovill, Justin (ed.), *Notable Historical Trials*, vol. 2, *Galileo to Admiral Byng*, Folio Society, London, 1999.

McArthur, John (ed.), *The Naval Chronicle*, vol. 27, *January–July 1812*, Cambridge University Press, New York, 2010.

Macaulay, Rose, *They Went to Portugal*, Cape, London, 1946.

Macaulay, Thomas Babington, *The History of England in the Eighteenth Century*, Folio Society, London, 1980 (1848).

MacClure, Victor, *She Stands Accused*, Cosimo, New York, 2005.

McCulloch, David, *John Adams*, Simon & Schuster, New York, 2001.

McGuane, JP, 'Old Government House, Sydney', *The Australian Historical Society Journal and Proceedings*, vol. 1, part. 5, 1902, pp. 73–82.

McIntyre, Kenneth Gordon, *The Secret Discovery of Australia: Portuguese Ventures 200 Years before Captain Cook*, Souvenir Press, Adelaide, 1977.

——*The Rebello Transcripts: Governor Phillip's Portuguese Prelude*, Souvenir Press, London, 1984.

Mackaness, George, *Admiral Arthur Phillip: Founder of New South Wales, 1738–1814*, Angus & Robertson, Sydney, 1937.

Mackay, David, *A Place of Exile: The European Settlement of New South Wales*, Oxford University Press, Melbourne, 1985.

McLynn, Frank, *1759: The Year Britain Became Master of the World*, Jonathan Cape, London, 2004.

'Manuscript Book Listing Appointments to the 1798 Establishment, Instructions (Financial), Widows' Charity, Other Appointments, Leave of Absences, Expense of the Service & Promiscuous. Index', 1798–1810, ADM 28/147, National Archives, London.

Marcus, Geoffery Jules, *A Naval History of England Vol. 2: The Age of Nelson*, George Allen & Unwin, London, 1971.

Mari Nawi: Aboriginal Odysseys 1790–1850, curated by Keith Vincent Smith, State Library of New South Wales, Sydney, 20 September–12 December 2010.

Martin, Ged (ed.), *The Founding of Australia: The Argument about Australia's Origins*, Hale & Iremonger, Sydney, 1978.

Martin, Peter, *Samuel Johnson: A Biography*, Weidenfeld & Nicolson, London, 2008.

Mathew, KM, *History of the Portuguese Navigation in India, 1497–1600*, Mittal Publications, Delhi, 1988.

Meehan, JF, 'Admiral Arthur Phillip, First Governor and Founder of New South Wales', *The Beacon* (Bath), April 1911.

Melville, Herman, *Moby-Dick: or, The Whale*, Penguin Books, New York, 2009 (1851).

Moore, Wendy, *Wedlock*, Weidenfield & Nicolson, London, 2009.

Mori, Jennifer, *William Pitt and the French Revolution 1785–95*, Keele University Press, Edinburgh, 1997.

Murray, Stuart, *Atlas of American Military History*, Facts on File, New York, 2005.

Nagle, Joseph, *The Nagle Journal: A Diary of the Life of Jacob Nagle, Sailor, from the Year 1775 to 1841*, ed. John C Dann, Weidenfeld & Nicholson, New York, 1988.

Name of Register: Fountain Quire Numbers: 512–58, 1792, PROB 11/1224, National Archives, London.

Name of Register: Marriott Quire Numbers: 782–838, 1803, PROB 11/1399, National Archives, London.

Nash, MD (ed.), *The Last Voyage of the* Guardian: *Lieutenant Riou, Commander, 1789–1791*, 2nd series, no. 20, Van Riebeeck Society, Cape Town, 1989.

Navy Board, Lieutenants' Logs, ADM/L/S/447, National Maritime Museum, London.

Neal, David, *The Rule of Law in a Penal Colony: Law and Power in Early New South Wales*, Cambridge University Press, Cambridge, 1991.

Neale, RS, *Bath: A Social History 1680–1850, or A Valley of Pleasure, Yet a Sink of Iniquity*, Routledge & Kegan Paul, London, 1981.

Nelson, RR, *The Home Office, 1782–1801*, Duke University Press, Durham, NC, 1969.

Nepean Papers, William L Clements Library, University of Michigan, Ann Arbor.

Nicolson, Adam, *Men of Honour: Trafalgar and the Making of the English Hero*, Harper Perennial, London, 2006.

Nicolson, Nigel, *The World of Jane Austen*, Weidenfield & Nicolson, London, 1991.

O'Brian, Patrick, *Desolation Island*, Harper Collins, London, 2003 (1978).

——*HMS Surprise*, Harper Collins, London, 2002 (1973).

——*Joseph Banks*, Harvill, London, 1994.

——*Master and Commander*, Harper Collins, London, 1996 (1970).

——*Men-of-War: Life in Nelson's Navy*, WW Norton & Co., New York, 1995.

——*Post Captain*, HarperCollins, London, 2002 (1972).

——*The Reverse of the Medal*, Harper Collins, London, 2003 (1986)

——*The Yellow Admiral*, Harper Collins, London, 1997.

Officers Commanding Sea Fencibles—1805, Ancestry.com, http://freepages.genealogy.rootsweb.ancestry.com/~pbtyc/Navy_List_1805/Officers/Sea_Fencibles.html.

O'Neill, Richard, *Patrick O'Brian's Navy: The Illustrated Companion to Jack Aubrey's World*, Running Press, Philadelphia, 2003.

Oldham, Wilfrid, *Britain's Convicts to the Colonies*, Library of Australian History, Sydney, 1990.

Ollivier, Blaise, *18th Century Shipbuilding: Remarks on the Navies of the English and the Dutch from Observations Made at Their Dockyards in 1737*, ed. & trans. DH Roberts, Naval and Maritime Books, London, 1992 (1737).

Otterness, Phillip, *Becoming German: The 1709 Palatine Migration to New York*, Cornell University Press, Ithaca & London, 2004.

Papers of Sir Joseph Banks, State Library of New South Wales, Sydney, online at www2.sl.nsw.gov.au/banks/.

Papers Relating to Waterhouse Family and Bass Family, Aw 109, Mitchell Library, State Library of New South Wales, Sydney.

Pares, Richard, *War and Trade in the West Indies 1739–63*, Frank Cass & Co., London, 1963.

Parker, Keiko, 'What Part of Bath Do You Think They Will Settle In? Jane Austen's Use of Bath in *Persuasion*', *Persuasions: The Jane Austen Journal* (Jane Austen Society of North America), no. 23, 2001, pp. 166–76.

Parkin, Ray, *H.M. Bark Endeavour*, Miegunyah Press, Melbourne, 2006.

Peschak, TP, *Currents of Contrast: Life in Southern Africa's Two Oceans*, Struik Publishers, Cape Town, 2005.

Phillip, Arthur, *The Voyage of Arthur Phillip to Botany Bay*, Stockdale (1789), facsimile edn, Hutchinson, Sydney, 1982.

——'Journal', n.d., box 17, Correspondence and Documents, Thomas Townshend, 1st Viscount Sydney Papers, William L Clements Library, University of Michigan, Ann Arbor. (In the Clements holdings the journal is listed as 'Diary'.)

'Phillip's Instructions', 25 April 1787, in *Historical Records of New South Wales*, vol. 1, part 2, *Phillip*, Government Printer, Sydney, 1892, pp. 84–91.

Phillips, Maberly, *A History of Banks, Bankers and Banking in Northumberland, Durham, and North Yorkshire ...*, Effingham Wilson & Co., London, 1894.

Picard, Liza, *Dr Johnson's London*, Weidenfield & Nicolson, London, 2000.

Pike, ER, *Britain's Prime Ministers from Walpole to Wilson*, Hamlyn, London, 1968.

Pitt, William, *The Speeches of the Right Honourable the Earl of Chatham in the Houses of Lords and Commons*, Aylott & Jones, London, 1848.

Pocock, Tom, *Battle for Empire: The Very First World War 1756–63*, Caxton Editions, London, 2002.

Political and Other Departments: Miscellanea, Series 1, FO 95/4/6, National Archives, London.

Pool, Daniel, *What Jane Austen Ate and Charles Dickens Knew: From Fox Hunting to Whist—the Facts of Daily Life in 19th-Century England*, Simon & Schuster, New York, 1993.

Pope, Dudley, *At Twelve Mr Byng Was Shot*, Weidenfield & Nicolson, London, 1962.

Port Jackson, 1786–87, CO 201/2, National Archives, London.

Porter, Roy, *England in the Eighteenth Century*, Folio Society, London, 1998.

——*Enlightenment*, Penguin Books, London, 2001.

Pottle, Frederick A (ed.), *Boswell's London Journal 1762–63*, Folio Society, London, 1985 (1950).

Proudfoot, Helen, Anne Bickford, Brian Egloff & Robyn Stocks, *Australia's First Government House*, Allen & Unwin & New South Wales Department of Planning, Sydney, 1991.

Ribeiro, Aileen, *The Art of Dress: Fashion in England and France 1750–1820*, Yale University Press, New Haven, 1995.

Rickard, J, *Sea Fencibles, 1798–1810*, 25 January 2006, Military History Encyclopedia on the Web, www.historyofwar.org/articles/weapons_sea_fencibles.html.

Rigby, Nigel & Pieter van de Merwe, *Pioneers of the Pacific: Voyages of Exploration, 1787–1810*, UWA Press, Crawley, WA, 2005.

Roberts, W, *F. Wheatley, R.A.: His Life and Works*, Otto Ltd, London, 1920.

Rodger, NAM, *The Wooden World: An Anatomy of the Georgian Navy*, Collins, London, 1986.

——'Le Scorbut dans la Royal Navy pendant la Guerre de Sept Ans', in Alain Lottin, Jean-Clause Hocquet & Stéphane Lebecq (eds), *Les Hommes et la Mer dans l'Europe du Nord-Ouest de l'Antiquité à Nos Jours*, Revue du Nord, Lille, 1986.

——*The Insatiable Earl: A Life of John Montague, 4th Earl of Sandwich*, WW Norton & Co., New York, 1994.

——*Command of the Ocean*, Penguin Books, London, 2005.

——(ed.), *Articles of War: The Statutes which Governed Our Fighting Navies, 1661, 1749, and 1886*, K Mason, Havant, 1982.

Rudé, George, *Hanoverian London 1714–1808*, University of California Press, Berkeley & Los Angeles, 1971.

Russell, Nelson Vance, 'The Reaction in England and America to the Capture of Havana, 1762', *Hispanic American Historical Review*, vol. 9, no. 3, August 1929, pp. 303–16.

Sanger, Chesley W, 'The Origins of British Whaling: Pre-1750 English and Scottish Involvement in the Northern Whale Fishery', *Northern Mariner*, vol. 5, no. 3, 1995, pp. 15–32.

Savelle, Max, *Empires to Nations: Expansion in America, 1713–1824*, University of Minnesota Press, Minneapolis, 1974.

Schama, Simon, *Citizens: A Chronicle of the French Revolution*, Alfred A Knopf, New York, 1989.

——*Rough Crossings: Britain, the Slaves and the American Revolution*, Random House, London, 2005.

Schiebinger, LL, *Plants and Empire: Colonial Bioprospecting in the Atlantic World*, Harvard University Press, Cambridge, Mass., 2004.

Scorgie, Michael & Peter Hudgson, 'Arthur Phillip's Familial and Political Networks', *Journal of the Royal Australian Historical Society*, vol. 82, no. 1, 1996, pp. 23–39.

Secretaries of State: State Papers Naval, Lords of the Admiralty (Supplementary), 1 January 1776 – 31 December 1782, SP 42/66, National Archives, London.

Simms, B & T Riotte (eds), *The Hanoverian Dimension in British History, 1714–1837*, Cambridge University Press, Cambridge, 2007.

Sir James Harris and W. Gomm., January–April 1785, FO 37/6, National Archives, London.

Sir James Harris, May–September 1786, FO 37/11, National Archives, London.

Smith, Keith Vincent, *Bennelong*, Kangaroo Press, Sydney, 2001.

Sobel, Dava, *Longitude*, Fourth Estate, London, 1995.

Southey, Robert, *History of Brazil*, vol. 3, Longman, Hurst, Rees, Orme & Brown, London, 1819.

Spain, Edward, *The Journal of Edward Spain, Merchant Seaman and Sometimes Warrant Officer in the Royal Navy*, St Marks Press, Bankstown, 1989.

Spate, OHK, *Paradise Found and Lost*, Australian National University Press, Sydney, 1988.

Stanbury, Myra, 'The De Saint Aloüarn Voyage of 1772', in Jeremy Green (ed.), *Report on the 2006 Western Australian Museum, Department of Maritime Archaeology, Cape Inscription National Heritage Listing Archaeological Survey*, Report 223, Special Publication 10, Australian National Centre of Excellence for Maritime Archaeology, Western Australian Museum, Welshpool, 2007.

Stanhope, PH, *Notes of Conversations with the Duke of Wellington, 1831–1851*, Longmans, Green & Co., New York, 1888.

Stanner, WEH, 'The History of Indifference Thus Begins', *Aboriginal History*, vol. 1, no. 1, 1977, pp. 3–26.

Stevenson, Robert Louis, *Travels with a Donkey in the Cevennes*, Folio Society, London, 1967 (1879).

Stonehouse, Bernard, *British Arctic Whaling: An Overview*, 5 October 2007, BAW [British Arctic Whaling], www.hull.ac.uk/baw/overview/overview.htm.

Strong, Roy, *Visions of England*, Bodley Head, London, 2011.

Summerson, John, *Georgian London*, Pimlico, London, 1991.

Syrett, David, *The Siege and Capture of Havana 1762*, Navy Records Society, London, 1970.

——& RL Di Nardo (eds), *The Commissioned Sea Officers of the Royal Navy 1660–1815*, Scolar Press for the Navy Records Society, Aldershot, 1994.

Tench, Watkin, *Watkin Tench: 1788*, ed. & introduced by Tim Flannery, Text, Melbourne, 1996.

The A to Z of Georgian London, Publication 126, London Topographical Society, London, 1982.

Thomas, Hugh, *The Slave Trade: The History of the Atlantic Slave Trade 1440–1870*, Picador, London, 1997.

The Thomas Jefferson Papers, Series 1: General Correspondence, 1651–1827, Library of Congress, Washington, DC, online at http://memory.loc.gov/ammem/collections/jefferson_papers/mtjser1.html.

Thomas Townshend, 1st Viscount Sydney Papers, William L Clements Library, University of Michigan, Ann Arbor.

Tink, Andrew, *Lord Sydney*, Australian Scholarly Publishing, Melbourne, 2011.

Tipping, GR (ed.), *The Official Account through Governor Phillip's Letters to Lord Sydney*, GR Tipping, Beecroft, 1988.

Toll, Ian W, *Six Frigates*, Michael Joseph, London, 2006.

Tunstall, Brian, *Admiral Byng and the Loss of Minorca*, Phillip Alan & Co., London, 1928.

Turner, HD, *The Cradle of the Navy*, William Sessions, London, 1990.

van der Merwe, Pieter, *A Refuge for All: A Short History of Greenwich Hospital*, National Maritime Museum, London, 2010.

Vickery, Amanda, *The Gentleman's Daughter: Women's Lives in Georgian England*, Folio Society, London, 2006.

Voltaire, *Letters Concerning the English Nation*, J. and R. Tonson, London, 1767 (1733).

——*Candide, or All for the Best*, J Nourse, London, 1759.

Walpole, Horace, *Letters from the Hon. Horace Walpole, to George Montagu, Esq. from the Year 1736, to the Year 1770*, Rodwell & Martin, Henry Colburn, London, 1818.

——*The Letters of Horace Walpole, Earl of Orford*, vol. 6, ed. Peter Cunningham, Richard Bentley, London & Dix, Edwards & Co., New York, 1857.

Watling, Thomas, *Letters from an Exile at Botany Bay to His Aunt in Dumfries*, ed. George Mackaness, DS Ford (printer), Sydney, 1945 (1794).

Webster, Mary, *Francis Wheatley*, Routledge & Kegan Paul, London, 1970.

White, Gilbert, *The National History & Antiquities of Selborne*, Folio Society, London, 1994 (1788).

White, John, *Journal of a Voyage to New South Wales*, Angus & Robertson, Sydney, 1962 (1790).

William Petty, 1st Marquis of Lansdowne, 2nd Earl of Shelburne Papers, William L Clements Library, University of Michigan, Ann Arbor.

Williamson, Jeffrey G, 'The Structure of Pay in Britain, 1710–1911', *Research in Economic History*, vol. 7, 1982, pp. 1–54.

Wilson, AN, *The Potter's Hand*, Atlantic Books, London, 2012.

Winchester, Simon, *Outposts: Journeys to the Surviving Relics of the British Empire*, Penguin Books, London, 2003 (1985).

——*Atlantic*, Harper Press, London, 2010.

Worden, Nigel, *Slavery in Dutch South Africa*, Cambridge University Press, Cambridge, 1985.

Worgan, George Bouchier, letter to Richard Worgan, 12–18 June 1788, First Fleet Collection, c. 1786–1802, Mitchell & Dixson libraries, State Library of New South Wales, Sydney, online at http://acms.sl.nsw.gov.au/album/albumView.aspx?acmsID=41292 1&itemID=823462.

Wulf, Andrea, *The Brother Gardeners: Botany, Empire and the Birth of an Obsession*, Windmill Books, London, 2009.

ACKNOWLEDGEMENTS

The writing of this book has involved research across numerous disciplines and resulted in many debts of gratitude. My first acknowledgment must be to the scholars and writers who have preceded me, without whom my task would have been so much more onerous. I am indebted in particular to Professors Alan Frost and George Mackaness for their invaluable historical works. I am also transparently indebted to the magnificent naval novels of Patrick O'Brian, the delightful Bath novels of Jane Austen, the insightful analysis of early Sydney by Grace Karskens and the considerable body of work on the Georgian navy and its history by Professor NAM Rodger.

Those writers and scholars provided the bedrock but I could not have attempted to take Phillip's story further without the assistance of the numerous librarians who answered my requests for books, journals and historical records ranging over three centuries. Foremost was Debbie Bennett from the Law Courts Library, Sydney who kindly procured many materials for me. I am also much indebted to the staff of the State Library of New South Wales, the National Library of Australia, the National Archives, Kew, the National Library of South Africa, Cape Town and the Library of the Royal Australian College of Physicians.

Museums as well as libraries were a considerable source of information and inspiration. I never ceased to be impressed by the unfailing patience, courtesy and assistance shown to me by the many curators who attended to my queries and requests. Like Patrick O'Brian, I can say that 'I never turned to any learned society, any library or any scholar without receiving the most generous and disinterested assistance'. Principal among those who gave me such generous assistance were Myra Stanbury from the Department of Maritime Archaeology at the Western Australian Museum, Pieter van der Merwe and Dr Kevin Fewster from the National Maritime Museum, Greenwich, Kieran Hosty from the Australian National Maritime Museum, Tanya Sladek and Sandy Ingleby from the Australian Museum, Dr Clare Brown from the Victoria and Albert Museum and Joy Kremmler and Laurie Benson from the National Gallery of Victoria. My thanks also go to the many staff from the Museum of London; the Fashion Museum, Bath; the National Portrait Gallery, London; the Royal Naval Museum, Portsmouth; the Museum of Sydney; and the Slave Lodge Museum, Cape Town who attended to my enquiries. The models of the first fleet ships at the Museum of Sydney created by Lynne Hadley and her husband Ray are of matchless beauty and attention to detail.

At a more particular level, I owe numerous individual debts. On questions of French maritime exploration and Anglo–French rivalry in the Indian and Pacific Oceans, I received valuable direction and guidance from Ib Barko, Professor Ed Duyker, Pierrelouis Berard, Myra Stanbury and Dr Clive Probyn. On the culture and fashion of eighteenth-century England, Dr Sophie Gee graciously gave me the benefit of her knowledge and expertise. On Jane Austen and her era, Dr Susannah Fullerton, President of the Jane Austen Society of Australia, was my touchstone. On Bath in general, and Phillip's house in Bennett Street, Sir Roger Carrick, Richard Pavitt and Pauline Lyle-Smith kindly provided much assistance and information. On St Nicholas' Church at Bathampton, Robin Donald was my guide. On the present value of sums of money in Georgian England, David Feetham of Gresham Securities generously provided me with calculations and explanations, as did Ian Maxton of Nomura Securities. On the politics and personality of Lord Sydney, Andrew Tink shared with me his knowledge.

On traditional methods of navigation and sailing in the Atlantic Ocean, Philippe Odouard gave me the benefit of his remarkable firsthand experience. On the botany of Sydney Harbour, Professor David Mabberley and Doug Benson from the Royal Botanic Gardens and Domain Trust informed and assisted me. On Aboriginal anthropology, Denise Donlon and John Ralston gave me the benefit of their accumulated knowledge and showed me their treasured artefacts. On issues of naval and military ordnance, armaments and gunfounding, Paul Duffy answered my questions and gave me access to his considerable library. On eighteenth-century silverware, Victoria Greene was my oracle. On spear wounds in classical Greece, Dr Christopher Allen, George Harris and Dr Robert Harper shared their knowledge of Homer. On matters of colonial architecture, James Broadbent and Howard Tanner provided inestimable assistance. On issues of forensic pathology and naval medical techniques in the eighteenth century, Dr Michael Kennedy and Professor Jo Duflou instructed me. On the effects of stroke, Dr Stuart Renwick advised me.

As well as being able to have recourse to persons possessing individual expertise on diverse subjects, I was privileged to have access to a number of substantial private libraries, including the naval library of Dr James Renwick and the early Australian history library of Ms Sue Snepp. Noel Dan also gave me access to his private collection of original letters, including letters between Phillip and Sir Charles Middleton. Among the many friends whom I besieged with queries, Diccon Loxton, George Harris, Anna Clark and Stuart Read never failed to assist. As for research, I was fortunate to have the services at all times of the highly skilled Dr Joanna Penglase, whose expertise far exceeds my own. I simply could not have written the book without her. Other clever and capable researchers who provided assistance included Kevin Tang, Christopher Parkin, Edward Einfeld and Katherine McCallum. In London, Lynne Leveson generously carried out research for me at the National Archives, Kew. Lyn Ferguson also deserves special mention. She shared her enthusiasm for the subject and generously supplied me with copies of several letters that were the product of her own research in the National Archives. And my parents, as always, provided valuable commentary and support.

From the outset, my publisher Pam Brewster has shown unswerving faith in the project and contributed dozens of inspired textual suggestions. She has skilfully guided the book to completion with consummate professionalism. Penny Mansley's editing was insightful and searching. She pushed me quietly and persistently to go deeper and closer to the bone. Nadia Backovic designed the superb jacket, for which I am immensely grateful. And Dale Campisi improved the final product with his careful copy-editing. My friend and agent, James Erskine, has smoothed the way forward in every respect with his renowned expertise. And Sue Page, my personal assistant for so many years, has done more than could have been expected, without complaint or demur. She knows how grateful I am. When the end was in sight, Geraldine Brooks, Simon Winchester, NAM Rodger, Geoffrey Robertson QC and Michael Parkinson all kindly agreed to read the book in proof form. I was surprised and delighted by their generosity and will remain indebted to each of them. Finally, my wife Gillian, to whom this book is primarily dedicated, has travelled with me from the beginning. I am fortunate to have had the benefit of her counsel, on this book and everything else – always wise, usually right and invariably loving.

CONVERSION TABLE

acre	=	0.404 hectares
degree (°)	=	$\frac{1}{360}$ of the circumference of a circle
fathom	=	1.82 metres or 6 feet
foot	=	0.305 metres
gallon	=	4.55 litres
knot	=	1 nautical mile per hour
league	=	$\frac{1}{20}$ of a degree or 3 nautical miles
mile	=	1.61 kilometres
minute	=	$\frac{1}{60}$ of a degree
nautical mile	=	1 minute of latitude or 1.852 kilometres
ounce	=	28.35 grams
pound	=	0.45 kilograms
ton	=	1.016 tonnes

INDEX